THE MASTER GUIDE FOR SPEAKERS

Other Books by Lawrence M. Brings

Clever Introductions for Chairmen

The Master Stunt Book

Humorous Introductions for Emcees

The Modern Treasury of Christmas Plays

The Golden Book of Church Plays

The Master Pep Book

The Christmas Entertainment Book

Choice Comedies for Junior High Schools

The Master Banquet Book

THE MASTER GUIDE FOR SPEAKERS

A COMPILATION OF PRACTICAL MATERIAL TO AID
SPEAKERS IN RESPONDING TO INTRODUCTIONS,
USING REPARTEE, TELLING STORIES, STYLING
THEIR SPEECH OPENINGS, AND IN USING EFFEC-
TIVE CONCLUSIONS.

By

LAWRENCE M. BRINGS, M.A.

Formerly, Director, Department of Speech, Teachers College, Aberdeen, S. D.; Instructor in Speech, the University
of Minnesota; President, Northwestern College of Speech
Arts; professional lecturer and entertainer.

PUBLISHERS

T. S. DENISON & COMPANY
MINNEAPOLIS, MINNESOTA

© 1956 by

T. S. DENISON & COMPANY

PRINTED IN THE U. S. A.

BY THE BRINGS PRESS

International Copyright Secured

Library of Congress Catalog Card Number: 56-13435

TO MY WIFE

For thirty-five years
My faithful associate and
Source of inspiration

FOREWORD

This is an unusual book designed to meet the special needs of speakers, students, and speech instructors. It is generally accepted fact that a speaker's favorable impression upon an audience hinges upon his ability to know **how to begin** his speech and **how to end** it. Oftentimes his success or failure before an audience is determined by seemingly inconsequential approaches to his subject and his listeners.

Aside from a speaker's reputation or personal appeal, much of his success is based upon the clever treatment of his opening remarks, or the spontaneous response to an introduction, or the gift of repartee, or an ability to use appropriate stories, or a skill in delivering an effective conclusion.

During my thirty years of experience in teaching courses in public speaking for college students, as well as for business and professional people, there were many times when I would have found a book of this type a valuable supplementary instructional aid. Recognizing the lack of a suitable collection of illustrative examples to aid students in acquiring skill in the aforementioned phases of speech making, ten years ago I began to gather excerpts from classical and contemporary speeches, actually delivered by experienced and accomplished speakers, that I could use in my classes to show students the best procedures and styling to follow. I used a filing system and classified the excerpts into categories, similar to the chapters in this book, which would make them easily accessible when needed for specific speech situations. All the material has been tested in my courses. I provided mimeographed copies of each category of the material when it was needed. It was found to be an excellent teaching device.

As a result, I have decided to share my collection of illustrative speech material with all students of the public speaking art. This accounts for the publication of this book. It is my hope and anticipation that high schools, colleges, speech clubs, and individuals will find it a valuable addition to their libraries and that the book will be used constantly for consultation and study. I realize that there exist many other illustrations perhaps more selective than those I have chosen for this volume. This fact, however, is a challenge to the user to begin his own research for additional material. By doing so, he will enhance his ability as an effective speaker.

Grateful acknowledgement is made to the many individuals, as well as publishers, who granted permission to us to use these excerpts. Without this cooperation, it would have been impossible for this specialized book to become available to you with all the variety you will discover in the five sections of the volume. In addition, many speakers contributed material that has never appeared in print before. To each of them, I extend my sincere appreciation for this service in the advancement of better speech performance.

We have omitted an index to the specific items given in this book because we suggest that no one should attempt to make a partial study of only one or two sections. It is important that the book be studied in its entirety in order to develop an all-around proficiency as a speaker. In fact, upon careful analysis you will discover that the main emphasis is upon how to make an effective beginning and ending of a speech. Usually it is here that speakers "fall flat" and miss their best opportunity to win an audience's favorable reaction. If I have contributed something to help speakers accomplish their objectives in this area, I will be well repaid for the effort I have made to assemble the material for this book.

—Lawrence M. Brings

CONTENTS

"Always have something to say. The man who has something to say, and who is known never to speak unless he has, is sure to be listened to. Always know before what you mean to say. If your own mind is muddled, much more will the minds of your hearers be confused. Always arrange your thoughts in some sort of order. No matter how brief they are to be, they will be better for having a beginning, a middle, and an end. At all hazards, be clear. Make your meaning, whatever it is, plain to your audience. In controversial speaking, aim to anticipate your adversary's argument. Reply to his jests seriously and to his earnestness by jest. Always reflect before hand upon the kind of audience you are likely to have. . . . Never, if you can help it, be dull."—Lord Bryce.

Section One

THE SPEAKER'S RESPONSE TO AN INTRODUCTION

THE SPEAKER'S RESPONSE TO AN INTRODUCTION

Chapter One

How To Make Successful Responses

The speaker's control of his audience can be predetermined during the first minute after he arises to acknowledge the chairman's introduction. His immediate and quick response to the introduction in the form of repartee, a story, a joke, or a pun, will win the attention of his listeners and he will have made a good start in securing acceptance of the ideas in the main body of his address. But of course much depends upon his manner of presentation. It is hoped that the illustrations given in this section will re-inforce many speakers with methods and ideas to attain the best possible results. Naturally it is assumed that the speaker will use his ingenuity in adapting this material to the situation to give his treatment the appearance of timeliness and originality.

THE SPEECH PRELIMINARY

Before a speaker begins his speech or engages in the actual introduction, he should make some preliminary remarks. Aside from acknowledging the introduction and giving an expression of pleasure for being called upon or for being the speaker, he should respond to the particular remarks of the chairman. This is what is known as the preliminary part of the speech—and is quite aside from the introduction.

This response to the remarks of the chairman is really in the category of the unexpected or the impromptu and, depending upon the way it is given, can affect the whole speech of a speaker.

It is the first impression made upon the audience and it requires planning in the mind of the speaker, if it is to be definitely impressed upon the audience. As one speech authority puts it, the beginning remarks of any speech must be "clear, compact and concrete."

Speakers who know their business always establish an immediate worthwhile impression by using carefully thought-out remarks in the beginning. Those who wish to attain audience acceptance should strive to do likewise. Very often the cue for making a good beginning may rest within the remarks the chairman has made. Listen carefully to the remarks of the chairman for such a cue and then attempt to build a novel response around it.

Here is a good example of a speaker taking the lead from the comments of the chairman to set up his preliminary response:

Actor Anthony Quinn Responds to the Chairman

It is reasonable to assume that this story is authentic. It is reported that at a recent Hollywood gathering Anthony Quinn, the movie actor, was welcomed after his return from Europe where he had been making some pictures. The chairman of the occasion referred to Quinn's work in the Italian pictures he had made, and what an unusual privilege it was for him to play love scenes with those beautiful Italian actresses. And then he was called on to tell something about his trip to the continent and his picture-making experience.

He arose, and after acknowledging the welcome, he said: "I think it was Edward Robinson who I once congratulated for his having played in a picture with the great Russian actress Ouspenskaya. 'Yes,' Robinson replied, 'it is true I appeared with Marie Ouspenskaya and I'm glad, because if I hadn't, I should never have known how to pronounce her name.'"

"It is true I appeared in or made pictures with the leading Italian actresses of the screen. I played scenes with"—and then he hesitated—but promptly enthralled and amused his audi-

ence by naming in rapid-fire order, and in clear perfect pro-
nunciation, with his exotic quality, the names of the beautiful
current cinema stars of Italy, who have caught the fancy and
gained the admiration of the American public—"Anna Mag-
nani, Gina Lollobrigida, Silvano Mangano, Lea Padovani, Ros-
sano Podesta." And then he added, "Of course I'm thrilled with
the experience, and I know exactly what Edward Robinson
meant, how else could I have learned to pronounce their
names?"

He smiled and with easy transition entered upon the more
prosaic parts of his speech.   —V. Spencer Goodreds

OUT OF THE WAY

My Lords, Ladies and Gentlemen: When I was a young
man in India, I used to report criminal cases for the newspaper
that employed me. It was interesting work because it introduced me to forgers and embezzlers and murderers and enter-
prising sportsmen of that kind. (Laughter) Sometimes, after I
had reported their trials, I used to visit my friends in jail when
they were doing their sentences. (Laughter) I remember one
man who got off with a life sentence for murder. He was a
clever, smooth-speaking chap, and he told me what he called
the story of his life. He said: "Take it from me that when a
man gets crooked, one thing leads to another until he finds
himself in such a position that he has to put somebody out of
the way to get straight again." (Laughter) Well, that exactly
describes the present position of the cabinet. (Laughter and
cheers.)   —Rudyard Kipling

*In one of his political talks in England, Mr. Kipling used
this humorous response to an introduction by drawing upon his
past experience and observation. It illustrates how important
it is for a speaker to use the right kind of material for a humorous treatment.*

NO TIME FOR CEREMONY

"Mr. President: No man thinks more highly than I do of the patriotism, as well as the abilities, of the very worthy gentlemen who have just addressed the house. But different men often see the same subject in different lights; and, therefore, I hope it will not be thought disrespectful to these gentlemen, if, entertaining as I do opinions of a character very opposite to theirs, I shall speak forth my sentiments freely, and without reserve. This is no time for ceremony. The question before the house is one of awful moment to the country. For my own part, I consider it as nothing less than a question of freedom or slavery. And in proportion to the magnitude of the subject ought to be the freedom of the debate. It is only in this way that we can hope to arrive at truth, and fulfill the great responsibility which we hold to God and our country. Should I keep back my opinions at such a time, through fear of giving offense, I should consider myself as guilty of treason towards my country, and of an act of disloyalty toward the Majesty of Heaven, which I revere above all earthly things.

Mr. President, it is natural for man to indulge in the illusions of hope. We are apt to shut our eyes against a painful truth, and listen to the song of that Siren till she transforms us into beasts. Is this the part of wise men, engaged in a great and arduous struggle for liberty? Are we disposed to be of the number of those who, having eyes see not, and having ears hear not, the things which so nearly concern their temporal salvation? For my part, whatever anguish of spirit it may cost, I am willing to know the whole truth; to know the worst and to provide for it."   —Patrick Henry

Here is a striking example of the use of tact in winning the opposition at the very beginning of a speech. Patrick Henry knew that there was opposition to him, yet he used this psychological approach to weaken their position at the outset of his famous "Give me liberty, or give me death!" speech.

TIRED

The following response is particularly apropos for a commencement talk. Traditionally the average commencement speech has been characterized as scholarly, dry, and long. That state of mind has to be counteracted, hence this type of introduction is necessary to create a psychology of receptivity toward both the speaker and his message. It also helps to dissipate other forebodings.

This is a type of response that can be planned because it ties into the subject matter. The immediate response to the chairman's remarks should preferably take note of some spontaneous observation by the speaker, or tie in with one of the specific statements of the chairman. Then would follow this type of introduction of the theme:

"If I were asked to choose the occasion most intriguing to me as a speaker, I would have to reply, commencement. It's a target day for the seniors; a rather imminent goal for the juniors; and certainly a day of anticipation for the sophomores and freshmen. It's a juncture in the lives of all students when perspectives change, and decisions have to be made that can become momentous. Personal yearnings, dreams, and capabilities have to be weighed in the light of the complex and grave problems—domestic and international—that form the backdrop in the lives of all of us. Yes, the commencement theme is so big, so broad, so challenging, both to the graduating seniors and parents alike, that I stand confounded with respect to where to begin.

"That's a big order, isn't it? But don't be alarmed. I'm not going to try to measure up to that assignment. The fate of the old North Carolina Negro preacher haunts me. He had talked for over an hour on the major prophets. In the course of time he came to Hosea. Unmindful of his audience, he became more and more eloquent in his classification of the prophets as time passed on. Introducing Hosea in his best oratorical fashion, he shouted 'Where shall we put Hosea?' Just then an old Negro in one of the back pews woke up and said, 'Hosea can have mah seat; ah's so doggone tired ah's goin' home.'

"Friends, you may rest assured that I won't lay myself open to a similar rebuke."

The specific nature of the comment made about Commencement isn't important. In this instance I simply grabbed a few thoughts that would illustrate a setting for the story. The story can be introduced smoothly and easily without laboring it into position.   —*Hugo A. Carlson*

THE USE OF TACT

"This is a red-letter day in my life. It is the first time I have ever had the good fortune to meet the representatives of the employees of this great company, its officers and superintendents, together, and I can assure you that I am proud to be here, and that I shall remember this gathering as long as I live. Had this meeting been held two weeks ago, I should have stood here a stranger to most of you, recognizing few faces. Having had the opportunity last week of visiting all the camps in the southern coal fields and of talking individually with practically all the representatives, except those who were away; having visited in your homes, met many of your wives and children, we meet here not as strangers but as friends, and it is in that spirit of mutual friendship that I am glad to have this opportunity to discuss with you our common interests.

"Since this is a meeting of the officers of the company and the representatives of the employees, it is only by your courtesy that I am here, for I am not so fortunate as to be either one or the other; and yet I feel that I am intimately associated with you men, for, in a sense, I represent both the stockholders and the directors."   —John D. Rockefeller, Jr.

This introduction was used by Mr. Rockefeller when he appeared before an audience of striking employees who were bitterly opposed to management. It is an excellent example of how the use of tact and good judgment will win an audience to your side as it did for Mr. Rockefeller.

UNACCUSTOMED AS I AM

Your Honor and gentlemen of the jury—oops! Sorry, I've been getting so absent-minded! I've been asked to make a speech, and well, I'm not used to talking. I'm a married man. H-rrrumph! You know how that is, you married men. Don't you? Seems the only chance we get to open our mouths is when we yawn. Right, fellers? Fact is, I once had lockjaw for six months before I found it out.

It seems the women, bless their little hearts, like the strong, silent men. And a lot of us are—strong, silent men. Not just because the women like strong, silent men, but because we don't get a chance to get a word in!

There are two kinds of men. Those who quarrel with their wives, and those who have learned to say, "Yes, dear." Only I usually say, "Yes, my lamb." That got me into trouble the other day. I was reading my newspaper, and so was she. She was reading some science article and remarked, "Honey, aren't sheep the stupidest creatures?" I said, "Yes, my lamb." You can imagine how **that** went. . . . Well, what is home without a mutter? You know why the good Lord made man first—it was to give him a chance to say something.

What should one really talk about? If you talk about yourself, you're conceited. If you talk about others, you're a backbiter. If you talk about your business, you're a shop talker. If you talk about other people's business, you're a gossip. If you haven't anything to talk about, you're uninteresting; if you do talk, you're gabby. If you talk about **things** like your club, your house or your church, you're a Babbitt; if you talk about **people,** you're a knocker. If you talk sweetly about your friends, you're a log roller; if you don't you're a sourpuss. If you talk about art, you're a high-brow; and if you don't talk at all, you're a high hat. What a life!

I've got a confession to make. I'm not exactly a rank amateur at this. I took a course in public speaking years ago. I'll never forget the first time I got up to speak. They laughed when I got up there to speak. Titters ran all around the place.

But let me tell you, by the time I got through they were speechless. Yes, sir. They were asleep.

I can remember—I see it plain as day—the sergeant-at-arms reaching over with a little gavel he had, to conk one sleeping fellow over the head. And the way that fellow raised his head and said, "Hit me harder; I can still hear him." . . . No appreciation!

My instructor had told me to make sure that when I spoke my voice filled the hall. I guess it did. I noticed people leaving the place to make more room for it.

After a while I learned a few tricks of the trade. To control that habit of people leaving the place while I was talking. For instance, here's one I would use to open my speech: "Ladies and gentlemen, there's a laundry woman outside with a bill she's been trying to collect for some washing she did for one of you folks here. She says the linen was very dirty and it took her longer than she thought. She doesn't want to disturb the meeting by coming in here so after I've talked a while, will that person just quietly slip out and meet her back there?" . . . And, you know, not a person left after that!

That reminds me of what they tell me actually happened in a theater in Cucamonga, California. There was a hysterical man who rushed into the theater one day, brandishing a revolver and shouting to the proprietor: "There's a man in your show with my wife! I'm going in there and start shootin'!" And while the manager was arguing with the man, his assistant slipped out and hurried to the stage of the theater, called for attention, and said to the audience: "There's a man with a gun out there in the office who came here to kill his wife and her lover who came to this show. To give them a chance to get away without embarrassing them, we'll put out the lights for a while." . . . And you know, when they put on the lights again, more than half the theater was empty! Well, so they say!

Come to think of it, there was something I wanted to talk about. No, we're not going to dim the lights! (Chuckle and look down at your notes, and then go into the body of your address).   —George A. Posner

A GOOD RESPONSE — PREMEDITATED OR UNPREMEDITATED

Some years ago, I attended the annual dinner of Buffalo's Gridiron Club at the Hotel Statler. This organization is the counterpart of Washington's notable Gridiron Club. Their annual affair of both groups is dedicated to the business of "giving the business" to well-known personalities. They are the targets for ridicule and the buffoonery is at their expense.

On this particular occasion, Joe McCarthy, the ex-major league baseball manager, was the main speaker. Joe's home was in Buffalo and this was the off season in baseball. It was also the winter after he had been unceremoniously released as manager of the New York Yankees by the fireball Larry MacPhail, and before he had taken up the managership of the Boston Red Sox.

A young Buffalo lawyer, who was visiting home after a service stretch with O.S.S. and Washington duty, was one of an array of speakers called upon before McCarthy was introduced.

He remembered McCarthy's experience with MacPhail and the Yankees. He was also mindful of the number of people being called upon, including himself, and he deftly employed these two items in the remarks of his response. He began by saying:

"There have been a number of people called on to speak tonight and now I am added to the array, and as I am not the speaker, I have a little story which I think is appropriate.

"Last year, 1946, was the year most of us came back from the service. In baseball, it was said it was the year the men came back. Last spring, our speaker here today was managing the Yankees and he was awaiting the veterans to return to replace the rookies who had been playing. Before he was able to use the new strength and bring a pennant to the Yankees, our friend, Mr. Larry MacPhail, upset the apple cart and Joe McCarthy resigned.

"Now on May 24th, the same MacPhail made a surprise

move. He appointed Bill Dickey, the team's catcher, to succeed McCarthy. No one had ever thought of Bill as a manager. Possibly as a coach when his catching days were over, but as a manager, no one had ever thought of that. No one save Mac-Phail.

"Bill handled the team for a series in Boston and then the Yankees were at the Stadium.

"A reporter approached Bill and said to him: 'Now that you've had at least a few days on the job, how does it feel to be a manager?'

"Bill answered, 'Funny thing, I keep looking around for McCarthy.'"

To which the young lawyer added: "If Bill Dickey were here tonight, he would still be looking around for McCarthy. I understood McCarthy was going to be the speaker tonight. But I've heard everybody else, including myself. I feel as Bill Dickey did and I say, 'McCarthy, where are you?'"

He was a howling success and it got McCarthy off to a good start when he was introduced.

—V. Spencer Goodreds

IN RESPECT TO THE ACKNOWLEDGEMENT

Upon rising, pause before you begin to speak. It will give you poise and you will improve in the estimation of the audience. As you recognize the chairman call him by name; then recognize the honored guests, in order, by name and then the guests in general. But don't as a general practice say, "Ladies and gentlemen." Use your imagination or ingenuity and employ something new. Don't call upon more guests by name than is necessary. After these acknowledgements, pause before you begin your remarks. When you finish, pause before you sit down.

DISARMING THE OPPOSITION

"Your Excellency, Ladies and Gentlemen, my Fellow Americans:

"I am largely indebted to President Lowell for this opportunity to address this great audience. He and I are friends of many years, both Republicans. He is the president of our great university, one of the most important and influential places in the United States. He is also an eminent student and historian of politics and government. He and I may differ as to methods in this great question now before the people, but I am sure that in regard to the security of the peace of the world and the welfare of the United States we do not differ in purposes.

"I am going to say a single word, if you will permit me, as to my own position. I have tried to state it over and over again. I thought I had stated it in plain English. But there are those who find in misrepresentation a convenient weapon for controversy, and there are others, most excellent people, who perhaps have not seen what I have said and who possibly misunderstood me. It has been said that I am against the League of Nations. I am not; far from it. I am anxious to have the nations, the free nations of the world, united in a league, as we call it, a society, as the French call it, but united, to do all that can be done to secure the future peace of the world and to bring about a general disarmament."

—Henry Cabot Lodge, Sr.

Senator Lodge used excellent tact in opening his argument in a debate with President Lowell on the League of Nations. The public had come to identify Lodge with complete opposition to the League and his remarks in this introduction had the effect of disarming both his opponent and the audience.

BE BRIEF

Franklin D. Roosevelt's advice to his son, James, on the subject of speech making: "Be sincere; be brief; be seated."

—V. Spencer Goodreds

LET US REASON TOGETHER

"Fellow citizens of Southern Illinois, fellow citizens of the State of Kentucky, fellow citizens of Missouri. I am told there are some of you here present who would like to make trouble for me. I don't understand why you should. I am a plain, common man, like the rest of you; and why should I not have as good a right to speak my sentiments as the rest of you? Why, good friends, I am one of you. I am not an interloper here. I was born in Kentucky, and raised in Illinois, just like the most of you, and worked my way along by hard scratching. I know the people of Kentucky, and I know the people of Southern Illinois, and I think I know the Missourians. I am one of them, and therefore ought to know them; and they ought to know me better, and, if they did know me better, they would know that I am not disposed to make them trouble. Then, why should they, or any one of them, want to make trouble for me? Don't do any such foolish thing, fellow citizens. Let us be friends, and treat each other like friends. I am one of the humblest and most peaceful men in the world. I would wrong no man, would interfere with no man's rights. And all I ask is that, having something to say, you give me a decent hearing. And, being Illinoisans, Kentuckians, and Missourians—brave and gallant people—I feel sure that you will do that. And now let us reason together, like the honest fellows we are."   —Abraham Lincoln

The above introduction was used by Mr. Lincoln during his campaign for the U. S. Senate in 1858 in southern Illinois. Information had been given him that there were many antislavery men in the audience who had threatened to kill him. Threats were changed to cheers by the tactful use of this clever introduction.

WHERE AM I?

(A Response by a Major League Umpire)

Last spring I attended a bowling banquet as a guest. Another guest was Bill McKinley, an umpire in the American Baseball League. Before the main speaker was introduced McKinley was called on for a few remarks. Bill responded by telling this story:

"There was a young umpire who was working games in the South during the training camp season of the ball clubs. The beginner was working under the wily and experienced eye of the veteran umpire Bill McGowan. They had been working games together. One afternoon, during pre-game practice, it began to rain quite hard. Expecting it would continue, a few of the fans made for a nearby hotel and the young umpire did likewise. He made for the grill and proceeded to get himself pleasantly drunk, or wet inside, as the rain continued for about an hour, outside. When it stopped, chief umpire McGowan decided to play the game, when he suddenly missed the young arbiter.

"He had a suspicion where he might be, and hurried off to the hotel grill and found him in a condition not fit for umpiring. As he was badly needed, McGowan instructed him to take a cold shower and report. Very shortly after the young fellow made his way to the ball park, but still showing the effects. He took his place at first base to umpire the base decisions, and the game got underway. On the first play a ball was hit to the infield and the throw caused a close play at first base, arriving about the same time as the runner. The young umpire looked at the play in a blurry-eyed manner, without calling the runner out or safe. The opposing team's coach and the first baseman descended on the bewildered umpire and yelled, 'What is he?' 'What is he?' said the umpire, still confused, 'What is he?— Where is he?'"

After telling the story, McKinley continued, "the young umpire said, 'Where is he?' As I stand up here I respectfully ask you, my friends, 'Where am I?' I have no speech, and I'm as lost as he was. I do, however, appreciate the chairman's kindness in calling upon me, so I may say I am happy to be with you. You have a fine bowling league and your weekly get-togethers has made possible, I know, a fine fellowship—the great value of all games. Thank you for asking me. I hope I may join you again sometime." He sat down. He made a hit.

—V. Spencer Goodreds

PEACE

Tonight I ask the privilege of coming into your homes to talk with you on some serious national subjects—without the noise and extravagance usual during a political campaign.

I want to talk of one word—and of many things. The word is—peace. And the many things are its many and momentous meanings.

The force and impact of this one word—peace—reach all persons, all problems, in all our land. Its meaning embraces past achievements, present problems, future hopes. It touches all things in our life and knowledge: from home and school, factory and farm, to the most distant points on earth—a frontier in Europe, an island in the Pacific, a canal in the Middle East. And this meaning ranges, too, from the highest kind of principle to the most personal kind of fact.

Let me begin with a personal matter. It is a personal kind of peace that I possess—granted to me by the mercy of the Almighty. It is this firm conviction: I am confident of my own physical strength to meet all the responsibilities of the presidency, today and in the years just ahead. If I were not so convinced, I would never have accepted renomination to this office.

I hope this conviction—this peace of mind—may bring assurance to many others, as I stand ready to serve as your president for another four years, if this be your will.

Let me now speak of greater matters. Peace, like all virtues, begins at home. So examination of our problems and achievements should likewise begin here.

—Dwight D. Eisenhower

A GREAT EVENT

Ladies and Gentlemen: I am but human, and when you give me a reception like that I am obliged to wait a little while I get my voice. When you appeal to my head, I don't feel it: but when you appeal to my heart, I do feel it.

We are here to celebrate one of the greatest events of American history, and not only in American history, but in the world's history. Indeed it was—the application of steam by Robert Fulton.   —Mark Twain

TWO GREAT MEN

I came here in the responsible capacity of policeman to watch Mr. Choate. This is an occasion of grave and serious importance, and it seems necessary for me to be present, so that if he tried to work off any statement that required correction, reduction, refutation, or exposure, there would be a tried friend of the public to protect the house. He has not made one statement whose veracity fails to tally exactly with my own standard. I have never seen a person improve so. This makes me thankful and proud of a country that can produce such men— two such men. And all in the same country. We can't be with you always; we are passing away, and then—well, everything will have to stop, I reckon. It is a sad thought. But in spirit I shall still be with you. Choate, too—if he can.

—Mark Twain

Chapter Two

General Responses By Speakers

There are occasions when the introduction is so abstract and general that the speaker is obliged to respond with the same type of treatment. We have attempted in this chapter to provide an assortment of general responses to serve as patterns. It is possible that some of these examples may be adapted to actual use. However, we must emphasize that the speaker must use his own originality by adjusting the material to his own style and phrasing.

There is nothing unusual or different about the general response. In fact, it probably is the most prosaic of all the possible types of responses that a speaker might use. Yet we are including this classification because it is a common type of response.

BETTER MOUSETRAP

I am happy to come to Middlebury again, where I have always been most graciously received by all you good people. First, by your fine president, Dr. Moody, and then by your distinguished faculty, those of you of the student body, and by the friends of the town.

And now your good chairman honors me with his gracious welcome and praise, for which I am grateful. He does me unusual honor in suggesting I preach a better sermon (smile), and make a better mousetrap. I shall try to give a talk worthy of your confidence in me, but I am afraid I can't make a better mousetrap. Good heavens! I have difficulty setting one. Mrs. Brown always has to show me how. So if it is something to do with a mousetrap, you will have to send for her.

—John Mason Brown

FATE WILLED OTHERWISE

Ever since I have come to this country, about two months ago, I have received nothing but the most profound and charming kindness and hospitality, which has culminated in this unique banquet tonight. I appreciate it all the more because I know it is given at a time when the greatest storm in the world's history is raging, and when nobody in this country or great city feels inclined to indulge in any festivities or banquets. When I return home, I shall be able to tell the people of South Africa that I have been received by you not as a guest, not as a stranger, but simply as one of yourselves. Speaking with a somewhat different accent, and laying a different emphasis on many things, as no doubt becomes a barbarian from the outer marches of the Empire—and one whose mind is not yet deeply furrowed with trenches and dugouts—I would like first of all to say how profoundly thankful I am to Lord French for the words which have fallen from his lips. Your expressions in regard to myself are largely, I feel, undeserved. At any rate, I accept them as coming from an old opponent and comrade in arms. I know they are meant in the best spirit, and I accept them as such.

Your words recall to mind many an incident of those stirring times when we were opposing commanders in the Boer War. I may refer to two. On one occasion I was surrounded by Lord French—and was practically face to face with disaster. Nothing was left me but, by the most diligent scouting, to find a way out. I ventured into a place which bore the very appropriate name of Murderers' Gap—and I was the only man who came out alive. One account of that stated that one Boer escaped, but he probably had so many bullets in him that he would be no further danger. I survived to be your guest tonight.

Two days after I broke through and on a very dark night, I came to a railway, which I was just on the point of crossing, when I heard a train. Some of us felt inclined to wreck and capture that train, but for some reason or other I said, "No, let it pass." You can imagine my feelings when some time afterwards I learned that the only freight on that train was Sir John French with one or two A. D. C.'s, moving round from one part of his front to another to find out how I had broken through. If I had not missed that chance, he would have been my guest, no doubt very welcome, though no doubt embarrassing. Fate has willed otherwise. I am his guest.

—Jan Christian Smuts

This response was given by Jan Christian Smuts when he was introduced by Lord French at a banquet given in his honor by members of both Houses of Parliament in London on May 15, 1917. It is an excellent example of the speaker's ability to utilize a situation to gain a total audience acceptance and response.

NOT AN ORATOR

President Dwight D. Eisenhower, awarding the Medal of Merit to a group of war correspondents at ceremonies in the National Press Club, said he regretted he was not enough of an orator to do justice to the medal's recipients.

"It reminds me of my boyhood days on a Kansas farm," Ike related. "An old farmer had a cow that we wanted to buy. We went over to visit him and asked about the cow's pedigree. The old farmer didn't know what pedigree meant, so we asked him about the cow's butterfat production. He told us that he hadn't any idea what it was. Finally we asked him how many pounds of milk the cow produced each year.

"The farmer shook his head and said: 'I don't know. But she's an honest old cow and she'll give you all the milk she has!'

"Well," the President concluded, "I'm like the cow; I'll give you everything I have."   —Dwight D. Eisenhower

This story can be related when the speaker wishes to admit that he is not a talented orator, and asks the audience to accept his message on its merits.

CANNOT TALK ON COMPLIMENTS

I think I ought to be allowed to talk as long as I want to, for the reason that I have cancelled all my winter's engagements of every kind, for good and sufficient reasons, and am making no new engagements for this winter, and, therefore, this is the only chance I shall have to disembowel my skull for a year—close the mouth in that portrait for a year.

I want to offer thanks and homage to the chairman for this innovation which he has introduced here, which is an improvement on the old-fashioned style of conducting occasions like this. That was bad. Under that old custom when the chairman got up and made a speech, he introduced the prisoner at the bar, and covered him all over with compliments, nothing but compliments, not a thing but compliments, never a slur, and sat down and left that man to get up and talk without a text. You cannot talk on compliments; that is not a text. No modest person, and I was born one, can talk on compliments.

A man gets up and is filled to the eyes with happy emotions, but his tongue is tied. He has nothing to say. He is the condition of Dr. Rice's friend who came home drunk and explained it to his wife, and his wife said to him, "John, when you have drunk all the whiskey you want, you ought to ask for sarsaparilla." He said, "Yes, but when I have drunk all the whiskey I want I can't say sarsaparilla." And so I think it is much better to leave a man unmolested until the testimony and pleadings are all in. Otherwise he is dumb—he is at the sarsaparilla stage.   —Mark Twain

HAPPY TO BE HOME

Governor Coolidge, Mr. Mayor, Fellow Citizens: I wonder if you are half as glad to see me as I am to see you. It warms my heart to see a great body of my fellow citizens again, because in some respects during the recent months I have been very lonely indeed without your comradeship and counsel, and I tried at every step of the work which fell to me to follow what I was sure would be your counsel with regard to the great matters which were under consideration.

I do not want you to think that I have not been appreciative of the extraordinarily generous reception which was given me on the other side in saying that it makes me very happy to get home again.

I do not mean to say that I was not very deeply touched by the cries that came from the great crowds on the other side. But I want to say to you in all honesty that I felt them to be a call of greeting to you rather than to me.

—Woodrow Wilson

This easy and friendly narrative response was used by President Wilson upon his return from the Paris Peace Conference when he addressed an audience in Boston.

THE OLDEST CORPORATION

I was asked to say something about the relation of colleges to business, but if I may be permitted I should rather talk about business—my business—for I am a manufacturer, as my forebears were before me, and I want to advertise. No, that is not the proper word. I want to let people know the quality of the goods that we produce.

My forebears made cotton goods. The concern that I belong to has a different kind of product, but it is an old and well-established concern; it is the oldest corporation now existing in the United States. In eight years the business will be three hundred years old, which is more, I think, than any here.

What we produce is men. I am speaking not of the professional schools, but simply of the college. We make men. It is a curious product, one that we cannot standardize, because it is a biological product and therefore it cannot be wholly standardized. Nevertheless, there are different grades in the goods we produce and one of the difficulties we find is in marketing —that business men are very apt to prefer our second-class goods and then complain that they are not first rate.

—A. Lawrence Lowell, former
President of Harvard University

THANKS FOR THE HONOR

I return you gentlemen my sincere thanks for the honor you have just conferred upon me. For I esteem it a very great honor to be President of the New York Central and Hudson River Railroad Company. It is always and under the most favorable circumstances a place of grave responsibility, but in the present critical conditions of the railway business of the country, the boldest might shrink from assuming the task.

It is, however, your unanimous expression of confidence which inspires confidence, and I shall devote to the work all the ability and experience I possess.

—Chauncey M. Depew

A MISSION OF PEACE

Mr. Mayor, Your Excellencies, Ladies and Gentlemen: How is it possible for me this morning to convey to you the deeply stirred emotions of my heart as the result of your welcome? I cannot do it.

I have come on a mission of peace. I believed, when I was still far away from you, that there was a desire in your hearts to bless the world by a common understanding between your people and the people of Great Britain, so that you and we together should give an example to the whole of the world of how to pursue peace earnestly and sincerely.

—J. Ramsay MacDonald

WOMEN

Mr. President, I do not know why I should be singled out to receive the greatest distinction of the evening—for so the office of replying to the toast of woman has been regarded in every age. I do not know why I have received this distinction, unless it be that I am a trifle less homely than the other members of the club. But be this as it may, I am proud of the position, and you could not have chosen anyone who would have accepted it more gladly, or labored with a heartier good-will to do the subject justice than I—because, sir, I love the sex. I love all the women, irrespective of age or color.

—Mark Twain

CUT DOWN TO SIZE

They say familiarity breeds contempt. The very fact that your chairman and your speaker have been pals ever since childhood, that he is aware of all the mistakes I have made during my lifetime, that he knows all my weaknesses, perhaps does give him a basis for introducing me to you in such a revealingly frank manner.

When Katharine Hepburn was assigned to her first role at MGM opposite Spencer Tracy, she was frightened over acting with a star who had already won two Academy Awards. But Katie wasn't going to let anyone know it—particularly Mr. Tracy. Breezing onto the set with her mind made up that she'd get in the first word, she stared at Tracy for a moment, then brashly trilled, "Oh, Mr. Tracy, I'm really afraid I'm too tall for you."

Spencer measured the upstart with a face devoid of all expression. Then he said calmly, "That's all right, dear. I'll soon cut you down to my size!"

—Motion Picture Magazine

A RESPONSE GIVEN TO AN INTRODUCTION

The occasion was the All-University convocation at the University of North Dakota.

"Mr. Chairman, Ladies and Gentlemen. That introduction was considerably more complimentary than one which I had last week in Chicago where the chairman leaned over to me during the dessert course and said: 'Would you like to begin now or shall we let them enjoy themselves a little longer?'

In listing these awards and accomplishments your chairman very kindly omitted one qualification about which I think you should be told before I begin. It was most dramatically illustrated recently when in another state I was acting as judge of a national forensic contest. The superintendent of schools of the city in which the contest was being held was acting as chairman. He was trying to assure the members of the audience as well as the contestants that not only was I unfamiliar with the individual contestants, but that I had not even been informed of the states or communities from which they came. After a long explanation he turned toward me with a flourish and said, 'and so ladies and gentlemen, here sits our Honorable Judge, completely ignorant.' I thought it only fair that this audience should be informed of that qualification which your distinguished chairman was far too gracious to mention. I shall probably remove any doubt which you may have on that score in just a few moments. And to keep the record straight I should add that on another occasion a couple of weeks ago the chairman who called upon me for an impromptu response, said, (perhaps deliberately, I have never been quite sure,) that although I was not scheduled to address the group, he felt quite confident that I would be willing to say a few **appropriate** words.

The words which I wish to speak to **you** today, however, are by no means appropriated. It is my hope that they may be appropriate, and that they may do something to awaken your interest in, and bring you information about, one of the most dramatic and threatening international problems of our time."

—Dr. E. W. Ziebarth,
Dean of the Summer Session, University of Minnesota

THANK YOU, PROFESSOR

You know, when I finished my last talk, a man came up to me, and said:

"Professor, would it be an insult if I called you an ass?"

"Why, of course," I said.

"And if I called an ass a professor would it be an insult?"

"No."

So he says, "Thank you very much, professor."

—George A. Posner

IT PLEASES ME

Friends: I have been assured that I could use that phrase here, thus far from election. You are very hospitable people, as much as they are in Pennsylvania. I was many years ago impressed with the fact that in Pennsylvania I was very cordially received on every day of the year except one, and I do not know of any place in the country except in Boston, where I have been more eulogized by Republicans in between campaigns. It impressed me; and I was speaking one day over there, after a very gracious eulogy, and I told them I could not explain the way they welcomed me in the state, knowing my views, except on the theory of a story I once heard. There was a very large man who had a small wife, and she used to beat him, and some one said, "Why do you allow it?" "Oh," he said, "it seems to please her, and it does not hurt me."

And so they seemed to welcome me over there, and just turned me loose on the theory that it might please me and would not hurt them. And I told them how discouraging it was for a Democrat to come into that state and talk as much as I did without converting people, and if it were not for an illustrious example in history I would probably have given it up. But I have been very much encouraged by the experience of Noah. It is said he preached righteousness for a hundred years and never made a convert outside of his own family. But at the end of the time a flood came and drowned all the Republicans. And so I go on talking, and I enjoy the opportunity such as is presented tonight.   —William Jennings Bryan

PAINTED VIVIDLY

Mr. Chairman: In my sixty years on the platform, I have been introduced by all sorts and kinds and conditions of men and women, but never in my life have I been frescoed and rubbed up and down and painted so vividly and multifariously as I have been by the chairman tonight.

—Chauncy M. Depew

FORCED UPON HIM

Do not begin your remarks by saying that you have not had time to prepare a speech, or that you are unaccustomed to public speaking. If your speech is good your auditors will not care whether it has been prepared or not. If it is bad they will know it without being told.

At a wedding breakfast recently the guests insisted upon the bridegroom making a speech. He was evidently not prepared and he did all he could to get out of it but they were not to be denied. Seeing that he would have to make some sort of an attempt he struggled to his feet and in a shaky voice began:

"Ladies and gentlemen, I—I—don't know what to say. This thing was forced upon me—" At this point the entire table let out a roar of laughter. The bewildered groom looked around. What were they laughing at? He couldn't understand it. He hadn't intended to say anything funny. He hastily reviewed his words but still failed to see the joke until, happening to look down, he noticed that he was standing with his hand on the shoulder of the bride.   —Arthur L. Kaser

GREASE HER KNEES

Well begun is half done, and you will find that once you have conquered the nervousness incident to facing your auditors and making your opening address it will be a comparatively easy matter to speak entertainingly. "Therefore," in the words of Mark Twain, "rise up on your hind legs, open your mouth and throw yourself into it."

Twain himself realized early in life that a weak attack makes for disaster. At the age of twelve he was slated to make his first appearance on any stage. It was the commencement exercise of the Hannibal public school and young Clemens had elected to deliver those noble lines beginning:

"When Greece her knees in suppliance bent."

The teacher called his name. The budding orator rose to

his feet, fell over them and staggered on to the platform where he stood at bay, glaring into the faces of his grinning classmates, terror in his heart and a lump in his throat. Making a supreme effort he swallowed the lump and in a low husky voice began:

"When Greece her knees . . ."

He stopped, took a long breath and made a fresh start:

"When Greece her knees . . ."

He could get no further; like a hunted hare he doubled back:

". . . Greece her knees . . . Greece her knees . . ."

It was no use. He just couldn't make the grade. He quit cold.

"Don't give up, Sam," said the teacher encouragingly. "Grease her knees a couple of times more and she'll make it!"

—Arthur L. Kaser

SUBJECT OF SPEECH

Your chairman came up to me this evening and asked for the title of my speech. I said to him that I hoped that he would be as agreeable in that respect as some country fellows I ran into on the way over here.

As I was driving along the highway on my way to Pottsville tonight, I became lost, and somehow or other found myself on a lonely country road. I proceeded down this desolate lane for about a mile, when I came to a country crossroads store. A group of local fellows were loitering in front of the store. Stopping my car, I cried out: "I want to go to Pottsville."

One of the country lads sauntered slowly up to my car, chewing on a piece of straw. When he got within proximity of my car, he slowly withdrew the piece of straw from his mouth, looked up at me and quietly said: "We've no objection."

—Sylvester McGovern

AWAKENS MANY OLD MEMORIES

Mr. Speaker: I am very much tempted to say "Fellow members of Parliament." You really do me a very great honor in allowing me to come up and stand here and address you for a minute or two. To me it awakens many old memories of early visits to Washington.

But it does more than that. It makes me feel when I look at you, when I stand to address an assembly like this, how very much alike are our democratic institutions, and how much akin we are in our democratic purposes.

You honor, however, not me. Precious as your honors are to me, I am sure you regard me as the representative of my country. And you wish me, when I go back to my own fireside and to my own House of Commons, to tell how very kind, how very generous, how very hospitable you were, and I pledge myself that I will do so.   —J. Ramsay MacDonald

This response was used by Prime Minister MacDonald when he was introduced to the U. S. House of Representatives in 1929.

BUSINESS AND FUN

Mr. President, Ladies and Gentlemen: I am very much gratified to be present here with you tonight. Your invitation was an agreeable change from the daily health routine of a summer health resort, but I am at a loss what to say to you. What I do not know about fertilizer, and what you do put together would fill a library. I attended your business meeting this morning in search of points. From the addresses I gathered two ideas in the way of advice. Certainly you have mingled business and fun in a way most instructive to tired workers in any line of life.   —Chauncey M. Depew

NOTHING BUT FIGURES

(Speaker tells what guests said about him in the lobby before the meeting)

I arrived early this evening, as I usually do when meeting a group for the first time, and did a little snooping out in the lobby. I no sooner stepped off the elevator than one fellow took a look at me and said to another fellow: "I hope that guy isn't going to read that bundle of papers he has in his arms and bore us with a windy speech besides."

Then when I looked the other way, I heard a guy say: "What! If it isn't that guy again." "What guy?" a second fellow asked. "That guy over by the post with a bundle of papers under his arm. I've heard that guy speak four times in the last four weeks."

"Oh, that guy!" exclaimed a third. "I know that guy," he added, craning his neck and looking me over. "I heard him at the Lions Club in Punkin Center last month. It was pitiful. Figures. Figures, figures! Nothing but figures!"

"And the stories he told!" said the first fellow. "Yellow with age."

"Our arrangement committee's slipping," said the first fellow.

"It certainly is," replied the second, and then both men elbowed their way through the crowd.

I moved over to where several ladies were chatting like magpies. "It's a disgrace," said one lady to the three others.

"What's a disgrace?" asked a second lady.

"Our speakers. I just for the life of me can't figure out why we have such peculiar characters addressing our meetings. Why, last month we had that little shrimp of a Professor Evans—such a dry, withered-up spectacle. And the month before, it was that horrid-looking Mr. Bangs who did nothing but stand up there all evening, drinking glass of water after glass of water, telling stories."

"And some of those stories were not just what they should be before a club like this," said a third.

"Who have we got tonight?" asked a third.

"We got that!" said one lady, nodding her head in my direction.

"Oh, that!" replied another.

"Who is that?" asked the second lady.

"That's what we got!"

So there's no mistake about what you've got tonight, I am going to illustrate with a little story about a Yankee straggler, who became lost after one of the toughest battle of the Civil War. This Yankee straggler was limping along the road, his clothes tattered to ribbons, half-starved, parched and half-dead. As he was traveling along in a snail-like pace the butt of his gun trailing in the rut of the dusty road, three Confederate soldiers dashed out of a clump of bushes, and pointing their rifles at the poor Yankee, cried out: "We git you!"

The Yankee stood still in his tracks threw down his gun and replied in a panting voice: "Yes, you git me, you git me all right. But what a hell of a git you got!"

—Hugh Lincoln

HOWLING WILDERNESS

A politician had prepared a speech and tried to commit it to memory. The opening sentence was as follows:

"Ladies and gentlemen, one hundred years ago tonight the place where I now stand was a howling wilderness."

Here he paused and tried in vain to recall the next sentence of his prepared speech. Sparring for time, he said:

"I repeat it for the sake of emphasis. One hundred years ago tonight the place where I now stand was a howling wilderness."

He paused again and tried to recall the next lines of his prepared speech, but they simply would not come, and then he said: "And I wish the Lord that it was a howling wilderness now and I was in the middle of it." He then sat down.

—A. F. Sheldon

TRIMMED DOWN TO SIZE

A man in Boston, two generations ago, came bursting into the home of the famed Edward Everett one fine afternoon. Everett was the polished orator, perhaps the greatest of his day, who broke into the history books by virtue of his two-hour long oration at Gettysburg on the afternoon of the day Lincoln delivered himself of the classic eulogy of the war dead. One of the papers had published a story about the man that was full of uncalled-for criticism, snide references, possible libel. Should he demand an apology, or sue the guy, or what should he do, the man wanted to know of his erudite friend Everett.

"What should you do? My dear sir," said Everett, "do nothing! Half of the people who read that paper never saw the article. Half of those who did see it, failed to read it. Half of those who read it did not understand it. Half of those who understood it, did not believe it. Half of those who did believe it were of no consequence anyway!"

Mr. Everett did what might be called a precision job of taking the conceit out of the editorial writers. He could have said about the same if a speaker had been involved.

Bob Williams, Minnetonka Record

ON MY OWN

Churchill's gift for the light touch was an important factor in winning friends and influencing legislators. On one of his first visits to the United States before he addressed a joint session of the Congress, Franklin D. Roosevelt was worried about the reception. The Prime Minister soon dispelled all doubts about his welcome. He even made isolationists cheer and chuckle when he said: "I cannot help reflecting that if my father had been an American and my mother British instead of the other way round, I might have got here on my own!"

—V. Spencer Goodreds

NOT TO BE TRUSTED

Some years ago in a western state, then a territory, a popular citizen became involved with an influential and overbearing character and killed him.

Public sentiment leaned toward the defendant, but the law was against him. When the day of trial came the defendant, his counsel and friends held a consultation, and, fearful of the consequences, they decided that the defendant should plead guilty and beg the court's mercy.

The jury was charged by the court and retired. Presently it returned, and the foreman said:

"We find the defendant not guilty."

The judge viewed the jury in surprise and said:

"Gentlemen of the jury, how be it? This defendant pleads guilty, and you find him not guilty?"

"Well, your honor," answered the foreman, "the defendant is such a liar we can't believe him under oath."

—The Progressive Grocer

This story may be used when the chairman has gone overboard in giving an exaggerated outline of the speaker's achievements, many of which are not exactly true.

DENIED HIMSELF NEEDLESSLY

When your chairman remarked that I had declined to eat your palatable dinner tonight I am reminded of the nervous young minister who dined one Sunday noon with a farmer and expressed his great sorrow that because he was about to preach at two o'clock, he could eat none of the chicken, or other "bounties of a kind Providence," but would take only a cup of hot water. The farmer was grieved and his women folks almost wept. After the service, the host joined his guest and said with a sigh as they started for home, "Well, pastor, you might as well hev et, mightn't you?"

—Rev. Dillon Bronson

A RESPONSE WITH A QUOTATION

Recently I was the main speaker at a dinner given by a credit men's association. A guest who was called upon for a few words responded in this fashion.

"I have attended many meetings of this group and I had hoped my presence alone would have conveyed my sincere interest in you without the necessity of talking. Not to think too highly of myself but the idea is expressed in the words of Emerson, "What you are speaks so loudly, I can't hear what you say." Or expressed in plain prose, "Actions speak louder than words." And it is quite possible, that I can say nothing of interest.

Anything I may say is in respect to my high regard for this organization. Emerson again said, "An institution is the lengthened shadow of an individual." I'm sure the fine work your organization is doing toward stabilizing credit in this area is a reflection of the energies and capable direction of your executive secretary. Extending Emerson's observation it may be said, an institution is the lengthened shadow of many individuals. The work of this group is a credit to the zeal of every one of its members.

It is a well established fact that through your concerted and organized efforts you are making an important contribution to the business life of this town. Congratulations upon your accomplishments for the past year."

—V. Spencer Goodreds

THE FIRING SQUAD

City Councilman Harry Davenport of Pompton Lakes, N. J., got a letter from the local American Legion Post: "You are invited to be one of the speakers at our Memorial Day meeting. The program will include a talk by the Mayor, recitation of Lincoln's Gettysburg speech by a high school pupil, your talk and then the firing squad."   —Time

NOTHING TO UNLOAD

A farmer was driving to town one day with a wagon load of apples. The way was long and the road was filled with mudholes, and the driver, dozing in his seat, failed to notice that a board came loose in the bottom of the wagon. The apples started rolling out, one at a time, two at a time, a whole peck at a time, until there wasn't an apple left. Finally they came to one mudhole that was worse than all the mudholes put together. The wheels sank down to their hubs in the serpentine mire, the horses sank down—to their alimentary canals. They frothed at the mouth as the farmer laid on the whip, but to no avail. The wheels and the horses only sank deeper. So the farmer got out to see what he had better do with the apples. You can imagine his amazement and dismay when he noticed the emptiness of the wagon box. He threw up his hands and said: "Stuck, by heck, and nothing to unload!"

Now I say that sometimes happens to a speaker. I know that it has happened with me tonight. So if anyone's really stuck it's your chairman who's responsible for my presence here tonight. —Strickland Gillilan

WOODEN DINNER BELL

One day in Iowa I came upon a large field surrounded by a board fence with hog wire around the bottom. There were about fifty hogs in the enclosure, whose actions were most unusual. They ran to one end of the field and looked up, then would run over to the side of the field and would look up, then run to the other side of the field and look up. When I reached the farmhouse I asked the owner if there wasn't something peculiar about his hogs. He replied in a whisper:

"Yes, you see I lost my voice a few weeks ago. When I wanted to feed the hogs I would pound on the fence. Now the durn woodpeckers are running them to death."
—Edward T. Hall

ANOTHER MAN'S WIFE

In New York, Dr. Stires was a very popular after-dinner speaker. He was delivering a speech at a banquet one night. At the outset, he gave a toast to the ladies present in these words: "To the ladies. To the ladies. To the ladies. The best part of my life I spent in the arms of another man's wife—my mother!"

There was an Englishman on the platform who was to be the guest at a banquet a week later. About ten minutes later, the sentiment which Dr. Stires had uttered reached him and he applauded. Then he whispered to his neighbor: "Next week I am going to be a guest at a banquet. That is a great toast the doctor has given, and I will repeat it in his very words when I am called upon to speak."

The banquet was held as scheduled. He was praised by the chairman and was finally introduced to the audience. He said: "Ladies and gentlemen, before I take up the text of my address, I wish to offer a toast that I heard in New York about a week ago," and said: "To the ladies. To the ladies. To the ladies. The best part of my life I spent in the arms of another man's wife —(hesitation) By jove, I forgot her name!"

—Max D. Steuer

ARE YOU AWAKE?

A famous lecturer uses this method to arouse the attention of his audience as he begins his address:

"I am certainly glad to be invited to speak in the beautiful city of St. Paul ..."

At this point usually the chairman or someone in the audience interrupts:

"Not St. Paul! You're in the city of Minneapolis."

"I know it, but I just wanted to see if you were alert and awake. Now I hope you will all stay awake until I've finished."

—James Nolan

MOTHER HIM

Whenever I am honored by the presence of ladies I like to recall the six ages of womanhood. First there is the infant. Then comes the little girl. Then the miss, which is followed by the young woman, which is also followed by the young woman and the young woman. I recited this transitory evolution of the female at a meeting in Peoria last week, which was attended by a number of ladies of the last three categories. I must admit that it didn't take so well, as I was pierced by some reproachful stares indeed.

I tried to smooth over the troubled waters by giving out some advice to the ladies. "Ladies," said I, "the best way to live agreeably with your husbands is to mother them." Then hoping for an audience participation, I said: "Which one of you ladies is willing to accept my advice?"

One woman of huge proportions arose to her feet, grabbed her half-pint husband by the coat collar and started for the door.

"Aha!" said I, "At least there is one noble lady present who is willing to take her husband home and mother him."

Immediately the ponderous woman let go her husband, pointed a menacing umbrella at me and yelled out indignantly: "Did you say, 'Mother him?' I thought you said 'smother'."

—Rome Roberts

FULL OF BULL

A lion was roaming through the jungle when he suddenly came upon a herd of bulls. One of these bulls he promptly killed and ate. After feasting upon the bull he felt so fine the lion roared and roared.

This noise attracted a hunter who approached with his gun. The hunter, upon viewing the lion, raised his gun and shot the lion dead. The Moral: "When you are full of bull keep your mouth shut."

—Bindery Talk

SPECIAL TERMS FOR DEMOCRATS

I am indeed happy to visit with you here in Pulaski, in an area which combines great natural resources and industrial vigor with some of the most delightful scenery and recreational facilities in the country, not to mention, of course, the charm and grace of Southern hospitality. I remember the last time I was here a few years ago, on a short vacation, I was looking around for an inexpensive place to stay, and I walked up to a house that had a card in the window advertising rooms for rent. Now, I'm not exactly a Northerner, having been born in South Dakota. But I had the somewhat old-fashioned idea, like many Northerners, that there might be some advantage in being a Democrat in this part of the world. So I very slyly said to the landlady, "You wouldn't by any chance have special terms for Democrats, would you?" She answered: "I certainly have, but I'm too much of a lady to use them."

—Arthur Larson, Under Secretary of Labor

WAKE HIM YOURSELF

A speaker at a luncheon meeting noticed that three elderly gentlemen in the front row had fallen asleep. Turning to the chairman, he requested:

"Mr. Chairman, will you please wake up these men?"

"Do it yourself," was the speedy reply. "Probably you don't realize it, but you put them to sleep." —James Nolan

SPEECHLESS

Yes, when I got up to speak, there was a snicker ran through the crowd; everyone seemed prepared for a big laugh. Little did they know I had taken a course in Public Speaking. But when I had finished, they were speechless. They were asleep. —George A. Posner

SENSIBLE MAN TALKS

I congratulate you, Mr. President, on having such a noble, such a generous, such a patient, such an appreciative audience to preside over. I congratulate you, gentlemen, on having a president who combines in himself in a marked degree these two great traits of a presiding officer—confidence in himself, and distrust of all who are to come after him.

I remember forty years ago to have heard a Senator of the United States, making a stump speech in a quiet town in Vermont, amuse his audience with a story of a wood sawyer who had worked for him and who had the habit of accompanying the movement of his saw with talking to himself. He asked him one day why he did so. "Why," said he, "for two reasons. The first is, that it is a great pleasure to hear a sensible man talk, and the second is that it is a great pleasure to talk to a sensible man."

—William M. Evarts

BLESSED EVENT

(If the emcee or the chairman fluffs his lines, or is nervous)

"Thank you for that introduction, sir. Ladies and gentlemen, you must understand he's a little nervous tonight. He had a blessed event at his house ... (applause) ... his mother-in-law went home!   —George A. Posner

HIT ME HARDER

I got onto my favorite topic in an after-dinner address the other night, and noticed several of those present beginning to look a bit drowsy. One fellow near me I noticed was resting his head on the tablecloth. The chairman reached over and tapped him lightly on the head with his gavel.

He roused a little and said: "Hit me harder, sir, I can still hear him."   —George A. Posner

CONSIDERABLE WIND

A few weeks ago I was invited to address an open-air celebration in southern Illinois. Two reviewing stands had been built, and there were thousands of people in the audience, but, five minutes before I was due to speak, a violent windstorm came up and blew down the stands and completely wrecked the proceedings. I never had a chance to give that speech. My next speech was up in Boston, and last Tuesday I headed in that direction. Perhaps you recall what happened last Tuesday. A hurricane hit Boston and most of New England. It's getting now so that when people see my name on a program they begin to issue warnings to be prepared for a considerable amount of wind. Perhaps this is why I've been invited to the Compressed Air and Gas Institute.

—Arthur Larson, Under Secretary of Labor

TEDIUM

Last month in the southern part of the state, I was highly honored by the mayor. He classed me with some of the greatest scientists in history. After I had concluded my performance as emcee, the mayor of the town came up to me and said: "Brown, it took Bill Ramsay sixteen years to produce helium. It took Madam Curie thirty years to produce radium. But you've got them all beat. Tonight you set a world's record — in five minutes you produced tedium."

—Sylvester McGovern

IN THE LION'S DEN

You know, this kind of reminds me of Daniel, in the lion's den. He looked around at those lions, and I imagine he thought to himself: "Well, whoever's got to do the after-dinner speaking, it won't be me." —George A. Posner

NEAR THROUGH

I'm not going to talk very long because I am informed by your chairman that your meeting closes promptly at 1:30— You see, I've been cured of speaking overtime.

The other day I was talking to another group like this when a man came into the banquet room and sat down near the speaker's table.

I had spoken about 40 minutes when I observed that he was becoming very fidgety. Suddenly he jumped up and asked:

"Mister, how long have you been lecturing?"

"About six years, sir."

"Well, I'll stick around. Maybe you're about through."

—Robert Smith

HARD TO DELIVER

This is a new experience for me. All of you know that I have never made a speech to an audience before. If you're patient with my feeble efforts, perhaps I'll be able to get some of my ideas over to you.

I am reminded of the famous doctor who made the comment about public speaking:

"Speeches are like babies—easy to conceive—but hard to deliver!"   —James Nolan

BORING

After an acknowledgement of the situation that made me the featured speaker for a certain state convention, substituting for Governor Sigurd Anderson of South Dakota, I responded with this statement:

"I caution you, ladies and gentlemen. Men are different from guns—the smaller the caliber, the bigger the bore."

—Hugo A. Carlson

WONDERFUL CHAIRMAN

In a small New England city the community fund campaign had just gone over the top. The secretary of the campaign, a prim, gray-haired little lady, was called upon to say a few words about the chairman, a Mr. Smith, at a victory dinner.

"Ladies and gentlemen," she said, "in China there is an ancient custom that parents must kiss their offspring on that part of the anatomy through which they hope the children will become famous. If they want their child to be an orator, they kiss him on his mouth. If they want their child to be a philosopher, they kiss him on the forehead. If they hope that he'll be a singer, they kiss him on the throat. Now, I don't know on what part of his anatomy Mr. Smith's parents kissed him — " she paused an instant for effect — "but he certainly makes a wonderful chairman."   —V. Spencer Goodreds

If a chairman of a speaking program wishes to use the story, the last line could be changed to read: "Now I am not quite sure my parents kissed me on the proper part of the anatomy, as I am not a very good chairman."

A SANDWICH, PLEASE!

The after dinner speaker had talked for fifteen minutes. "After partaking of such a meal," he continued, "I feel if I had eaten another bite, I would be unable to speak." From the far end of the table came an order to the waiter: "Give him a sandwich."   —Mountaineer

ENTERTAINMENT?

I recall an introduction given me the other night in Sioux City when the chairman said: "The gentleman I am about to introduce tonight is our only speaker. The rest of the program is entertainment."   —Lawrence M. Brings

LOST OR FOUND

I feel much like the country gentleman who used to go to town every Saturday in his farm wagon drawn by two mules. On each occasion he would come home in an intoxicated condition, but the mules knew just what to do. They stopped in front of the house, and the farmer's two sons would come out, unhitch the team and put the old gentleman to bed.

One Saturday night, the boys thought it was time to teach their father a lesson. They put the mules in the barn, but left him in the wagon. As the sun came up over the horizon, he aroused himself, stood erect and rubbed his eyes. Then he saw his plight. As he looked out over the muleless tongue and hind gate of the wagon, he observed to himself, "I have either lost a damn good pair of mules or I have found a damn good wagon!"   —Alben W. Barkley

BORED BY MY TALK

About a month ago I addressed a meeting at which a number of ladies were present. My subject was on feminine styles, and I dwelt at great length on the fashion of piercing ears. Just before I concluded, I asked a stylish matron at one of the front tables if she ever had her ears pierced.

"No," she replied. "But right now I'm having them bored."   —Rome Roberts

OLD FORMULA

Gentlemen, there is an old formula, it is said, that applies either to giving a speech or writing a love letter. That formula is to begin without knowing what you are going to say, and to leave off without knowing what you have said. I am going to follow that formula this evening.

—Sylvester H. McGovern

FOOLS

I'm reminded of the experience of a friend of mine who is a celebrated doctor of laws. His talk was to be on fools. The chairman, who was somewhat of a wit, stood up to introduce him:

"Ladies and gentlemen," he said, "We are now to have a lecture on fools by one" . . . he paused, and there was loud laughter before he resumed . . . "of the wisest men in the country."

The lecturer then rose to speak.

"Ladies and gentlemen," he said, "I'm not half as big a fool as the chairman" . . . he paused, and again there was loud laughter . . . "would have you suppose."

—George A. Posner

SILENCE IS GOLDEN

A tourist spending the night in a small Vermont town joined several men sitting on the porch of the general store. They were a close-mouthed bunch and, after several vain attempts to start a conversation, he finally asked, "Is there a law against talking in this town?"

"No law against it," answered one of the men, "but there's an understanding no one's to speak unless he's sure he can improve on silence."

—Margaret Schooley in Reader's Digest

MAKING FACES

Gentlemen, it is said that the Brazilians interchange thought to a surprising degree by facial motions and gesticulations. At this moment I wish I were a Brazilian and could stand up here and just wave my hands and make faces at you.

—Sylvester H. McGovern

HOW LONG?

When I sat down beside your chairman today, I asked him: "How long do you want me to talk?"

His quick reply was: "You can talk all afternoon if you want to, but we usually leave here at 1:30."

So I'll heed his advice and you may be assured now that I will close my address promptly at 1:30.   —James Nolan

NOTHING!

My opponent, who has just talked to you, is a cunning and plausible speaker. He has blinded you by his sophistry. He has dazzled you with his rhetoric and he has attempted to capture you with his honeyed accent. But what has he said about the issues in this campaign? Nothing! Absolutely nothing!   —Sylvester H. McGovern

SQUEEZED ORANGE

(For a speaker appearing on the tail-end of a program)

Being the sixth speaker on the agenda this evening, I find that my thunder has been stolen, and the subject of my talk in the condition of a squeezed orange.

—Sylvester H. McGovern

DISAPPOINTED

Oscar Hammerstein 2nd, New York writer and producer, was introduced at a banquet given in his honor. "I came here hoping to hear a brilliant speech," he flipped. "I was hoping to hear it from my own lips. But I'm afraid I'm going to be disappointed."   —Billy Rose

FEAR AND PREJUDICE

I return my gratitude for the honor done me by the Peabody Committee. Mr. Weeks, in his generous and gracious citation, employed two words—fear and prejudice. I confess to an abiding fear—a fear that has been my companion at many microphones in many countries. It is a concern lest this mechanical device which magnifies the voice, inflate the speaker in his own eyes, cause him to believe that his knowledge, wisdom and understanding increases in direct proportion to the range of his voice. It is a fear of failing always to remember that a great many people think they are thinking when they are really rearranging their prejudices.

—Edward R. Murrow

THE BANQUET

The American institution of the banquet has been described by a well-known after-dinner speaker as "an affair where a speaker first eats a lot of food he doesn't want and then proceeds to talk about something he doesn't understand to a lot of people who don't want to hear him."

—V. Spencer Goodreds

GOOD SPEAKER

A good speaker is a fellow who says the things you would like to have thought of in the way you would like to have said them had you thought of them. —V. Spencer Goodreds

WHY I WENT INTO POLITICS

Your chairman has asked me to speak to you on the reason why I have gone into politics. I have entered politics because there is too much politics in the administration of criminal justice. To put it another way, I have become a candidate in the judicial forum because there is too much of the wrong kind of politics in the prosecution of crime.

—Thomas E. Dewey

SIX BLIND HINDOOS

This modern treatment of an old story can be used effectively by a speaker who wishes to clarify the audience's impressions of his corporation or a governmental department.

Six blind Hindoos were led up to the elephant and asked to tell what it was like. One of the blind Hindoos caught hold of the elephant's trunk and said: "An elephant is like a big snake."

Another blind Hindoo got hold of the elephant's tusk and he said: "An elephant is like a spear."

Another blind Hindoo got hold of the elephant's ear, and he said: "An elephant is like a fan."

Another blind Hindoo got hold of the elephant's leg and he said: "An elephant is like a tree."

The next blind Hindoo ran his hand over the big flat side and he said: "An elephant is like a wall."

And the last blind Hindoo, who took hold of the elephant's tail, said: "It is plain to be seen that an elephant is like a whip."

Now each of the blind Hindoos judged the whole of the elephant by the small part with which he came in contact; and each employee and stockholder in a big corporation is likely to judge the whole of the corporation by the small part with which he comes in contact.   —C. M. Ripley

SMALL CHANGE

Not long ago the worth of a man was reckoned at 98 cents —based on the value of the chemical content of his body. Now, with atomic power in view, this is all changed.

Some smart fellow—or wise guy—has figured out that the atoms in the human body will produce 11,400,000 kilowatts of power per pound. If they could be harnessed, that is. At $570 for that amount of power, a man who weighs in at 150 pounds is worth $85,500. All too often these days, the boss can't get enough energy out of a man to make him worth a day's wages.

—Convoy's News Roundup

This is a good opening to use for a salesmanager in addressing a group of salesmen when his main objective is to persuade them to exert more effort in selling.

Chapter Three

When The Speaker Is Introduced Without Warning

The inexperienced speaker is usually embarrassed whenever he is called on without previous warning. The examples given in this chapter are aimed to help such speakers to hurdle the hazards involved in uncomfortable situations forced on them by inconsiderate chairmen.

WHEN INTRODUCED WITHOUT WARNING

For the speaker who is called on without warning it is suggested that while making an effective impromptu speech is not an easy job, it is possible. When the chairman or toastmaster calls on you unexpectedly try to show composure and not nervousness.

Think about the situation and the people concerned and express a definite idea or two about them. This will get you started. If you have cultivated a few stories which seem appropriate, use them.

Cultivate the habit of knowing a few quotations from the writings of those men who knew human nature and institutions. The great speakers always quote them. There are gems for every occasion in the essays or writings of Emerson, Pope, Bacon, St. Paul and Shakespeare. "Bartlett's Familiar Quotations" is a valuable book which contains them all. He who would use quotations well should own a copy of this fine collection.

Don't talk too long. Try to tie your remarks together, and as you talk keep in mind a definite ending. Don't at any time make any suggestion of an apology. You are not called on for that reason, so don't indulge in it. Never say, "I did not expect to be called upon this evening."

THAT UNEXPECTED TALK

It is an unwise and unfair speech chairman who calls on a person to speak without warning him in advance and expects an adequate response. Likewise, it is only a novice in the field of speaking who attends such an occasion, and occupies an important place, in respect to the program, who does not anticipate being called on and does something about it. The truth is, the experienced chairman knows in advance whom he is going to call on and advises the speaker. Conversely, the experienced speaker anticipates in advance if he is likely to be called upon. So let it be set down as fundamental, that in the realm of public speaking there are few speakers called on unexpectedly, and, therefore, the typical impromptu speech is a rarity.

The remarks, on this subject, made over twenty years ago, in a radio speech, by Mr. Henry Roberts, a speech teacher, are still of interest. They have been repeated enough to have become a classic and are in no way trite, unless the Twenty-third Psalm is trite. Here they are in part:

"Now, have you ever heard a polished after-dinner speaker, a veritable magician with words, astound an audience with the brilliance of his wit, the penetration of his ideas; a skillful talker who made every phrase fit the occasion and who left the impression that he had waited until coffee had been served before giving the least thought to his remarks? You probably went away greatly impressed and not a little mystified at his uncanny ability to make a speech with little or no warning— what you called 'his ability to think on his feet.' Yet, you should have realized that the tricks of the impromptu speaker were probably quite simple once you got onto them.

"In the first place, that brilliant impromptu speech of the polished after-dinner speaker probably wasn't impromptu at all. Certainly, if every example of polished and effective impromptu speaking were analyzed, we would find that the speaker had, at one time or another, given considerable thought to his subject matter and had enjoyed such a long apprenticeship at the task of preparing speeches that he had been able to employ the short time at his disposal to the greatest advantage. Such a speaker has learned the first important lesson of thinking on your feet—only the occasion should be impromptu, not the thought . . . *

There are tricks to all trades and it is certain the adept impromptu speaker or the effective spur-of-the-moment speaker, if and when there is such a person, has mastered most of them. He has, in his storehouse of knowledge, material which serves a suitable response for various occasions. He may have a few good stories which are appropriate. In addition, he considers the occasion and the people concerned about which he makes a few remarks without getting off the track or losing a sense of terminal facility; that is, he doesn't talk too long. From experience he knows how to adapt his material to the occasion. He cuts his cloth to suit the pattern or better, he makes the punishment fit the crime.

*Quoted from speech, "Thinking On Your Feet," Henry G. Roberts "Effective Speaking For Every Occasion," Williard Hayes Yeager, Prentice-Hall.

SHE'LL DO THE TALKING

There was a man who went to a clairvoyant, for a seance. And after a while, after the usual meditation and concentration, and hand holding and table wiggling, the medium intoned: "Ah, at last, behold! Before you is the spirit of your late wife!"

And when the client just sat there, still and dumb-looking, saying nothing, the medium cried: "Don't you understand? It's your wife! Speak to her."

The gent replied: "Don't worry, feller. If that's her, she'll do all the talking." . . .

And that's about as good an alibi for not talking as any I can think of . . . Say, isn't that my wife there in the audience? . . .

—George A. Posner

NEVER BETTER PREPARED

(When a speaker is called on suddenly, without preparation)

When your chairman asked me to come up here and make a speech this evening, for the moment I was stunned. The idea, I thought, of asking me to come up to the platform and address such a distinguished gathering without any preparation.

Then as I wound my way through that maze of tables and chairs, my confidence came back. Heck, I said to myself, I never could give a speech at any time, preparation or no preparation.

Then I was reminded of the story of a rugged old settler out in Montana who made moonshine whiskey. There was a question of which member of the family, the settler or his wife, was the more addicted to drinking whiskey. So in order that he would be sure of getting his share of the brew, the old settler hid the jug out in the woods, where he journeyed frequently to quench his thirst.

One day, while the old settler was taking the cork off of his jug, he saw a big bear charging through the brush, directly at him. The old man hoisted the jug to his lips, took a healthy swig, and then turned and faced the bear. "Come on, you brute!" he yelled. "Come on and charge! I was never better prepared than I am right now!"　　　　—Hugh Lincoln

THE MISTAKE

Once, when asked to make a speech in England, John G. Winant stood in agonized silence for four minutes, then finally said, softly:

"The worst mistake I ever made was in getting up in the first place."　　　　　　　　　　　　　—Time

This item may be used when the speaker is caught off guard and is unable to express himself adequately. He realizes that the audience recognizes his predicament.

WHEN YOU GET IN A PINCH

Then there was the fellow who had taken a course in public speaking from a self-styled genius of the art. And one of the tricks of the trade this genius had taught him was this: "When you get in a pinch, always turn on Patriotism—speak of **your** country, **my** country—the heroes of history—then finally mention the flag. Rant and shout. The less you have to say, the louder you shout. On those topics, in loud tones, you're sure to get applause!"

Fine. He was well-equipped with a couple of sure-fire stories on patriotic topics which he had well memorized, but in the spot he was in that evening—called upon suddenly to talk on the subject of breeding **mules**—how could he fit **those** in? If it had only been **horses,** he could have brought in Paul Revere. But **mules!** So he thinks for a moment, inspiration strikes him, and he comes out with this:

"Mules are temperamental creatures, you know; and you know how temper will affect the digestion. So here we have a typical mule, in his typical mean tantrum, which brings on ulcers and gas in his alimentary canal. This gas rushes down to one end of the colon and is blocked there, and it rushes back to the other end, and is similarly blocked—back and forth, back and forth—and finally it is crying out, so to speak, 'Give me Liberty, or give me Death!'—the same expression used by our illustrious Patrick Henry. And speaking of Patrick Henry . . ."   —George A. Posner

KEEP YOUR MOUTH SHUT

At an evening function, a gentleman was unexpectedly called upon to make a speech. Obviously embarrassed, he arose and opened his remarks as follows:

"It is indeed kind of the chairman to have honored me by calling on me to speak. I must confess, however, that I am totally unprepared and I am reminded of a striking verse in the book of Jonah. You all remember the story and no doubt you remember Jonah's expostulation to the fish. To you, Mr. Chairman, I would quote Jonah's closing words to the fish: 'I wouldn't have been in this hole if you had kept your mouth shut.' "

—Rabbi de Sola Pool

THE WORST WAY

Being called on to speak by your chairman comes in the nature of a surprise. I came here today prepared to listen to everything you had to say, without saying anything you'd have to listen to.

But your worthy chairman has willed otherwise; he even intimated just a few moments ago that you wished to hear me the worst way. Well, probably that is how you will hear me.

At that, I trust your experience will prove more satisfactory than that of a man who recently entered a cheap restaurant and became thoroughly disgusted with the steak he had ordered.

After slashing it with a knife for ten minutes, he beckoned the waitress and said, "I can't make a dent in this doggone steak, and I'll be darned if I'll try any more. Take it out to the cook and tell him to ram it down the boss' throat."

The waitress gave the man a fishy stare and ankled off with the steak. Pretty soon she came back and said, "I'm sorry, mister, but you'll have to wait. There's two orders of pork chops ahead of you."

—James Madison

NO WARNING

(When the speaker has been called upon without warning)

There was a certain minister who stood up to give his sermon one Sunday, and found he had forgotten his notes. So he said to his congregation: "It seems I've forgotten my notes, so this time I shall have to rely on the Lord for guidance. Next time I'll come better prepared."

I'm afraid I'm a bit unprepared myself. And perhaps a little nervous. So you'll have to bear with me while I stall around until I can think of something to say.

Luckily the spot I'm in seems to have reminded me of a story or two of people in similar situations.

There's the case that occurred in a big Washington hotel recently. The speaker, it seems, was slated to go on in a little while, and he was walking up and down, lost in deep thought, when a woman entered the room. She asked him: "Is anything wrong?"

"Not a thing," he answered, rather acidly. "I'm supposed to go on and make a speech in the Banquet Room in a few minutes and I'm just mentally rehearsing my lines out here."

"Are you nervous?" she asked him.

"Of course not!"

"Then," said she, "What are you doing in the Ladies Room?"   —Arthur L. Kaser

WHO PUSHED ME?

(A response made by a college president)

A college president was called on by a chairman to say a few words. Upon responding he said he was reminded of a story which seemed appropriate.

"During a recent ocean voyage, a storm blew up and a young woman, leaning against the rail, lost her balance and was thrown overboard into the rough sea.

Before the ship could be halted, another figure plunged overboard into the water beside her.

To the astonishment of everyone, it was the oldest man on the cruise—an octogenarian. He held the girl above the water until a lifeboat picked them up.

That evening the old man was given a party in recognition of his bravery. "Speech! Speech!" cried everyone enthusiastically.

The old gentleman rose and looked around the gathering carefully. "I have just one thing to ask," he said testily. "Who pushed me?"

The president said, "I am not asking who pushed me into this vertical position, I am merely saying, don't push me into making a speech. I paid my way to this affair, which entitles me to hear some one else speak, not to hear myself. I am happy to be here." He sat down. He made an impression.

—V. Spencer Goodreds

NO WARNING

When the chairman calls on you to speak without a previous warning, one of the following tested retorts will "save the day" for you:

"See my agent and agree on a fee first!"

* * *

"Sorry I can't stay, but there's a sundial that needs winding."

* * *

"No speak English."

* * *

"They're converting to buses and I've got to catch the last streetcar."   —George Grim, News Commentator

YINGLE! YINGLE!

There are emergencies which bring out the speech in a man. There's the case of Svenson, who was running from a pack of officers. Svenson was a Swede, in case you don't get my dialect.

Well, he came running into the general store run by a friend of his, and shouted: "Hansen, old friend, vill you safe me? I'm running from the sheriffs, but I'm innocent, I svare! Hide me, kvick, Oley!" (Any resemblance between this dialect and Swedish is, of course, purely coincidental.)

So Oley looked around, and all he could figure out is to put Svenson into a big burlap bag, and tie up the top.

So in came the sheriffs, and they asked: "Did a big Swede run in here?"

And Hansen said: "No, on my honor, officers, I bane seen no one."

Then one sheriff saw the big burlap bag, he thought he saw it move, and said suspiciously: "What's in there?"

"Oh, yust sleigh bells," says Oley.

"That so?" says the officer, and delivers a big kick to the bag.

And from inside the bag comes: "Yingle, Yingle!!"

—George A. Posner

WORDS TO SAY

When your chairman called on me without warning, I feel that I am in the same position as the colored minister from down South who was about to address a large congregation of colored worshippers in Chicago. He asked the host pastor what he should say to the group and was advised to pray to the Lord for inspiration.

Whereupon he replied: "No, Bruther Johnson, it is not inspiration Ah needs, but words to say to your people."

—John Melton

NEVER COULD PLAY BEFORE

It is disconcerting to be called upon unexpectedly this way. The chairman says I am going to make a speech. He reminds me of the medical man who was attending a young man whose hands had been badly cut up. After his hands had been treated and bandaged, the young man looked them over and then asked the doctor:

"Doc, do you think I'll be able to play the piano when I get well?"

The doctor said, "Sure!"

"That's funny," the young man remarked, "I never could play before."

I don't know whether I am going to make a speech or not.

—The Kablegram

BREAKING IN SHOES

I am just like the average person who when called upon unexpectedly to "say something" feels about as comfortable as an individual breaking in some shoes for a friend.

—James Madison

DOING WHAT COMES NATURALLY

(When an individual is called on to speak unexpectedly.)

I am happy for the confidence placed in me, which allows you to call on me to say a few words.

The question which always arises in one's mind on such an occasion is, what shall I talk about? The reply one quipster made to the question was, "talk about a minute." In more specific language, or in the language of Franklin Delano Roosevelt to his son, "Be sincere, be brief, be seated." I can try to follow these three points.

Actually, I do not consider myself a public speaker, and yet when one hears some people speak with perfect ease and unusual appeal, speaking seems to be a simple matter.

I don't mean to moralize or instruct, but I am reminded of an incident, from the world of sports, about which I read, and which I think establishes my point.

"Some years ago 'Hoot Evers, the Detroit outfielder, was having a bad afternoon playing center field; he had made two or three errors. An enthusiastic fan jumped from his seat in the outfield bleachers, ran out into the field and stood next to Evers. He nudged him, and as the story goes, said, 'move over, I can play this position better than you.'"

That's about it. To the average fan after watching the smooth, easy play of Joe DiMaggio, playing the outfield, like many other things, it looked easy.

Ethel Barrymore talking to some young hopefuls of the theatre said, "Yes, acting appears to be easy. You watch an actress on the stage as she goes through her part, so gracefully and with such perfect naturalness that it looks easy. But that grace and naturalness is the result of years of training and practice in technique, and hard work. Yes, good acting appears to be the natural thing, the easy thing, but don't try it unless you are trained to be natural."

Yes, as the saying goes, "doing what comes naturally" is what it amounts to. Since I don't think speaking is easy and doesn't come natural to me, I am going to sit down and listen to the main speaker for whom it is, apparently, the natural thing.   —V. Spencer Goodreds

STATUS QUO

As the discussion has developed upon this topic of "Status Quo," I am reminded of a story which Irvin Cobb told in one of our evening papers the other day, of a debate held in a certain colored community upon "Status Quo," and somebody finally got up and asked the colored preacher who was presiding just what this status quo was. The gentleman thought and then said, "Well, brudder, status quo is de Latin name for de mess dat we'se all in."   —Francis H. Sisson

Chapter Four

To Counteract The Longwinded Introduction

The most disconcerting experience that a speaker can have is to be forced to wait while the chairman encroaches on his allotted time by never using his terminal facilities. The audience, too, will feel that they are being taken advantage of and will resent it. The speaker can usually win a sympathetic response from his listeners if he is able to use an effective and appropriate story or repartee.

TWO SPEECHES PREPARED

Recently a presiding officer began to introduce the speaker of the evening by starting out on a speech of his own. He consumed nearly one-half hour and incidentally made no reference to the principal speaker. When he had at last concluded, the principal speaker began by saying: "I have prepared two speeches for this evening. The chairman has already delivered one of them, and if you will bear with me I will attempt to give a brief resumé of the second one."

—Paul R. Brees

WHAT'S TIME TO A HOG?

It was in the hills of Kentucky that a traveler saw a farmer holding a pig in his arms so that the creature could eat the apples right off the tree.

"Won't it take a long time to fatten your hog that way?" asked the traveler.

"I suppose so," replied the farmer. "But what's time to a durned old hog?"

—Joe Miller

LONG-WINDED

Pardon me if I take a drink of water! It reminds me of the long-winded lecturer who had been holding forth for over an hour, except for brief pauses from time to time to gulp a hasty drink of water. Finally, during one such "intermission," an old man in the audience leaned toward his neighbor and announced in a loud whisper: "First time I ever saw a windmill run by water!"

—Mrs. E. G. Covington in Reader's Digest

LAVISH WITH TIME

Trapped with that painful bore, the master of ceremonies who hogs the limelight and most of the speaking time, former Vice-president Alben Barkley has been known to tell this one:

"Years ago when I was a county judge, I sentenced a chronic offender to 20 years in jail. 'I'm giving you 20 years because you deserve it,' I told him. 'Have you anything to say?'

" 'All I has to say, Jedge,' drawled the culprit, 'is that you sho' is mighty lavish with my time!' "

—Alben Barkley

35 MINUTES LATE

The rather lengthy introduction given to me tonight reminds me of the citizen who burst into the office of a railroad official and demanded: "I want you to give orders that the engineer of the express train that passes through Elm Grove at 11:15 be forbidden to blow the whistle on Sunday mornings."

The railroad official responded: "Why, that's impossible! Why do you make such an unreasonable request?"

"Well, our preacher preaches until he hears the train whistle blow—and that confounded express was 35 minutes late Sunday."

—John Sheldon

THE LONG-WINDED CHAIRMAN

This is how I would respond when introduced by the long-winded chairman.

"I wouldn't dare interrupt your utterly fluent chairman. Continue, sir." (You sit down to no applause at all.)

* * *

"There is just time for me to change my address. It is now 3485 Conostoga Boulevard. I thank you."

* * *

"May we all rise and drink a toast to your fulsome chairman?" (When everybody has stood up and, as they touch glasses, you slip out. When they sit down again—no speaker. The chairman then makes the speech.)

—George Grim, News Commentator

FOR POSTERITY

Ladies and gentlemen, for a few minutes I have been worried that the chairman had forgotten to introduce me. I am reminded of the political orator who was taking an exceedingly long time for his speech. He bellowed forth over his hearers' weary heads:

"I am speaking for the benefit of posterity."

"A heckler promptly shouted: "Yes, and if you don't be quick about it, they'll be along to hear you!"

—John Sheldon

KEEP YOUR MOUTH SHUT

"After a long-winded introduction, I tell about the mounted fish hanging over the doorway of an oil station with the inscription on it: 'If you'd only kept your mouth shut, you wouldn't be in this position.' "

—Judge Luther W. Youngdahl, Washington, D. C.

ENDURED FOREVER

As I listened to the rather lengthy introduction by your chairman, I was reminded of the experience of a well-known eastern judge who was visiting in California and went to church on Sunday even though he knew that the preacher had a reputation for being long-winded.

After the service the preacher met the judge in the vestibule and asked: "Well, your Honor, how did you like the sermon?"

"Oh, it was wonderful," replied the judge. "It was like the peace and mercy of God."

"Oh, I scarcely hoped to achieve that," said the preacher who was much flattered. "How can you make such a comparison?"

"Why, very easily. It was the peace of God, because it passed all understanding, and, like His mercy, I thought it would have endured forever."   —Henry Thompson

TRESPASSING ON ETERNITY

After a long-winded introduction, the chairman remarked to the speaker, "I hope I haven't been encroaching on your time."

When the speaker got up, he replied: "You may not have been encroaching on **my** time, but you certainly have been trespassing on Eternity!"

—Judge Luther W. Youngdahl, Washington, D. C.

HARDLY A CHANCE

I have often used this response when the chairman has used too much time in introducing me:

"I am in the position of the man who said, 'Last night my wife and I had words, but I didn't get a chance to use mine.' For a time it looked as though I wouldn't have a chance to use mine this evening."   —Dr. E. S. Hjortland

1170 DELAWARE AVENUE

The chairman insisted on making a speech. Then he thought it necessary to introduce two or three prominent citizens and each of these people indulged in extended remarks without purpose. Finally, with the audience tired and the hour late, the speaker who had been engaged for the principal address was introduced. The chairman took it upon himself to make a long-winded introduction, and concluded by saying, "We will now have the address of the distinguished gentleman."

The speaker arose and said: "My address is 1170 Delaware Avenue. Good night."   —V. Spencer Goodreds

THINK TO STOP

If I make my remarks brief, it is largely because I do not wish to duplicate an experience that recently befell a long-winded speaker.

After talking for over an hour, he finally brought his fist down on the table and inquired of the bored listeners, "Did you ever stop to think?" And a weary voice responded, "Did you ever think to stop?"

When a speaker holds the floor for too long a period, he is inconsiderate, totally unlike the young man who took his sweetheart to a roller rink and told the attendant to provide her with three skates.

She looked at him reproachfully as she remarked, "Why do I need three skates when I only have two feet?"

"Very true," said her sweetheart, "but you may not always be on your feet."   —James Madison

MY ADDRESS

I remember once when I was in politics, or I thought I was—one of my friends said I did not know I ever had been in politics—we had one of these occasions on which there was to be one of these preliminary addresses, and one of these preliminary gentlemen got the platform and held it, but when he finished finally I said, "I will now present Mr. So-and-So, who will give you his address." Mr. So-and-So arose and said, with some apparent heat, "My address is No. blank, 22d Street, New York City, where my train goes in fifteen minutes. Good night."

—William Howard Taft

A COMPLETE EXPLANATION

Last year right here in Washington I was at a banquet. There were about eight hundred big, successful business men from all over America present. They had been in convention for four days with three sessions per day, morning, afternoon, and night. They had ended this orgy of conferences, this debauch of meetings, with a banquet at this very hotel, in this very room. They had secured somewhere, I don't know where on earth they found him, a toastmaster. He was a curly wolf for oratory.

He put in half an hour at the beginning of this meeting telling these successful business men from all over America, who had been in convention for four days, with three sessions per day, what they were in Washington for! It would have been a dirty trick if he had let them go back home and never know what they came for. He knew, and he was a good sport and he could conceal it from them no longer, so he told them what they were in Washington for.

Having relieved their suspense and satisfied their curiosity about what had been puzzling them all the time they were in Washington, he proceeded to introduce speakers. He would put in twenty minutes introducing a speaker, and, when the speaker got through his few faltering and utterly negligible remarks, this fellow, in words of one syllable, for fifteen minutes would explain to the assembled morons what the man meant.

—Strickland W. Gillian

Chapter Five

When The Chairman Flatters
The Speaker

The chairman who uses honeyed phrases and flattering statements when introducing a speaker usually places him at a disadvantage. The audience expects more from the speaker than he is able to deliver—and is disappointed if they accept the chairman's remarks on their face value. It is important that a speaker be prepared to counteract the flattering statements with an appropriate story or illustration. The examples given in this chapter are aimed to supply the speaker with ammunition to protect himself against chairmen who take unfair advantage of him.

THE WRONG MAN

The flattering introduction that your chairman has given me tonight reminded me of the Irishman who died after a rather tempestuous existence. He was a mean Irishman, who got drunk often, never gave a cent to charity, never went to church and would beat up his wife and family whenever he drank to excess.

At his death, his wife decided to make a good showing and hired the best preacher in town to conduct the services. The widow with her young son Mickey took a front seat and the preacher, who had never known the deceased, began his sermon by explaining how the late deceased had been a model citizen, related his wonderful generosity and his beautiful home life, and how great the loss would be to the community.

This was entirely too much for the widow, who leaning over, nudged her son, and in a hoarse whisper said: "Mickey, take a look at the body in the coffin. I think we've got in on the wrong funeral."

—John L. Bacon

WHOSE DOG WAS IT?

(When a speaker is given credit for something that he didn't do.)

I certainly want to thank Bill Smith for that wonderful compliment that he just paid me. But I think that Bill is stretching a point, as I do not consider that my efforts were responsible for the success of the undertaking. In fact, I had little to do with it, which recalls a story:

One day last summer a decrepit old bum in tattered clothes, his personal belongings wrapped in a red handkerchief and dangling from a stick over the man's shoulder, was walking along Highway number 10. Following on the heels of the bum was a mangy dog, full of fleas and cockle burs. As the two replicas of dereliction progressed down the highway at a leisurely pace, a speeding automobile rounded the curve simultaneously with the mangy dog's decision to cross the road. The car struck the dog, abruptly finishing its existence.

The motorist excitedly stepped on the brakes, and when the car came to a screeching stop, he rushed out and approached the bum. "My good man," said the motorist. "I am awfully sorry. Will $15 help toward alleviating your sorrow?"

"Yes," said the bum. "It'll be sufficient."

As the car sped away over the hill, the bum looked down at the dead animal and said, "I wonder whose dog it was?"

—Horton Smith

I CAN HARDLY WAIT

It was a dinner commemorating the 25th anniversary of a college organization, and the toastmaster introduced the speaker with great fervor, stressing her years of faithful service to the club and eulogizing her ability and charm. Somewhat overwhelmed, the speaker faced the audience. "After such an introduction," she said disarmingly, "I can hardly wait to hear what I'm going to say."

—Adnelle H. Heskett, in Reader's Digest

BLIGHT ON THE BEAN

It is unfortunate that the chairman has given me such a flattering introduction. As you will soon discover, it is entirely unmerited. In fact, I am here tonight at a disadvantage because you see I am suffering from "keetactus." It's a strange malady and one that can only be controlled periodically. I've been afflicted with this disease a long time.

It's quite a universal disease, too. It strikes in many varied situations and conditions. I remember that I first discovered it years ago when I made a lecture trip through the West. One evening as I sat in the lobby of a hotel in North Dakota I engaged in a conversation with the owner and queried him about the status of the wheat crop in that area. "Well," he said, "the yield is normal south of here, but north of town the crop is a complete failure because of keetactus." Now that word was a new one to me; I had never heard it before. But rather than reveal my ignorance to him, I changed the subject.

Again in eastern Montana when I discussed the cattle raising situation with a rancher, the word popped up again when he commented: "Keetactus is certainly ruining the cattle business around here."

On this same trip when I visited a large irrigation project in Wyoming I heard the government engineer in charge assert: "I hope now that keetactus will disappear from this region as soon as this arid land is irrigated."

So I resolved to learn the definition of the word, keetactus, when I returned home. Associating it with something agricultural, I called one of my friends at the agricultural college. Even he couldn't give me the desired information immediately but said he would look it up and call me back. And when he did, I knew that I, too, had been afflicted with the same disease on that trip. In fact, I know that I am suffering from it tonight, for you see he defined the word as BLIGHT ON THE BEAN.

—Lawrence M. Brings

The effectiveness of this story lies in prolonging the details to create suspense until the surprise phrase is given at the end.

A LITTLE BULL

At a recent dinner Professor Robert Graham Caldwell of William and Mary College was introduced by a chairman who poured on compliment after compliment. The embarrassed professor said the introduction reminded him of the story of the three bulls—a big bull, a medium-sized bull and a little bull. As they trotted down a road together they passed a green field full of Conover model cows. After one look at these beauties, the big bull said "Good-bye" and jumped over the fence. The middle-sized bull and the little bull kept going until they reached another field full of Powers model cows. The middle-sized bull shouted "Farewell" and jumped over the fence. Then the little bull went on and on and on and on. . . .

The moral of this tale, Professor Caldwell explained, is that a little bull goes a long way.

—Fulton Oursler in Reader's Digest

EXAGGERATION

(Where the speaker fears the chairman has given him too elaborate and enthusiastic a build-up.)

If I thought I deserved all that, I'd go right home and ask my wife for more privileges . . . maybe even ask her to do the dishes.

No, I appreciated the introduction, of course, but I hardly think I deserved much of it. It was exaggeration; well meant, of course.

It reminds me of something that happened down in Texas —San Antonio. Incidentally, someone just said to me, "Won't it be something, when Alaska is finally admitted to the Union, and we're able to call Texas, 'The **Second Largest** State'?"

Well, it seems a Britisher who was stopping over for a lecture tour, found himself in a bragging competition with a native Texan in a hotel bar in San Antonio.

"Yes, you have some fairly large cities, in a manner of

speaking, you might say," said the Britisher, "like New York, with its grotesque skyscrapers—but where does it compare with dear ol' Lunnon, with its nine million souls?"

He continued: "And perhaps you have a few—but beastly few—theatres, like Radio City Music Hall. But where does it compare with our immense Palladium in dear ol' Lunnon?"

Again he continued, before the Texan could get a word in: "And maybe you have a bit of a slightly historic spot, as it were, like the Alamo, or your Texas bum steers; but where do they compare with our historic places like Lunnon Tower, and our big bully beef?"

By this time the Texan gave up, frustrated, beaten and disgusted. He got some of the hotel help aside and cooked up a scheme.

That night, when the Britisher had retired, he awoke presently with a great start of fright. He turned on the light and found a 200-pound turtle in between the bedsheets.

"Help! Help!" he screamed. "Confound it, let me out! What is this fantastic, infernal beast? Help!"

In came the Texan, the manager and a crowd of guests. And the Texan said to the Britisher: "Fo' heavens sakes, man, you're not afraid of one of our lil' ol' bedbugs, are you?"

—George A. Posner

ONLY THE DOG

Of course much depends upon the speaker's own experience and the situation but I have often told the incident when I went to my son's bedroom to see if he was asleep. As I leaned over him, he half awakened and put his arm around my neck and gave me a good squeeze. Then he woke up and saw me and said: "Shucks, I thought it was the dog." So it is that oftentimes an audience has high anticipation of what is to come but it suddenly drops down to a much lower level when hearing the speaker. I trust that your reaction to this wonderful introduction and my speech will not be the same.

—Dr. E. S. Hjortland

NO GENTLEMAN!

(Response to a flattering introduction)

Thank you, sir, for that nice introduction. Perhaps I deserve it. I hope so. I wonder if those present realize, however, that a nice introduction is little more than a matter of form. Let's say like the salutation, "Gentlemen," at the beginning of a letter.

I am reminded of a morning in our office when the big boss called his beautiful secretary over to him and said: "Miss Gittlepuss, I have a letter to dictate which, you may be interested to know, is to a law firm you used to work for. Ready?"

And when she had assented he began: "Messrs. Gottrox, Schmendrick and Schnook, Esquires; Gentlemen: . . ."

At which point his secretary interrupted with: "I beg to differ, Mr. Brown! I've been out with those three jerks, and not one of them is a gentleman!"

Yes, there are formalities. It seems you can't always call a spade a spade, nor an old rake an old rake.

Which reminds me of another letter which an irate—a very irate—gentleman dictated to his stenographer. It went:

"Sir: My secretary, being a lady, would never take down the letter I should write to you. I, being a gentleman, couldn't say what I think of you. You, being neither, ought to be able to guess it!"   —George A. Posner

AMAZING PERSON

Whenever the chairman exaggerates his introduction of me, I use one of these responses:

"This is an unexpected pleasure, not to have to make a speech. Let me resume my seat and we'll all enjoy the amazing person you just introduced."

*   *   *

"I suggest we all move to the windows and look to the heavens for what your chairman just described. Ought to be arriving any minute."

—George Grim, News Commentator

TELESCOPIC VIEW

I fear that the chairman has been viewing your speaker tonight through the wrong end of the telescope. His flattering remarks overestimate my record, experience and ability. Such exaggeration reminds me of the Texan who, on a visit to Chicago, asked what he thought of the stockyards, replied, "Why, we got brandin' corrals in Texas bigger'n this."

"What do you think of the imposing sky-scrapers of the Chicago skyline?"

"Why, man, we got tombstones down thar bigger'n them." Not to be outdone, that night they put a brace of snapping turtles in the Texan's bed. When he turned back the covers and asked what they were, he was told that they were Illinois bedbugs. He peered at them a moment and agreed, "So they are, but young'uns, ain't they?"   —Press Proofs

NOT UP TO IT

The introduction by your chairman has overwhelmed me. It is impossible to find words at this moment to respond to his flattering and unwarranted remarks. It is appropriate that at this moment I recall old Mike Monaghan, a melter in the open hearths at U. S. Steel.

Mike was the envy and idol of every man on his crew. He had a colorful and apparently unlimited vocabulary; half a dozen times a day, when something incurred his displeasure, he would sound off until the air in the shop became a deep and satisfying purple.

On this particular day, however, nothing at all had gone wrong. Mike and his crew were melting steel faster than it had ever been melted in those furnaces before, and they were out to set an all-time record. They would have done it, too, except for one of those freak things that come once in a lifetime. The roof of the Number Two furnace cracked under the strain, and the bricks came tumbling down into the melt. It ruined the steel, it ruined the furnace, and it ruined Mike's chance for a production record.

For a full minute he stood there, staggered by the enormity of his bad luck, while his men waited breathlessly for the great explosion—the one magnificent outburst—that would fully express his feelings, and theirs. His face grew red; his bull-neck swelled with rage; he rumbled; he sputtered. Finally, with a gesture of utter despair, he spoke at last:

"Fellows," he said, "I just ain't up to it."

—Benjamin F. Fairless

EXAGGERATION

Your chairman's very flattering introduction brought to mind an experience my wife had with our little daughter, Mary.

Mary was given to exaggeration and was often reprimanded for the fault. One day she came rushing into the house and cried: "I have just seen a big black bear out in the yard."

Her mother remonstrated but Mary asserted that she was not telling a lie and that she knew it was a bear because God had told her so. Thereupon she was sent upstairs to the dark closet for meditation, prayer and repentance. Upon her release, her mother inquired: "Does God still say it was a bear?"

"No," replied Mary, "it was a dog, but God said that when he first saw it, it looked so big that he thought it was a bear himself." —Dr. C. E. North

FLATTERY

Thank you for the flattering remarks. Flattery, however, sometimes pays off. I was on a crowded bus not long ago when two ladies pushed their way in. One said to the other, "I wish those good looking men would give us their seats." Seven of us stood up. —Arthur L. Kaser

GOOD APPEARANCE

(When the chairman compliments you on your good appearance . . . such as "You look wonderful")

I want to thank your chairman for that very kind remark of his pertaining to my appearance. He no doubt was referring to my tan, which I acquired on a recent vacation in the southwest. But remember a suntan is only skin-deep. However, this generous compliment recalls an incident that happened in Brooklyn a few years ago.

Mrs. Morris Ginsberg was called suddenly to her reward, and the funeral was a most lavish one. As her friends passed by the bier one by one all remarked how wonderful she looked, shrouded with the best dress on Fifth avenue, and the rest of her toilet in corresponding fashion. At the tail end of the line was Mrs. Goldberg, an old friend of the family, who stopped to console the widower. Mrs. Goldberg looked down at Mrs. Ginsberg, and then turned to Mr. Ginsberg and remarked: "Mama looks just darling."

The widower thought for a moment, and then replied: "Why shouldn't she? She's just been spending the entire winter in Cuba."   —Rome Roberts

PREJUDICED INTRODUCTION

I'm afraid the chairman may be a little unfair and perhaps a bit prejudiced, too. I'm reminded of the story of the prize fight in the Irish Free State, between an Irishman and a Britisher. You know an Irish Free Stater is a bit prejudiced, let's say, against a man from England—a Limey, I believe the last is called.

The Britisher had much the better of the Irishman for round after round, and finally in the sixth, he floored the Son of Erin with a terrific swat which seemed assuredly to have enough power to keep him on the floor for the fatal ten seconds.

The referee (who also happened to be an Irishman) counted

over him thus: "1, n-n-n! Mike for God's sake, get up! 2, ooh, ooh, ooh! Mike, are ye hurt? 3, ee, ee, ee! If ye have any regard for yer family, get up, Mike! 4, or, or, or! Don't you see the Limey laughing at you? 5, v-v-v-v! Mike, do ye hear me? 6, icks, icks, icks! For the love of the old country; for the love of old Erin, get up! 7, n-n-n! If you have any red blood at all in ye, get up, Mike! 8, t-t-t—that's the boy, Mike! Get up now and kill the Limey!

Mike finally staggered to his feet at the count of eight, which had been plenty more than eight seconds ought to be; and summoning all his strength, made a terrific lunge at his opponent, hitting him with enough force to knock him down; and the referee counted over him:

"1—2—3—4—5—and 5 is 10. You're **out,** you Limey!"

—George A. Posner

DISTURBING THE ATMOSPHERE

The flattering introduction just given me by your chairman recalls a remark made by the late Dr. Cyrus Northrup, the beloved president of the University of Minnesota for more than a quarter of a century.

Dr. Northrup was the guest speaker at a church meeting. The organist, a show-off, saw the doctor as he took his place on the platform, and proceeded to put the organ through all the musical gymnastics of which it was capable. Later in the evening, fishing for a compliment, he said: "Well, Dr. Northrup, what did you think of that for music?" The doctor replied, "Simply disturbing the atmosphere does not necessarily constitute music."

So, Mr. Chairman, your flattering remarks mean nothing more than just "disturbing the atmosphere" because it really doesn't guarantee to this audience that I'm going to deliver the kind of speech you expect to hear. However, I liked your introduction. You were most kind and I wish that Mrs. Conant could have heard it.   —Edward M. Conant

BIG LIAR

That was a very nice introduction. I only hope I can live up to all the nice things he said about me. There are some flattering remarks that should be taken with a grain of salt, but what our friend said about me—Well, I like it.

Sandy, a Scotchman, came home after an absence of several years and looked up his former sweetheart. He found that she was still unmarried, and sweet memories began to surge through his romantic Scotch brain. "Ah, Mary," he murmured softly, "Ye're just as beautiful as ye ever were, and I ha'e never forgotten ye, my bonnie lassie." "And ye, Sandy," Mary cried, "ye're just as big a liar as ever ye were, and I believe ye just the same as ever I did."   —Arthur L. Kaser

NOT AN ORATOR

I want to thank the chairman for his remarks. I surely appreciate his introductory phrases. I would also like to emphasize, ladies and gentlemen, the fact that I may be a speaker, but not an orator. There is a difference as explained by a colored friend of mine. He said, "I'll tell you what oratory is and ain't. If you says black am white, dat's foolishments. But if you say black am white, and bellers like a bull, and pounds de table with yoh fists, and stomps de floor with yoh feet, dat am oratory."   —Arthur L. Kaser

PLEASE, NO FLATTERY

I want to thank our chairman for those beautiful things he said about me. It reminds me of the judge who started to lecture the prisoner before delivering a severe sentence. He began, "This robbery was consummated in an adroit and skilful manner." The prisoner blushed and interrupted, "Aw, come now, our Honor. Please, no flattery."
          —Arthur L. Kaser

OVERWHELMED

The chairman was a woman. Her introduction of me was embarrassingly complimentary. The audience was fairly well aware of our friendship and mutual regard.

My response was a deliberate, thoughtful silence indicating not embarrassment, but rather one of having been overwhelmed. Then I said:

"Now I know. Now I'm sure of it. Woman was made to be loved; not to be understood."   —Hugo A. Carlson

I'M DEAD

Um! Well! That was something listening to those fine compliments. I kept thinking, "Either he's lying, or **I'm dead!**"
—George A. Posner

TOO BIG A HONK

After listening to the flattering introduction of your chairman I am unable to recognize the speaker he refers to. Certainly he has used his characteristic blarney in his remarks about me. Surely I don't deserve them.

As I sat here listening to his attempt to inflate me in your presence, I thought of the experience of the farmer who was leading a calf to market. He came to a bridge spanning a river but the calf refused to cross it. The farmer pushed the calf and pleaded and finally used a stick, but the calf refused to budge from its position.

After several minutes of effort, a motorist approached and gave several loud honks on his horn to clear the roadway. The farmer jumped aside, dropped his grasp on the calf's rope, and to his dismay the panic-stricken calf broke away, made a wild leap over the side of the bridge and fell into the river below. The unfortunate calf was drowned before it could be rescued.

The wise farmer summed up the entire situation with this comment which really applies to me today: "The honk was too big for such a small calf."   —Richard Drummond

SEND ME FOR ANOTHER PAIL

I do not have words to express the appreciation which I feel on this occasion. Had I the words I am sure I would not have the voice. Yet I feel that I ought to say a few words at least.

For some reason or other my mind goes back to an incident sixty-four years ago this summer. My mother had sent me to a nearby spring for a pail of cool water because we had company for dinner. When I returned Aunt Sally discovered pebbles in the bottom of the pail and asked me about them. I told her I put them there. I thought they looked nice. I said it was fun to see them go down through the water. She was not pleased and called my mother's attention to them.

My mother looked into the pail and then with sympathy toward me. I tried to explain. "I am sorry," she said, "but I know you meant all right." A moment later she handed me a piece of pie which somehow I could not eat just then.

I heard my aunt say on the side, "Sarah, you are certainly spoiling that child." Finally, my mother thought we needed another pail of water and told me to run and get it. This was my opportunity. I soon returned and this time without the pebbles. I could then enjoy my pie.

I cannot help thinking that if Aunt Sally were here tonight to hear all these praises and to hear not one word about my faults she would say right out, "All you bug educators, you are certainly spoiling that child."

The pail I brought you, up to this evening, has the bottom covered with pebbles. But, Mr. Chairman, I beg you to give me the chance my mother did—I do wish you would send me for another pail of water.   —J. W. Crabtree

This illustration of the narrative type of response indicates what a speaker may do when the introduction has been flattering or when he recognizes the sincerity of the tributes given him by previous speakers.

HERE ON MY OWN

I feel greatly honored that you should have invited me to enter the United States Senate Chamber and address the representatives of both branches of Congress.

The fact that my American forbears have for so many generations played their part in the life of the United States, and that here I am, an Englishman, welcomed in your midst, makes this experience one of the most moving and thrilling in my life, which is already long and has not been entirely uneventful. (Laughter)

I wish indeed that my mother, whose memory I cherish across the vale of years, could have been here to see. By the way, I cannot help reflecting that if my father had been American and my mother British, instead of the other way around, I might have got here on my own. (Laughter and applause) In that case, this would not have been the first time you would have heard my voice. In that case, I should not have needed any invitation; but, if I had, it is hardly likely that it would have been unanimous. (Laughter) So perhaps things are better as they are.

I may confess, however, that I do not feel quite like a fish out of water in a legislative assembly where English is spoken. I am a child of the House of Commons. I was brought up in my father's house to believe in democracy. "Trust the people"—that was his message. I used to see him cheered at meetings and in the streets by crowds of workingmen away back in those aristocratic Victorian days when, as Disraeli said, the world was for the few, and for the very few. Therefore, I have been in full harmony all my life with the tides which have flowed on both sides of the Atlantic against privilege and monopoly and have steered confidently toward the Gettysburg ideal of "Government of the people, by the people, for the people." (Applause)

I owe my advancement entirely to the House of Commons, whose servant I am. In my country, as in yours, public men are proud to be the servants of the state, and would be ashamed to be its masters. On any day, if they thought the people wanted it, the House of Commons could by a simple vote remove me from my office. But I am not worrying about it at all. (Laughter) As a matter of fact, I am sure they will approve very highly of my journey here—for which I have obtained the King's permission—in order to meet the President of the United States and to arrange with him for all that mapping out of our military plans, and for all those intimate meetings of the high officers of the armed services of both countries which are indispensable to the successful prosecution of the war.

—Winston Churchill

Prime Minister Churchill used this effective response to a flattering introduction when he was presented to a joint session of Congress in 1941.

THANK GOD FOR THE RUMOR

That was a very flattering introduction which reminds me of the story of Miss Lucretia Sproggs. Once rumor was widespread that Miss Sproggs, the perennial spinster, was at last engaged to be married. Shortly thereafter, her minister met her on the street and congratulated her heartily.

"Oh, dear," said Lucretia, "there isn't a word of truth to it, but thank God for the rumor!"

And so I say "there isn't a word of truth in the kind remarks of the chairman, but thank God for the rumor!"

—Dr. Harry Emerson Fosdick

FLATTERED BY GUEST

I was highly honored this evening. As I walked across the room on my way up to the head table, I heard a lady refer to me as a handsome man. That is quite an unusual statement. I am generally referred to as something else. To the best of my recollection I have only been called handsome by one other person, and that is my wife. Upon occasions — occasions when she needs money, she brushes up to me and in a challenging voice, says: "Handsome — hand some over."

—Rome Roberts

AIN'T HE PLAIN?

Your chairman has certainly been flattering in his introduction which reminds me of the old lady who had always hoped that some day she would see a hippopotamus. At last her wish came true when a traveling circus came to town with a hippo as its main attraction.

The old lady bought a ticket and rushed in to see the animal that had always awed her. She gazed at him for a moment and then exclaimed, "My, ain't he plain!"

I believe that you are going to deprecate your chairman's introduction after you've listened to me for a few minutes and you'll be saying, "My, ain't he plain!"   —Arthur L. Kaser

BECAUSE OF THE FIRST ONE

Just after the war, I was in England, and I met a soldier one day, who was decorated with medals from one shoulder to the other, and I said, "Now, there is some great distinguished man whom I must meet and get his history," and going up to the man, I asked him if he would mind telling me the circumstances that led to all these honors that he possessed, and he said he would do so with pleasure.

He said, "Now, this one, the first large medal that you see on my left, I received by mistake, and I have had all the others given to me because I had the first one."

—Charles M. Schwab

This response was used by Mr. Schwab after he had received a very laudatory introduction and it had the effect of establishing a happy communication between the speaker and the listeners. The speaker had deflated himself and began his address in a modest manner.

Chapter Six

When The Speaker Arrives Late

The speaker can be placed in an embarrassing situation whenever he arrives late. The chairman will be perturbed and is obliged to make excuses to the audience while patiently waiting for the speaker to make his appearance. Moreover, the audience becomes impatient and the speaker must begin his address under unfavorable circumstances. These examples may be helpful to the speaker in overcoming the handicap.

ON TIME

They say Lincoln once borrowed a horse from a livery stable to attend a political convention in a town some thirty miles away. Unknown to Lincoln, the livery stable owner was a political adversary, and he gave Abe a very slow horse, hoping he would be late for his mission.

But Abe made it on time, and when he returned the horse, he said to the livery stable owner: "You keep this horse for funerals, don't you?" And when the stable owner denied it, Lincoln said:

"I'm glad, because he'd never get the corpse to the grave in time for the Resurrection."   —George A. Posner

NO CHANCE TO TALK

Speaking of being late—you know I never bother to invent any story or alibi when I get home late at night. I figure this way: "If the wife's asleep I won't need one; and if she's awake I won't get a chance to talk."   —George A. Posner

91

A CHANCE TO LEAVE

This reminds me of a fellow who was always late for work because he had a hard time getting enough sleep. He roomed downtown, and complained that the bright lights and the neon signs blinking on and off kept him awake.

Finally his friends got together and bought him a set of heavy draperies for his windows, got him a sleepshade to wear over his eyes, and wax ear stoppers to shut out the noises.

It seemed that ought surely to do it. But what happened?

We were hard at work in the office, when he came dashing in—late again, but bright and chipper. "Gee, I had a wonderful night's sleep!"

In a few minutes the boss came in and said: "Roger, you're fired!"

"But, boss," he expostulated, "look. I'm only six minutes late today. That isn't so bad!"

"Yes," returned the boss. "But where were you yesterday and day before yesterday?"

Late speaker: "I won't apologize for being late. Let's put it this way—you had your chance to leave, and you muffed it."

—George A. Posner

HE MADE IT

I regret that my train was so late that I barely arrived here in time for your chairman to introduce me. I realize that the sponsoring committee must have been pretty worried that I wouldn't make it. I am reminded at this moment of the woman who was driving on a highway at 70 miles an hour.

She happened to look into her rear view mirror (by accident, of course) and saw a traffic cop chasing her. She thought she'd shake him by increasing her speed up to 80, but when she looked into the rear view mirror later on she saw two speed cops after her. Then she shoved down on the accelerator and got up to 80. They were still there on her tail, however.

Suddenly she spotted a gas station, pulled to a stop, and dashed into the room marked "Ladies."

When she came out the cops were still there. Without batting an eye, the lady said coyly: "I'll bet you thought I wouldn't make it."
—George A. Posner

FORGET TO TURN AROUND

The cutest alibi I ever heard regarding being late was that of a private in my company in a training camp on one of those vast plains in Texas.

He was up on the carpet one morning, and asked to explain why he was late for reveille.

"I wasn't late at all," said he. "In fact, I had been up at least an hour before reveille, enjoying the sunrise. I found I had lots of time to take a walk in the woods. So I walked, and pretty soon I decided to light up my pipe. The wind was blowing pretty hard toward me, so I turned my back on this breeze to shelter the match while lighting up. Then I continued my walk. And presently, I decided to turn around and return to camp for reveille.

"And do you know, suddenly I found I was miles away? I had forgotten to turn around again after lighting my pipe!"
—George A. Posner

THE WRONG DIRECTION

A Negro, who was late for work, was asked what had detained him.

"Ah was kicked by a mule, sah," he replied.

"Well, being kicked by a mule shouldn't have made you late," said his boss.

"Ah know, sah," said he. "Ah wouldn't have been late if de mule had kicked me dis way—but he kicked me in de wrong direction!"
—George A. Posner

SORRY TO BE LATE

"Sorry I'm late but they're counting proxies today to see who runs the next train."

*　*　*

"Pardon my tardiness, but I thought a group like yours would meet in a better hotel than this. I tried the others first."

*　*　*

"Sorry, but they didn't flash the lights in the bar until 30 seconds ago."

—George Grim, News Commentator

Chapter Seven

When The Speaker Disagrees
With the Chairman's Point Of View

Usually the experienced chairman can control the audience situation and exercise his parliamentary perogatives which can place the speaker in a difficult position if he wishes to object to the chairman's point of view. It is important that in such a situation that the speaker be fortified with material that will help to switch audience support to him. These examples are intended to aid the speaker in such a situation.

WRONG POINT OF VIEW

(When the chairman has misjudged or has the wrong slant on the speaker's intent.)

I don't think the chairman got quite the right slant . . .

There was a man who had been a house guest at his friends place for a number of weeks before Christmas and his host was beginning to tire somewhat of the visitor. There can be too much of a good thing, even in the matter of a good friend's visit. So the weary host looked around for some means of getting rid of the fellow without offending him.

After remarking about the nearing holidays, he said: "Don't you think, old fellow, that your wife and your children will want you to be with them during Yuletide?"

The guest shook his host's hand, and in a voice filled with emotion, said: "Thanks awfully for the invitation—I'll send for them at once."

So I say there are a number of ways of looking at any given subject, and it is possible to get a wrong slant. We must watch that.

—George A. Posner

IT'S THE POINT OF VIEW

One man's meat may be another man's poison. And what's sauce for the goose may be apple sauce for the gander.

I am reminded of some lines in a zany act by those clever comedians, Martin and Lewis which, possibly unintentionally, contained some good serious reasoning.

Dean Martin straight-lined: "Let's sing some romantic songs."

And Jerry Lewis replied: "O.K. Let's sing, 'Hold that Tiger.'"

Said Dean: " 'Hold that Tiger' isn't a romantic song."

And Jerry answered: "It is to another tiger!"

Yes, it's all in the point of view.

—George A. Posner

WHERE'S THE DOG?

There are, of course, more ways than one of looking at most subjects, and it all depends on the point of view as to what is logical to deduct from a given circumstance. And just a little bit of added evidence can change things completely, as is often exemplified in real life as well as detective stories.

A woman had invited some friends over for a steak and mushroom dinner. When the cook opened a can of mushrooms for the sauce she was troubled at the appearance of a slight scum at the top of the can.

Time was short, so the lady said: "Try it on the dog, and if he likes it, it's probably all right."

Since the dog gobbled it and begged for more, that seemed to settle the matter and the dinner proceeded.

When dinner was over a white-faced cook gestured to the hostess from the kitchen, then whispered the dread words: "The dog is dead!"

There was but one thing to do, and the lady did it . . .

When the doctor had packed his stomach pump and departed, and eight guests lay around in various stages of recovery, the lady wearily asked her cook: "Where's the dog?"

"Lying outside where he fell when the auto hit him," she answered.

—George A. Posner

POOR WOMAN

A housewife, answering a ring at her door, found a gent with moist eyes who said: "I'm collecting for a poor woman and her children living on this block. She has no coal and no money to buy any, and they're freezing." He paused to wipe his eyes. "And the poor things have no dough to buy groceries. They haven't eaten for days; neither she nor her three kids. But worst of all, she hasn't paid her rent for three months and is about to be evicted. You could help, if only to pay the rent and keep a roof over their heads."

The housewife began to cry, too. And she said: "That was surely sweet of you to take it upon yourself to collect the money for this poor woman. Who are you?"

"I'm the landlord," the man answered.

—George A. Posner

NERVE CONTROL

There is a story of a town in the wild and woolly West where bedlam was reigning; guns blazing all over the place. But one mild gent came in the door, sauntered nonchalantly across to the bar and ordered a drink. Then he began to sip it leisurely while the bartender ducked back under the counter.

Soon the shooting died down, and then the bartender came out of hiding and began to congratulate the quiet man on his remarkable nerve control.

"Oh, podner, that was nothing," said the nonchalant one. "I'm quite safe. I owe everybody in the place money!"

—George A. Posner

THE PAINTER

There was a friend of mine who came home one day and found the painter he had hired, had done a beautiful job of painting his apartment.

So well pleased, indeed, was my friend that he told the painter, "You've certainly done a conscientious and thorough job. Here's an extra ten spot—you go and take the missus to a show and dinner."

The happy painter thanked him and departed, but a couple of hours later, the bell rang, and there was the painter back again, dressed to the hilt in a new suit, and with a box of candy in one hand and a bunch of flowers in the other.

"What's all this?" asked my friend.

"Don't you remember?" returned the painter. "You told me I could take your wife to a show."

—George A. Posner

NOW YOU KNOW

A young couple had received many valuable wedding presents when they wedded and established themselves in a new home in the suburbs.

To top their joy, they received, a day or so later, two tickets to a very popular and very-difficult-to-get-seats for a musical show in town, with the single line: "Guess who sent these."

The pair had much amusement in trying to identify the donor, but gave it up. They attended the theater and had a delightful time. On their return, late at night, they again took up trying to guess the identity of the unknown host, as they approached their home. But they remained pleasantly baffled. Then they entered their home and found it stripped of every article of value. On a bare table in the dining room was a piece of paper on which had been written in the same hand as the enclosure with the tickets: "Now you know!"

—George A. Posner

POINT OF VIEW

I'm thinking of a certain character who was brought up before a judge. The judge said:

"You say you've never been up before me? Well, your face looks very familiar to me. I'd say you're one of those habitual offenders—always in bad company, always in trouble—and I'll wager my robe I've seen you often."

His gaze then went into the ceiling in fixed contemplation, when the prisoner spoke up:

"Yes, Your Honor, you see me every day—I'm the bartender in the saloon across the street."

Yes, get the facts, by all means. They may mean a lot.

—George A. Posner

NOT WARM

Yes, just a bit of additional evidence or knowledge when added to what we already have can make a whale of a difference. A certain business man who often went on long business trips suspected that one of his office force was cheating on him, leaving before the customary five o'clock.

One afternoon he returned unexpectedly, and it seems he found his suspicions confirmed.

The next morning he called the offender to his desk, and the remaining members of the office force were treated to something like a shock as they heard him tell her:

"Miss Smith, I came into your office at five o'clock last evening and felt your seat and it wasn't even warm."

—George A. Posner

EXPENSIVE CIGARS

Another friend of mine (and I have a few characters among them, but God bless 'em, I love them) went to his fiancee's house and found a derby hat in the closet.

"Oh, that?" she shrugged. "That goes with my riding habit."

Then one day he found a walking stick in the hall.

"That?" she sniffed. "Used it once when I sprained my foot."

And later he found a Corona-Corona cigar in the ash tray.

When he told me the last, I asked: "Oh, oh, that was the end, eh?"

"You bet," he said firmly. "I sure don't want any girl like that—one that smokes such expensive cigars!"

—George A. Posner

Chapter Eight

Replies To Misinformation
And Exaggerated Statements

Whenever a chairman becomes over-enthusiastic in his praises of the speaker he may indulge in exaggeration and misstate the biographical facts and accomplishments of the speaker. Usually the audience will recognize the inflated statements and will respond to the speaker when he sets the record straight. The examples included in this chapter are selected to help the speaker to fortify himself with appropriate illustrative material to counteract the misinformation.

EXAGGERATION

Whenever the chairman misstates the facts about me, I have often used the little story of the speaker who highly altered the facts.

A certain speaker had a tendency to be carried away by his own emotions. Frequently he would handle the truth rather carelessly because of his intense feeling about a subject. His wife admonished him to be careful.

He said, "I get so excited and enthused I cannot control myself."

So she said, "Tonight when you are speaking and I note that you have exaggerated, I'll raise my hand and warn you," which he said would be agreeable.

That evening he was describing a visit to a large city and told of a big building he had seen. He said: "It was two thousand feet high." His wife, sitting in the back of the audience, immediately raised her hand. He saw it, and immediately said: "and the building was two feet wide."

This is the danger of trying to bring together too generous an expansion of the facts with the sudden reduction of them to a more reasonable size. —Dr. E. S. Hjortland

WHY KNOCK?

Your chairman was certainly frank and outspoken in his introduction of me. He omitted nothing in the information he gave you about my past life. All the details were given. But he forgot the most important part. He neglected to announce my subject. It reminds me of a story.

A man had just been admitted to the hospital when there came a sharp knock on the door of his room. He called, "Come in," and a snappy little woman entered. "I'm your doctor," she said. "Take your clothes off, please."

"All of them?" he asked.

"All of them," she said.

So he took off his clothes, and she examined him: nose, throat, chest, stomach, thighs, feet. When she had finished, she announced briskly, "You may get into bed. Do you have any questions?"

"Just one," said the patient. "Doctor, why did you knock?"

—Arthur L. Kaser

WHAT'S IN A NAME?

On vacation last summer we stopped for gasoline in a lonely mountainous section. When the proprietor responded to our horn, two bright-faced little girls came with him.

"What are your names?" my wife inquired.

They giggled, but wouldn't answer. Whereupon their father said: "That's Hassie Maude there. Lucy Jewel's the little one."

"Family names, I guess?" my wife said.

"Yes, ma'am," replied their father. "An' we got a newborn one in the house—came last week. Wife's gettin' fancy about names," shaking his head to show he'd never understand women, "an' she's callin' this one Lois."   —J. M. MacDonald,

The Training School, Vineland, N. J.

This story may be used when the speaker's name is not given or pronounced correctly.

ERRORS

(When the chairman is in error concerning the speaker's name, or other facts)

(After correcting the error.) "That's all right. We all make mistakes. This isn't nearly as bad as some I've come across. Yes, it could have been much worse."

A man named McGuire, a member of my lodge, made a business trip back East last summer. It seems this fellow is rather quiet by nature, not given to much bragging about his personal business, and so when he returned, there was a good deal of talk and speculation going on among the other members of the lodge as to the results of the trip. McGuire, taciturn Irishman that he was, said nothing, and this only served, of course, to pique the curiosity of his fellows all the more.

Finally a few of them got him cornered at the cocktail bar, and one of them said to him pointblank:

"Ah, McGuire, old fellow, we hear you made forty thousand dollars in a big business deal in Chicago on your trip East!"

"Where did you hear that?" quietly returned McGuire.

"Oh, the talk's going all around here. You can't deny it, can you? 'Fess up!"

"Well," said McGuire, "the story is substantially correct. Yes, substantially correct, outside of a couple of details. First, it wasn't Chicago, it was Minneapolis. And it wasn't forty thousand dollars; it was four thousand dollars. And also, I didn't make it—I lost it."

One stormy day, when time came for the kids to go home from school my boy's teacher saw him struggling to get into a pair of rubber galoshes. And after noticing that he had a bad time with them, his teacher came to the rescue. She pushed and pulled for several minutes, and as Churchill might have put it, it was almost a case of "blood and sweat and tears" before she finally got them on his feet. Then he thanked her and said: "Oh, by the way, teacher, did you know, these aren't mine?"

So the poor harassed woman groaned, set the boy down, grabbed hold of his feet and struggled until she got those galoshes off again.

"Now then," said she. "Who do these belong to?"

"My brother," explained my boy, "but my mother always makes me wear them."

A man rushed into a saloon and asked the bartender: "Quick, tell me how to stop a case of hiccups!"

The bartender without a word grabbed a big wet bar towel and slapped it smack across the man's face.

The fellow sputtered and gasped, half stunned, and when he could get his breath, asked: "What the devil did you do that for?"

"Well, you haven't the hiccups now, have you?" said the barkeep.

"It ain't me; it's my wife outside!"

Oh, there have been worse, more embarrassing mistakes.

For instance, when we were going to have our new minister for dinner, my wife thought she ought to give our little girl a few instructions ahead of time.

So she told her: "Now, darling, if he asks your name, tell him Betty Jane; and if he asks how old you are, remember it's five years. Then he'll probably ask, who made you, and of course in reply to that, you say God made you."

It turned out the clergyman did ask those questions—don't they all?—but he didn't ask them in that order, and there was the rub.

To the first two Betty replied correctly, but when he asked the other: "Who made you?" she hesitated and then said:

"Mummy did tell me the man's name; but, gosh, I've gone and forgot it!"

And speaking of that, reminds me of the woman who was confessing her sins to a priest one day. Said she: "I'm afraid

I'm guilty of the grevious sin of vanity. Each morning I stand before the mirror and keep thinking: 'What a beautiful creature I am!'"

"Is that all, daughter?" asked the priest.

"Yes, father," was her reply.

"Then be troubled no more, and go in peace," said the confessor. "For to be mistaken is surely not to sin."

—George A. Posner

WRONG INFORMATION

After listening to the lengthy introduction your chairman has given me tonight I am compelled to set him straight on the incorrect information he has given you about me. I am thinking of two men who had been boyhood chums that illustrates what I mean. They had not met for a number of years but chanced to be passengers on the same train and the following dialogue took place between them:

"Hello, Jim. How are you?"

"Oh, pretty good. You know I got married."

"That was good."

"Oh, not so good! My wife has nine children."

"That was bad."

"Oh, not so bad. She has a million dollars also."

"That was good."

"Oh not so good. She won't spend any of it."

"That was bad."

"Oh, not so bad. She had a nice house. I have no rent to pay."

"That was good."

"Oh, not so good. It burned down last night."

"That was bad."

"Oh, not so bad. My wife burned up with the house."

—Parkman B. Flanders

A HARD BLOW

The introduction given me by your chairman certainly flatters my ego but I'm afraid he has exaggerated many of the statements he made about my achievements. While listening to him tonight I recalled an experience I observed a few weeks ago while traveling on a Pullman to the West Coast.

A group of chamber of commerce boosters from Kansas City boarded our train and began to praise their city to a New Yorker who sat beside me, telling him of its beautiful boulevards, large industrial concerns, and its wonderful possibilities for growth. Finally the New Yorker became disgusted and said that the only thing that would improve their city would be to make it a seaport.

The enthusiastic Kansas Citians laughed at him and asked how they could make it a seaport, being so far from the ocean.

"That would be easy," he replied. "The only thing that you will have to do is to lay a two-inch pipe from your city to the Gulf of Mexico. Then if you fellows can suck as hard as you can blow you will have it a seaport inside half an hour."

—Charles Sheldon

MORE LIGHT AND LESS NOISE

The chairman has outdone himself tonight with his eloquent and enthusiastic introduction of your speaker. However much I do appreciate his remarks, which certainly have inflated me and no doubt have caused you to wonder what kind of a speaker I really am, it reminds me of a favorite Lincoln story:

"Some years ago, there was a gentleman traveling through Kansas on horseback. There were few settlements and no roads, and he lost his way. To make matters worse, as night came on, a terrific thunderstorm arose, and peal on peal of thunder, following flashes of lightning, shook the earth or momentarily illuminated the scene.

"The terrified traveler then got off and led his horse, seeking to guide it as best he might by the flickering light of the quick flashes of lightning. All of a sudden, a tremendous crash of thunder brought the man to his knees in terror and he cried out:

"'Oh, Lord! If it's all the same to you, give us a little more light and a little less noise!'" —Sheldon Brown

REGARDING MISUNDERSTANDINGS

The worthy chairman seems able only to see the material aspect of things; overlooking the fact that there are also spiritual values. And it's not so uncommon these days, is it? It reminds me of a certain character in my home town. The minister met him on the street one day and said to him: "Good morning, Mr. Jadorah. I haven't seen you in church for quite some time. What's wrong?"

"Oh," answered the worthy. "You know I haven't been working for a long time. And my clothes were getting so ragged, I was ashamed to go to church that way."

"Oh, my dear man," answered the minister. "You know the Lord doesn't look at the outward appearance; he looks within."

"Yes? Well, my underwear's just as bad."...

For the life of them, a lot of people can't see anything but the material side!

———

There was a traveling salesman who late one night knocked on a farmhouse door, and asked if he could stay over for the night. And the farmer said: "We're pretty crowded here, but if you wouldn't mind sleeping with the red-headed schoolteacher..."

To which the traveling salesman interrupted: "I'm sorry, but I'm not sleeping with any red-headed schoolteacher; I'm a gentleman!"

And the farmer answered: "So's the red-headed schoolteacher!"

So let's not be so quick in jumping at conclusions, eh? We could be wrong! —George A. Posner

WHITE LIES

(When the chairman has exaggerated the speaker's virtues)

Well, if the chairman's description of me is correct, my wife would have shot me long ago—too good for this world!

No, I'm afraid I'll have to say his description of me was, well, a little exaggerated.

It reminds me of my little daughter. She's rather scared of thunderstorms. So I took the trouble of explaining to her one day that thunder was nothing to worry about—it was just the noise the angels made when they went to bed; taking their shoes off and dropping them on the floor!

So one morning, after a storm, she said to me: "Daddy, I didn't mind the angels making all that noise dropping their shoes on the floor, going to bed. But what made me nervous is when they couldn't decide whether to turn the lights off or on!" . . .

So that gave me something else to work on. . . . Anybody got any suggestions?

———

Funny thing is, I've been bawling **her** out for exaggerating things. She came running into the house the other day, all out of breath, shouting: "Oh, Daddy, Daddy, I was passing the Jones house down the street just now, and a great big lion came out of the place, tried to jump on me, and then chased me home!"

I said: "Now you know very well that wasn't a lion! It was that big, yellow dog of theirs, and he wouldn't hurt a fly! How many times have I told you, you've got to curb that imagination of yours, of exaggerating everything? Now you go right upstairs and pray to God to forgive you."

So she went upstairs, and all was quiet for a while. A little later she came downstairs again, and I asked: "Well, is everything all right now?"

"Oh, yes," she replied. "When I prayed to God, He said: 'Oh, that's all right, dear; that dog was so big, for a minute I thought he was a lion, too!' " . . . So what can you do?

Oh, the little white lies have their uses. We just don't want to get **color blind!** Sometimes there are repercussions, too. Things turn out a little different than we anticipated. They work out with a little "reverse English," as it were.

A certain chap I know is of a careful and frugal nature. While dining at his Athletic Club he once lost a hat—oh, some of us still wear them.

So next time he stuck a note in a prominent place on his new Stetson as he put it on the hat rack. The note read: "The owner of this hat is a member of the boxing team and can deliver a knockout blow of 250 pounds. I shall return in a few minutes."

As an additional precaution, while dining, he sat in a chair facing the hat rack.

So what would happen, but some beautiful female passed, and his gaze was diverted for a few moments (even as would you and I!)

And when he returned to the rack, the hat was gone! And in its place was a ragged, beat-up top-piece, which he couldn't wear anyway, even if it had been wearable, because it was two sizes too small. And to top that, a sign on it read: "The owner of **this** is a member of the track team, and can do a mile in two minutes flat. I shall not return."　　　—George A. Posner

PRUNES WILL BE SERVED

"Once in Virginia," said a speaker who had received an introduction that promised more than he felt he could deliver, "I passed a small church displaying a large sign. It read: 'Annual Strawberry Festival' and below in small letters, 'On account of depression, prunes will be served.'"

　　　　　　　　　　　　　　　　—Boston Transcript

WRONG NAME

It is easy for any chairman to make an exaggerated statement that does belie the facts. After listening to your chairman's introduction, I recall the little old lady was having lunch with her granddaughter in the diner of a crack extra-fare express.

Hearing the waiter address by name a distinguished looking man across the aisle, she grew greatly excited, seized a menu, and murmured to her granddaughter, "I'm going to get his autograph." After a few words with the celebrity, the little old lady came back triumphantly, whispered, "I got it," and settled to her soup.

Presently, with a courtly bow towards grandmother, the man left the car and granddaughter inquired, "What did you say to him to get his autograph?"

"Oh," beamed grandmother, "I just told him how much our Chrysler car means to us and how pleased I was to make his acquaintance and he gave me his autograph right away."

Granddaughter had the grace to be silent, for the name written on grandmother's menu was "Fritz Kreisler."

—Orville E. Reed, in **Readers Digest**

Chapter Nine

Humorous Responses By Speakers

Audiences always rate a speaker on the basis of his ability to respond effectively to an introduction. There is no doubt that the humorous type of response always has a tendency to win an immediate audience reaction. It is essential, however, that the treatment be apropos for the occasion so that it will appear that the response is impromptu and spontaneous. It is advisable, therefore, that the speaker have a storehouse of appropriate material on hand. It is hoped that the responses given in this chapter will help speakers to build up a good library of adaptable numbers.

A B C's

I think you understand that I have been in the Office of Education only a very short time. I arrived in Washington just four weeks ago today. I have already discovered what the Washington whirligig is.

People frequently ask me what the Office of Education is and what it does, and so on. I have some notions about it, but I always have to say that because of the fact that I have come here so recently I am reminded of the story of the young lad, a little ragmuffin, who entered one of our schools in Des Moines, Iowa, where for fifteen years I was Superintendent of Schools.

The principal was trying to find out how to enroll him in the grades. She asked him questions and finally she said, "Young man, do you know your A B C's?" He said, quick as a flash, "Thunder, no, I have only been here three minutes!"

So I hardly know my A B C's about the work of the Office of Education.   —Dr. John W. Studebaker

INTELLIGENT AND WELL-EDUCATED

Mr. President and Gentlemen:

I was out in my old home about nine months ago, and I heard an after-dinner speech there by a gentleman who had some trepidation in making it; and he said he had consulted a friend of his, who had had a great deal of experience in making after-dinner speeches, which friend advised him that the best kind of audience to address, as an after-dinner speaker, was an audience intelligent and well-educated but half tight. (Laughter and applause) Now, all I can say is that this audience is one of the best audiences I ever saw for an after-dinner speaker. Something has made up for the absence of that element that the remark implied (applause), and I must think it is the spirit of the Metropolitan Life Insurance Company.

—William Howard Taft

In this response, Mr. Taft not only gives a humorous twist in his introduction but at the same time he compliments his audience for their attention.

MAKE A DIVE FOR IT

Because of the nature of my technical subject it will be necessary for me to indulge in the use of technical terms, charts, and statistics. For some of you this may be rather boring, but I have no choice in the matter.

I am reminded of the elderly college professor who had gone to the campus pool for a swim. As he was about to jump in a young female student standing at the pool accidentally dropped her compact into the water. There were several young fellows in swimming, but she called to the professor to rescue it for her.

Surprised, he said, "I'll be glad to dive for it, but why haven't you asked one of the young fellows who can do it much quicker?"

The young lady looked at him coyly and said, "Professor,

you don't remember me, but I'm in that large class of yours in statistics, and I know that you can go down deeper, stay down longer, and come up drier than anyone I know."

—Arthur L. Kaser

MIDNIGHT LUNCH

I'm rather surprised at being called on, because I came here today prepared to listen to everything you had to say and say nothing you'd have to listen to.

However, I shall not dodge my responsibilities, but inasmuch as your worthy chairman is the guilty wretch who has inflicted me upon you, I shall relate a little incident that occurred last August at a fashionable summer hotel, where he and I both arrived at the same time.

This was a very stylish hotel, the ladies changing their costumes for every meal. For breakfast they came down in ankle dresses, for dinner in knee dresses, while for supper they came to the table attired in bathing suits.

The first evening about eleven o'clock I noticed our worthy chairman hovering around the dining-room doors, and when I asked him the reason, he told me he was hoping they'd serve a midnight lunch.   —James Madison

AGAINST IT

In addressing you on my subject tonight I will endeavor to be brief and all the gingerbread will be omitted. In fact, I will try to follow the example of one of our former presidents of the United States, Calvin Coolidge. One Sunday he went to church alone and when he returned Mrs. Coolidge asked him:

"What did the preacher talk about?"

"Sin," replied her husband with his usual brevity.

"What did he say about it?" asked Mrs. Coolidge.

"He was against it," was the curt reply.

Well, I will follow his example and be brief.

—Arthur L. Kaser

HAVING A GOOD TIME

I know pretty well the attitude of banqueters about this time in the evening. It makes me think of an experience that I had over in Van Wert County, Ohio, within a year. I was attending a Grange supper—and, thank God, there are people in this country yet who eat supper in the evening. (Laughter) If we ever get to the place where everybody eats dinner in the evening, there is no hope for the country at all.

This was a good old-fashioned Grange supper. After the supper was over, the young people were playing games and having a perfectly delightful time. Finally the time came for the more serious part of the evening's performance. It had been threatened in the handbills that had been passed out that I was to make a speech. The presiding officer, not performing the duties of that office with delicacy and finesse, as the present presiding officer has done, but somewhat overcome by the importance of the occasion and the burdensomeness of the duties he was to perform, finally called the meeting to order and proceeded to introduce me in this somewhat questionable fashion. He said, "Now, ladies and gentlemen, we have been having a good time; shall we change the program now and begin the speaking?" (Laughter.)   —Senator Willis, Ohio

RESOURCEFULNESS

Although it has always been my ambition to be called upon to make a speech, now that I actually stand before you, I feel myself rather helpless.

What would I not give to possess the resourcefulness of our brilliant chairman, Mr. Rogers (substitute his real name), who in his younger years was a traveling salesman and once found himself, I believe, in the flourishing town of Colusa. (Substitute a real town)

The town boasted of a single hotel, although on second thought, I believe they merely had the hotel but never boasted of it. At any rate, there was a farmers' convention in Colusa at the time, so when Mr. Rogers arrived at the hotel at ten o'clock that evening the clerk told him that every room was taken and it would be impossible to accommodate him.

"You must put me up somewhere," replied Mr. Rogers. "I'm a regular customer here, and since I'm leaving again at six in the morning, I really require a good night's rest."

The clerk thought a moment and then said, "We always like to oblige our regular customers, and I think I have a plan. There's an empty church across the street, to which I have the key. I'll let you sleep over there tonight, and as you say you're leaving again at six tomorrow morning, no one will be wiser."

Mr. Rogers gladly agreed to this. The clerk took him over to the church and returned to his duties behind the hotel desk. In a few moments the church bell began to ring in a most violent fashion. It woke up all the people, who surely thought the town must be on fire. The clerk rushed over to the church and said to Mr. Rogers, "Why did you ring that church bell just now?"

Mr. Rogers replied, "Send a pitcher of ice water to pew thirty-seven."   —James Madison

LITERATURE'S LOSS

I am very glad indeed to be here and look into your faces. God knows there are faces here that ought to be looked into once in a while. As my father used to say when he led me to the woodshed with a barrel stave in one hand and me in the other, "It is going to hurt you a great deal more than it hurts me."

I lived on a farm until I became so familiar with it that I felt the contempt which comes from familiarity. I rather think I was the originator, at least I was always said to have been the originator, of a back-to-the-farm movement. I turned mine on ours at the first opportunity. I rather think that when I did this and gave up the plow for the pen, literature's loss was agriculture's gain. I came from Ohio, as did Senator Willis and everybody else who could.   —Strickland Gillilan

In this introduction Mr. Gillilan uses a humorous twist to words and phrases which always make an impression on an audience.

COME IN WITH THE NUTS

It was the great Bulgarian philosopher, Peter Zilch, who once remarked, "There is a reason for all things." But my having been called upon to address you, makes me question his infallibility.

Perhaps even the chairman had a few misgivings regarding my oratorical qualities, because just before I arose, he said to me, "What will you talk about?"

I said, "About a half a minute."

I understand that the purpose of this organization is largely to discuss important matters, pro and con. My remarks will be mostly con.

At that, I know I shall enjoy myself much better than I did at a recent similar function that I attended in New York, and where I was also called upon to speak.

Only that affair was arranged differently. Instead of having all the speakers address the helpless victims in a bunch, the chairman called us together just before we sat down, and said, "Mr. Jones will talk after the soup, Mr. Smith after the entree, Mr. Brown after the roast, Mr. Gray after the dessert, and so on.

Not having heard my name mentioned, I said, "Excuse me, Mr. Chairman, but when do I speak?"

He gave me a pitying glance and said, "Oh, you come in with the nuts.'"
                                                    —James Madison

IT PAYS TO BE HONEST

Gentlemen: I cannot address you as fellow citizens, because your voting power has been confiscated. I cannot address you as fellow convicts, because they're not on to me as yet.

I am glad to be here this morning for one day only. In fact, no doubt if you had your way all jails would be conducted as a one-night stand. I prefer appearing in this prison to any vaudeville theatre, because I know you can't walk out on me.

When a man secures accommodations here, I believe they ask him what his vocation is. If you are a tailor, they put you in the tailor shop. If you are a musician, they put you in the orchestra. If you are a shoemaker, they put you in the shoe shop. Take a tip from me. Next time they ask you your occupation, tell them you're a traveling salesman.

Men, remember it pays to be honest. Even if it keeps a fellow poor. I recall that one time the Governor of New York was making a tour of inspection through Sing Sing, and interviewed the inmates as to the cause of their incarceration. He asked every man what crime he had committed. Every man stated he was innocent—did not do anything. Next fellow said the same thing; claimed he was wrongly convicted and that he was a decent, honorable man. And so on.

The Governor finally approached one fellow who admitted he was a thief and had stolen ten thousand dollars, and the Governor said, "You get out of here right away. I don't want any crooks associated with all these honest men." So you see, it pays to tell the truth. —Loney Haskell

For many years Mr. Haskell was one of America's most talented vaudeville entertainers. In this response, when introduced to the residents of the federal prison at Atlanta, Mr. Haskell not only revealed his analysis of his audience's thinking, but at the same time he was able to use humor to sugarcoat his remarks.

AUDIENCE LEAVES

I had a sad experience last week over at Center City. I was giving my usual discourse on my usual subject. At the end of the first five minutes of my talk, a large group in the rear of the room got up and left. After ten minutes had passed, practically everyone in the hall arose and started to an exit. At that moment a large man rushed up to the front of the room, waving his arms. "Wait! Wait!" he cried. "Women and children first!" —Rome Roberts

SAY A FEW WORDS

In the time of Nero, sport-loving Romans crowded the Coliseum to see Christians tossed to the lions. For one victim who had given the authorities untold trouble, Nero had eleven of his most ferocious lions starved for a week.

When the first lion made a beeline for the Christian, the spectators wet their lips. But the Christian calmly bent down and whispered in the beast's ear. His tail between his legs, the lion slunk out of the arena. Six more half-starved kings of the forest followed the same performance, and the crowd started hollering for its money back. Then Nero summoned the Christian and said: "If you will tell me how you make those lions act that way, I will grant you a full pardon."

"It's very simple," explained the Christian. "I whisper in their ears: 'Remember, you'll be expected to say a few words after dinner!' "

—Francis Meynell

WARNED THREE TIMES

The young minister was in the pulpit for the first time — and a little nervous. He read the text: "Behold I come." The sermon was to follow immediately, but his mind went blank, and he repeated the text: "Behold I come," hoping to remember the opening words of the sermon — but with no success. Trying to be nonchalant, he leaned forward as he repeated the text for the third time. Under his weight the pulpit gave way and he landed in the lap of the wife of one of the elders. "I'm awfully sorry," he said, much embarrassed. "I really didn't mean for this to happen."

The lady smiled kindly and replied, "Oh, that's all right. I should have been ready after you warned me three times."

—C. L. Axtell

This story may be used when the speaker has been invited back to the same group to speak for the third time, or when the speaker has been able to accept only the third invitation.

IT NEEDS REST

Your hearty greeting tempts me to compliment you as one friend complimented another, when he said: "May you live to eat the chicken that scratches the top of your grave." When I rise to speak I remember that the most natural thing in the world for an American to do is to make a speech. When the genuine American is born and gets up on his feet, the first thing he does is to say "Fellow Citizens," and after he has got through with the world and is about to leave, he says, "One word more."

But silence sometimes is more agreeable than speech, as when the man said to the bird trainer: "I gave you fifty dollars to teach my wife's parrot how to talk. How much will you charge to teach the confounded bird to shut up?" And then there are times when silence is more restful than speech, as when the lady asked the physician for some medicine and he said: "Madam, all you need is rest." "Oh," she says, "just look at my tongue." "Ah," says he, "that needs rest, too." But who could keep silence when there is such an introduction as your chairman has given me, and I am asked to speak to you.

—T. DeWitt Talmage

SWEARING OFF

Almost all my life I have lived through a perilous life of after-dinner speaking, and now I have sworn off. I swore off about three years ago, but the way I swore off was like the way the Connecticut deacon swore off eating clams. He ate too many one day, and it made him feel very uncomfortable and pious, and he thought that he would have recourse to prayer, and he said: "Oh Lord, heal thy servant of this grievous illness, and I faithfully promise thee that he will never eat any more clams—very few, if any. Amen."

—Rev. Henry van Dyke

ANY EXPLANATION IS IMPOSSIBLE

Ladies and gentlemen, I regret exceedingly that there has been so much misunderstanding about my scheduled appearance here tonight. I suppose that if I were to explain all the reasons involved which caused the mix-up, you still wouldn't find the explanation a plausible one. I am reminded of the story about the married man who made an attempt to win back his wife's love.

A man who had trouble with his wife said to a friend: "I don't know what's the matter with her. We seem to have reached a stage where we have lost all interest in our wedded life." His friend suggested to him that he should make a pronounced demonstration of affection toward his wife. The man who was in trouble said he would try it, that he would do anything to have his home happy again.

He arranged that at four o'clock a box of candy should arrive for his wife, at five o'clock there should arrive a beautiful bouquet of flowers, and when he got home at six o'clock, he said: "Get your clothes on, darling, and we will go to the Ritz-Carlton for dinner. After dinner we will go to the theatre, and then have a dance or two, and come back in a taxi, just like old times."

She said: "Listen to me—the baby is cutting a new tooth, the servant girl has the grippe, the chauffeur has been arrested for speeding, and now you come home drunk."

—Robert H. Davis

THE CONSIDERATE TOASTMASTER

I am reminded of something the Hon. John Temple Graves told as happening to him in England when he was to be the first speaker. The toastmaster turned with extreme infelicity to the honorable gentleman on his right and said, "Mr. Graves, shall we let them enjoy themselves a little longer, or shall we let them have your speech?"

—Ernest M. Stires

PERSUASIVE POWERS

It is only a good friend like your chairman who could have persuaded me to take the time to come to your city to speak to this assembly of civic leaders. His outstanding persuasive powers can be well illustrated by this story.

A predecessor of mine as President of U. S. Steel was a man of unusual persuasive powers. His name was Charlie Schwab. One incident that illustrates this gift of his concerns a new steel mill. Company officials had collected all but one parcel of a large tract of land they needed. The farmer who owned this parcel stubbornly refused to sell. Vice-presidents, lawyers, the local mayor, everybody took a crack at trying to win him over. They offered him more money, company stock, double the acreage somewhere else. The farmer would not budge.

Then Charlie Schwab went to call on the farmer at his home. They sat down together on the parlor sofa and Charlie put his big, genial arm around the farmer's shoulder. Turning on the full voltage of his electric personality, he started to reason with him. Schwab had talked only a short time when suddenly the farmer jumped up.

"Mr. Schwab," he said, "I'll sell you the property, but thank God I'm not a woman."   —Benjamin F. Fairless

EQUAL TO THE OPPORTUNITY

A young boy was in the habit of going to the cellar where a large barrel of molasses was stored. He was in the habit of running his fingers on parts of the barrel to get drippings of the molasses. One day to his surprise he found the top removed from the barrel and upon investigating and finding it half full, he either fell or decided to get in the barrel. He stuck his head out over the top and was heard to say in a prayer-like manner: "Oh, Lord, make my tongue equal to this opportunity."

—V. Spencer Goodreds

MAKE ME TAKE IT

Regardless of the remarks your chairman has made in introducing me to you tonight, I feel that you are obliged to give me courteous attention. Try to accept what I have to say without too much mental or physical resistance. I am reminded of a story.

There was an old fellow in Mississippi who thought he was dying. As the sun sank slowly in the west, casting its benign rays over the horizon, he motioned to his wife to come over to his bedside.

"Mary!" he croaked. "You remember that old trunk in the basement?"

"Yes, John," she said tearfully. "I believe there is an old trunk down there."

"Well, Mary," he whispered, "there's a quart of bourbon—fine old bourbon—in it. Go and get it."

"Yes, John," she said. "What then?"

Well, John gave her specific instructions. He told her to fill a glass with finely crushed ice, to bruise some mint and stir it up in the glass, with just a pinch of sugar. Then he told her to pour the bourbon liberally over the concoction, and to decorate it with sprigs of mint and set it aside until a frost formed on the outside.

"And then, Mary," gasped the old man, his voice now all but extinct, "bring it up here—bring it up here to me. And when you bring it in here, Mary, no matter what I do or say—make me take it."   —Alben W. Barkley

COLLECT A BOUNTY

There is the incident about the man who came into the sheriff's office to give himself up because he had shot a toastmaster. The sheriff informed him he should go to the Auditor's office where they pay bounties!

—Judge Luther W. Youngdahl, Washington, D. C.

Section Two

OPENINGS FOR SPEAKERS

OPENINGS FOR SPEAKERS

INTRODUCTION

"In public address, it is all-important to make a good start. In the whole hard process of speech-making, there is nothing quite so hard as to make easy and skilful contact with an audience. Much depends upon first impressions and opening words. Often an audience is either won or lost by the first half dozen sentences of a speech."
—**Public Speaking Today,** by Lockwood-Thorpe

"The most important fact about speaking is to get an arresting opening, something that will seize the attention immediately."　　　　　　　　—Dr. Lynn H. Hough

"If you happen to be one of a circle of public speakers who are relating their experiences, you will often hear someone remark apropos of the proper construction of an address: 'Get a good beginning and a good ending; stuff it with whatever you please.'"　　　　　　　　—Victor Murdock

EFFECTIVE OPENING IS ESSENTIAL

The ultimate success of a speaker is invariably predetermined by his ability to use an effective opening. Experienced speakers devote considerable time and effort to the precise phrasing of their opening remarks because they realize that in the first two or three minutes of their appearance before an audience the listeners will appraise them and decide if they are interested or not.

It is important that the opening be direct, vital, and immediate. Otherwise, the audience will become impatient and lose interest. The whole spirit of the modern world is for fast action. A slow opening will spell disaster for any speaker. Be brief and to the point.

There are many ways to classify effective openings. I have tried to present the various types in the following chapters. I expect that the readers of this book will have sufficient background in public speaking to be able to analyze the various classifications and to use them as models in a training program, either in the classroom or through individual study.

Chapter One

The General Opening

Of all the various types of openings we have listed in this section, the most useable and practical is the general opening. Usually the average speaker is at the mercy of the chairman who introduces him. If he fails to properly name the subject, the speaker will have an opportunity to tell exactly what he is going to talk about. All misunderstandings are eliminated if there is a clear-cut statement about the subject at the very beginning of the talk. These examples will clearly illustrate what we mean by the general opening.

A CALL TO SPIRITUAL GREATNESS

My friend Roger is a typical American. At twenty-eight, he is married, has a down payment on a ranch-style home, a modest bank account, and an income pushing past five thousand dollars a year. Everybody considers Roger a success; everybody except Roger, that is. He is searching at present for some satisfying philosophy, some basic meaning which will make life worth while. For in spite of all his material success, Roger is losing his grip on life; Roger is dying spiritually.

J. B. Priestley analyzed Roger and the rest of us Americans when he gazed at New York's skyscrapers several years ago and commented that America was always giving the world something to look up to—except a state of mind! Cyril Connolly, editor of the English magazine HORIZON and loyal friend of America, says, "The American way of life is one of the most effective the world has known, but about the end of life Americans are more in the dark than any people since the Gauls of Tacitus."

If you wonder what these foreign critics mean, ask our own Dwight Eisenhower. He tells us that at the time during the last war when America most needed manpower, there were 6,000 of our soldiers in the hospitals of northern Africa. These men had not suffered wounds; President Eisenhower explains, "Their emotional stamina and spiritual strength had left them."

At this very moment, a leading national magazine points out, fifty-five percent of America's hospital patients are **mental** cases. In fact, one out of every ten people in our nation is suffering from some mental ailment.

—J. Ellsworth Kalas

An introduction to an address, "A Call to Spiritual Greatness," delivered by J. Ellsworth Kalas. This is an example of opening an address with a specific illustration, then shifting to a general statement of philosophy and in the last two paragraphs leading into a statement of the subject of the address.

SIMPLE FOOLS

During the years following the depression of 1921, the American people floating in the midst of paper profits and paper prosperity had no time to think; they had time only to buy and sell, and to scatter wealth to the winds. But during the last three years a change has come over this country, and with it a change in its people. Today want and misery in some degree permeate almost every home. Two hundred thousand youth tread our highways, a generation of hoboes. Chicago's unpaid school teachers march in protest. Closed banks vie with speakeasies in the number closed, but re-open with far less regularity. Seeing such misery and chaos, our people now start to think. Thinking, they discover something that has existed for years, but which has been permitted to thrive through the indifference of a satiated people. They realize suddenly, under the pinch of hunger, that their governments— national, state and local—are squandering their taxes.

—Paul Kenneth Howells

This introduction illustrates good thought progression in leading up to the statement of Mr. Howells' subject—the squandering of taxes.

THE VICTORY

We meet today to felicitate you, the members of the graduating class of Notre Dame University, who are now ready to go about your lifework. A sense of victory is attached to the occasion for you. About sixteen or eighteen years ago you began school. Out of each hundred boys and girls who started with you, forty-five finished the grammar school, five entered college, and one is now being graduated from college. In other words, the members of the class graduating today have been sifted out of several thousand students. You have won a great start for the adventure before you, having demonstrated that you have, in a reasonably large measure, persistence, courage, intelligence, and character, from which success is made.

The occasion is perhaps, more than you know, also one of victory for your parents. Many of them have made sacrifices in order that you might be here today. They may justly feel rewarded. They may justly be proud of you. But at this time they are not looking backward. They are looking forward, filled with the hope that you will now use to the best advantage your training, your ability to think, and your culture, for the achievement of civilization and, before all, for the welfare of the community in which you are to live.

The occasion is, again, a victory for the community and state. You are the young men who are to carry on the highest work of the state as those of us with gray hair let go. The idea that you are to do this work better than we touches the deepest feelings in us. You are our bond, so to speak, for the future prosperity and happiness of the people of the United States.

—Dr. William J. Mayo

The opening of a commencement address delivered by Dr. Mayo on June 7, 1936, at Notre Dame University illustrates the use of the informal and general beginning of a special address.

OTHERS

Major Booth died just a short time ago. He had spent his entire lifetime working for the welfare of others. If ever a man was the personification of unselfishness, Major Booth was that man. Others, not himself, was his primary thought, the basis for his every desire, action and motive. As the door opened for his soul to pass into the Everlasting, those who were with him heard him say one word, a word that expressed his entire philosophy of life, a word that most aptly charac-terized him—"Others."   —Eloise M. Wehner

The whole subject of Miss Wehner's address is introduced by this short paragraph. A simple declaration many times is effective in setting the foundation for the main body of the talk.

LEARNING TO LIVE

I am glad that I'm living today. Seldom has there been a time so filled with the drama of existence. Great battles are being waged, and waged not alone on the political front but in the home, the schools, the churches and in our shops. Our fight is for national well-being, and there never was a struggle more stirring than this which so completely involves us all. I'm glad that I am here today to watch the purging of national forces that must come from a sane and courageous attack of our great problems. I'm glad of the chance, tonight, to urge that we do not forget the place of education in the social order of the future.

Now, you and I of the universities know that every day of our lives, experiments are questioning the techniques of teach-ing. No hard and fast rules of learning are known, and there is no reason, then, for a blind worship of any system of learn-ing. But there are, on the other hand, many reasons why our schools are in need of the purging influence of the times.

—Russell W. Lembke

An introduction used by Mr. Lembke to open up his discus-sion of the trends in modern education to prepare students for a better program of practical living.

THE STRENUOUS LIFE

In speaking to you, men of the greatest city of the West, men of the state which gave to the country Lincoln and Grant, men who pre-eminently and distinctly embody all that is most American in the American character, I wish to preach, not the doctrine of ignoble ease, but the doctrine of the strenuous life, the life of toil and effort, of labor and strife; to preach that highest form of success which comes, not to the man who desires mere easy peace, but to the man who does not shrink from danger, from hardship, or from bitter toil, and who out of these wins the splendid ultimate triumph. —Theodore Roosevelt

In his famous address, "The Strenuous Life," delivered in Chicago on April 10, 1899, Mr. Roosevelt uses this type of opening to key the principal theme of this speech.

THE TRAGEDY OF INCOMPLETE THINKING

Cato the Elder stood in the Senate of Rome crying, "Delenda est Carthago." Carthage must be destroyed. Carthage was destroyed. Her fields were plowed with salt. Her ships disappeared from the seas and her glory became a legend. Fear mocked reason. A great civilization perished. Priceless learning was lost to man.

Two thousand years later at Versailles delegates from the leading nations of the earth composed a document that proclaimed, "Germany must be destroyed." A million corpses lay on Flanders Field, ten million men were mutilated, whole nations were ravaged by famine, and half the world was bankrupt. Selfish commercial policies and national military ambitions had plunged the world into a maelstrom of destruction. These nations usurped Germany's commerce, confiscated her ships; annexed her colonies. They stripped her of all means of payment, then imposed an indemnity in excess of her entire national wealth. But they left untouched the real causes of war.

—Jeannette Amidon

Miss Amidon in an address on the essentials of an adequate peace program keys her message with a very appropriate and basic introduction.

LET NO MAN PUT ASUNDER

This is a memorable week in the history of America, and I am honored to be here with you on this occasion which coincides so happily with the handing-down of the Supreme Court's decision on segregation in the public schools. I should like to say that the principle of that decision reminded me of one of the many stories that have to do with a Sunday School teacher and her class. The particular lesson had to do with the Ten Commandments, and the teacher was trying to see whether her pupils really understood how they applied to actual situations. She asked Johnny: "If you don't go to church, which commandment do you violate?" Johnny promptly replied, "The second." "That's right; and Eddie, which one do you violate if you don't mind your mother?" "Fourth." "Very good; and Frank, which is it if you steal an apple?" "The seventh." Finally the teacher said, "Now here is a hard one: who can tell me which commandment you violate if you cut the tail off your dog?" There was a dead silence. At last, little Henry tentatively raised his hand. "Good for you, Henry, which one is it?" "Well," said Henry, "I can't exactly tell you the number, but I can recite it." "All right, go ahead." So Henry stood up and announced: "What God hath joined together, let no man put asunder."

Well, my friends, for a long time now we have been putting asunder what God has joined together—the whole human family.

I suppose you have often wondered, as I have — and as generations of philosophers have — whether mankind is really moving forward or backward, and whether our cherished theories of the inevitability of progress are just an illusion. But just about the time we are almost ready to write off the whole concept of human progress, something like this decision comes along and dramatizes for us the fact that we are indeed, slowly and painfully, but with tangible and measurable success, working our way toward the ideals of human relationship that we know in our hearts to be right.

—Arthur Larson

This introduction was used by Mr. Arthur Larson, Under Secretary of Labor, in an address delivered at the annual banquet of the Capital Press Club in Washington, D. C., on May 22, 1954.

THE AMERICAN SYSTEM

Eight years ago it was my painful duty to present to the House of Congress an unexaggerated picture of the general distress pervading the whole land. We must all yet remember some of its frightful features. We all know that the people were then oppressed and borne down by an enormous load of debt; that the value of property was at the lowest point of depression; that ruinous sales and sacrifices were everywhere made of real estate; that stop laws and relief laws and paper money were adopted to save the people from impending destruction; that a deficit in the public revenue existed, which compelled the Government to seize upon, and divert from its legitimate object, the appropriation of the sinking fund, to redeem the national debt; and that our commerce and navigation were threatened with a complete paralysis. In short, sir, if I were to select any term of seven years since the adoption of the present Constitution, which exhibited a scene of the most widespread dismay and desolation, it would be exactly that term of seven years which immediately preceded the establishment of the tariff of 1824.   —Henry Clay

This opening was used by Mr. Clay in his address delivered in the United States Senate on Feb. 2, 1832, on the subject of the American system. It illustrates how the negative approach may be used. In the main body of his speech Mr. Clay outlined the accomplishments of the country under our democratic system.

THREE SCORE YEARS AND TEN

My subject this evening is an old and familiar one—racial discrimination in the United States. I realize that, as I begin, most of you are thinking: "That old theme! I can sleep through this. Let the speaker do the worrying. It's his affair, not mine." Yes, it is my affair. But it is vastly more. It is the deep concern of twelve million members of my race, twelve million Americans. That means one-tenth of our country's population. Can it be that the other nine-tenths can afford to grow weary of the effort to solve our common problem? It is a problem the Negro did not create alone; alone he can not solve it.

But tonight, my case against discrimination is not so much the old and familiar charge — unjust! Un-American! That charge we have heard over and over again. This evening it is another basis on which I urge that discrimination be ended. The record of the Negro's achievements, his progress, his contribution to world culture, argues powerfully for the abolition of discrimination based on race.

Three score and ten years ago, my fathers were slaves, uneducated, unpropertied, penniless. Today, after only two generations of freedom, we look back with genuine pride upon a glorious progress—a progress unmatched, unparalleled by any other group in history in a similar period.

—John A. Cobbs

This introduction by Mr. Cobbs is an excellent example of a speaker's appeal to the audience's sense of justice and fairplay. Rather than dwell upon the usual charge of discrimination, he uses a positive appeal by showing the accomplishments of the Negro over a short span of eighty-five years.

DEMONSTRATION OF COOPERATION

After such a magnificent and flattering reception and such a wonderful dinner as this, it would be difficult for any man to find in his vocabulary words to express the feelings in his heart. I would be unworthy of any attention from you whatever if I made the mistake of taking all or a major portion of this demonstration as intended for me personally. The time has gone by when a large piece of complicated work can be done by one man.

In the very nature of our art the vast system must extend over a continent and other continents, and many men and many minds must engage to do the work. It has been my good fortune, and perhaps I showed some skill in the selection of my subordinates; we are all together one family. I know I have the finest group of telephone engineers that exists in the whole wide world. And I know that without the work that they have done none of these things that you have participated in tonight would be possible. There is no other nation, no other combination of nations which has men such as compose our staff. In no other country in the world would it be possible to have a demonstration such as that given over the long line to San Francisco, nor a demonstration such as that given by wireless tonight. It is only in America that the men live who know how to do that.   —John J. Carty

This opening was given by Mr. Carty in his address on the occasion of opening of telephone connections across the continent to San Francisco in 1915.

HEART DISEASE

One hundred years ago a little man with a heavy beard was traveling extensively around Europe. Before 1848, he had been booted out of both France and Germany. He wasn't too welcome in England, either, but he was often seen in the British Museum, a poverty stricken recluse, poring over books. By the end of 1848, he managed to publish in Brussels a brief hundred-page document. The name of the document—the Communist Manifesto. The name of the little man who wrote it—Karl Marx. The document was, as Marx put it, "the birth cry of modern socialism." The newly-born child wailed in 1848: "Capitalism above all produces its own grave diggers."

Today, the child has grown up—he is a mature being, with

a gigantic frame and powerful extremities. He sits alone in the East.

In the West sits another colossus. His birth cry was heard in 1787, when in Philadelphia, 39 men signed the Constitution of the United States. This elder giant of the West faces the newly matured colossus of the East, and hears him cry defiance. The words are not cries from the mouth of a child any more; they are thunderous pronouncements spoken with authority.

The giant in the East is aggressive. His motive, as strong as our desire to preserve the American way of life, is to convince the world that we of the West must be destroyed.

—Charles Guggenheim

In this introduction, Mr. Guggenheim paves the way for his discussion of the gradual encroachment of the world by Russia. The use of the two contrasting philosophies are exemplified by the East and the West is effective.

THE GREAT REGIMENTER

Near the close of the tenth century, a hooded monk bent low over his newly perfected machine. He listened tensely to the rhythmic clank-clank of the works. He had created a clock. To this day, that clock has served as the taskmaster of men. It sits on a mahogany mantle, rides high over a city's traffic, or rests in a dirty pocket. But wherever it is, its silent hands wield more power than an army of dictators. It drags man from bed, sends him to work, serves his meals, tells him when to quit work, then puts him back to bed again. The clock is the Great Regimenter of mankind.

As these millions of time-pieces tick off the years, we can hear a chorus of triumphant laughter from their metallic throats. For just as the clock regiments man's actions, so there are many forces which regiment man's thinking—creed, dogma, institutions, and men and women themselves. Some bludgeon man's thoughts like mighty piledrivers. Others are cunning enough to woo man with poisoned sweetness and simplicity.

Tonight I should like you to examine with me these forces which regiment man's thinking.   —James A. Rahl

Here is a classic example of the use of a specific reference to an everyday object to make graphic a general theme to an audience who may not be particularly interested in a philosophical subject.

THE GRAVITY OF THE WORLD SITUATION

It is impossible to exaggerate the gravity of the world situation at the present time. Certainly not in the last five hundred years has civilization as we know it, and live it, been so threatened. The struggle now in progress is not merely a renewed attempt at conquest of the weak by the strong—although that is a part of it. It is not solely a fresh attempt to change, or correct, the balance of power in Europe, although that, too, is not absent. It is not primarily a contest over control of trade routes and the possession of colonies—although this frequent cause of war has played its part. Fundamentally it is a clash between two irreconcilable systems of living and governing, which apparently cannot exist in the same world, peaceably.

This is what makes this a different kind of war than most wars that history deals with. And this is why it will be fought to a conclusion, without compromise. It is as impossible to end the war in Europe by negotiation, as it was to end our war between the states—and for the same reason. The world, now so closely knit together, cannot continue to be half slave and half free. It will either become all slave, or all free. This can only mean a long war, a war of fearful costs, and fearful suffering, a war of exhaustion, leaving in its wake economic bankruptcy for the victors, and indescribable chaos for the vanquished.

—Frank Knox

In this opening Mr. Knox introduced his subject very effectively. The audience had no doubt about the speaker's attitude to his subject and could anticipate the full substance of his entire speech.

A FEW WORDS ABOUT DEEDS

A legislative session, Mr. Chairman, is like a baseball season. You don't really know where you stand until the season is over.

While the season is going on, you can say anything you like and get away with it. You can say your team hasn't got a chance, that its apparent success is phoney, and that it's sure to go into a slide at the end and lose the pennant. Or you can say that the pennant is as good as won on the Fourth of July, that it's only a matter of time, and that your team will win going away.

But when the season is over, either you've won or you haven't. The percentages are there, and there isn't anything more to argue about.

Now, we've been hearing for months from some people that President Eisenhower's program was all bogged down, that it would never get through by the end of the session, and that this, that, or the other bill didn't have a chance. We've heard from others that the main parts of the program would pass substantially as President Eisenhower proposed, and that when the session was over, it would prove to have been a winning season all along.

Well, let's see what the score is. I cannot cover the entire program so I shall discuss only those items that are of special interest to labor. I am not going to try to talk you into anything; I am merely going to summarize a series of simple historical facts about what has happened, and I shall leave it to you to draw your own conclusions.   —Arthur Larson

The opening of an address by Arthur Larson, Under Secretary of Labor, at the Ohio State Federation of Labor Convention, Cleveland, on Aug. 9, 1954.

TIME REQUIRED FOR PREPARATION

From time to time during the past two years or more I have been honored with invitations to address the Canadian Club of Ottawa, but, for one reason or another, it has not been my good fortune to have that privilege. Upon my return from Great Britain the invitation was renewed, and while I really do not intend to make an address to you today, because that would have required more time than I have been able, by reason of urgent and pressing public duties to devote to preparation, still I did consent to speak conversationally and intimately to you, my neighbors and friends in this city, with which I have been associated more or less for nearly twenty years, in which I have lived during the past ten years, and in which I hope that the remaining years of my life may be spent. Indeed, it is said that to prepare even an entirely extempore address requires a good deal of careful preparation. So you will thoroughly understand that I am not making an address to you today, but that I shall merely attempt to give you my impressions of some incidents of my recent visit to Great Britain and France.

I am throughly conscious that even if I took the utmost limit of time for preparation, and if I were most brilliantly and exceptionally gifted with expression, I could hardly hope to make you feel those incidents as they did impress me from time to time.   —Sir Robert Laird Borden

The Prime Minister of Canada uses this opening to discuss the fighting of Canadian troops in the first year of World War I. Sir Borden used an intimate style to win the attention of his audience.

WHAT IS A LIBERAL?

For the past several years we have heard a lot of talk about liberalism and liberals. Practically everybody claims to be a liberal. The New Deal phrase-makers cooked up the word "economic royalist," but when you interview a man who by common consent belongs to that category, you find that he has pretensions to liberalism. Then there are a lot of business-men whose business is in such a state that no one would call them economic royalists or even "Princes of Privilege." These men call themselves liberals. Then there are the New Dealers; they say they are liberals, and they say it so loudly that they have almost succeeded in appropriating the word. But then there are other "liberal" groups also. For instance, the Socialist group. They think they are liberals. Finally, the Communists, who want to set up a complete collectivist state, consider themselves the most liberal liberals of all.

So you have the picture of everybody in the United States calling himself a liberal, no matter what he believes. If he believes in concentrating industrial power in the hands of a few corporate giants and a few great bankers, he is a liberal. If he believes, on the other hand, in concentrating political power in the hands of one gigantic government, he is a liberal. If he doesn't believe in concentrating power in the hands of either one of these groups, he is a liberal. What is a liberal?

—Wendell Willkie

In his address on "Liberalism," Mr. Willkie began his speech with a definite statement of definition which gave a basis for the main body treatment of his subject. It is a type of treatment that can be used effectively when the audience must have a clear understanding of the speaker's viewpoint.

KEEP FREEDOM ALIVE

This is the seventh time I have had the high honor of addressing the conventions of the Republican Party. The last two times I have indicated I was making my farewell appearance. I have both a precedent and a request for this appearance.

Some of you may recollect that the great singer of yesteryear, Madame Adelina Patti, by request came to America six times to make farewell appearances. But do not get too alarmed over the possibility of three more from me.

The excuse for this third such appearance of mine is the special request of President Eisenhower and your chairman. No greater compliment could be paid to any Republican.

In each of my former addresses to the conventions I have stressed our responsibility to maintain the safeguards of free men. That still remains America's most vital issue.

—Herbert Hoover

Mr. Hoover used this effective opening at the San Francisco Republican convention to explain his third farewell appearance as a speaker on the program.

RELIGION AND THE SOCIAL PROBLEM

Samuel Rogers, the 19th century English banker and wit, was once asked, "Mr. Rogers, what is your religion?" "It's the religion of every sensible man," replied Mr. Rogers. "And what," continued his questioner, "is that?" "That," said Samuel Rogers, "is what every sensible man keeps to himself." But fools rush in where men of sense fear to tread, so I am going to offer you a few reflections on the place of religion in matters of social organization.

For Mr. Rogers and most of his contemporaries, religion was solely a private matter, a transaction between the individual and his Maker. Religion has always been at least that, but it has also been something more. Religion—man's basic beliefs about the universe and his place and destiny therein—has been a powerful factor in shaping men's thinking about their political and economic activities. Men cannot help adopting some basic premises which—even if they do not rise to the level of articulate thought—have unavoidable social consequences. It may have been difficult for our Victorian forebears to recognize this truism, but in our own day there is a growing feeling that social thought cannot deal with political and economic theory alone—it must show its credentials in the fields of ethics and religion as well.   —Edmund H. Opitz

In the opening of his address before a meeting of economists on July 16, 1956, Mr. Opitz used a quotation to provide the basis for his main theme.

WORLD PEACE

On behalf of Columbia University, I thank Mr. Leo Silver for the generous gift that will make the Gabriel Silver Lecture on Peace a recurring feature of the University calendar. His endowment will permit us at regular intervals to call on selected individuals for reports on peace. Perhaps there will be added new strength to the philosophical and social foundations of peace, and a stronger light thrown on the hazards within the international economy that endanger its permanence. Possibly there will be launched new attacks on inequities and injustices in which lurk some of the causes of war.

Mr. Silvers has established a worthy memorial to his father and we are grateful that he has chosen Columbia University as its home. On my own behalf, I want to thank him for the honor paid me in his request that I deliver this inaugural of the series. Without his intervention, I should not be so presumptuous as to appear in this role before a distinguished gathering of Columbia faculty and graduate students because you are, in our country, part of the great body especially qualified to be the architects of world peace.

—Dwight D. Eisenhower

SAMUEL GOMPERS

The number of labor executives who knew Samuel Gompers grows smaller each year. We are glad that this celebration of the hundredth anniversary of his birth in London, honoring the name and work of the founder of the American Federation of Labor, also permits those of us who knew and worked with him to share our experiences with newer members of our organization.

Though not a large man, Samuel Gompers had a magnetic personality and a commanding presence that forced him to the front as a leader. With a rich and powerful voice and a rare ability to plumb the mind and feelings of his listeners, his was a high crusading spirit that voiced the struggle of his fellow workers, urging them to join unions and to agitate, educate, and organize and enlist others in the battle for human freedom. There was a radiance in his gift for living and enjoying homely details, and this gift drew men to him in sincere comradeship.

—William Green

In this opening, Mr. Green begins his eulogy of Mr. Gompers at the beginning of his address in a direct manner. This is an effective way to attract the immediate attention of an audience.

THE COMMUNIST ECONOMIC OFFENSIVE

Mr. Chairman, honored guests, and Texans, it is always a privilege and a pleasure for a Latin American to be invited to speak in Texas, to any group of Texans. That is true not only because of the immense economic, political, and social importance of your great State, and of the kind hospitality of your people, but it is especially so because the people of Texas, bordering as you do on Latin America, are more acutely aware of our problems than are the people of many other sections of the United States.

However, Mr. Chairman, I must say that I feel a very special pleasure in being asked to address this particular group of Texans, the Dallas Council on World Affairs. Since I have been the Guatemalan Ambassador to the United States the one thing that has impressed me so much is the keen interest of your citizens in world problems, and of the splendid educational job that is being done in so many of your communities through such forums as this.

—Col. Jose Luis Cruz Salazar

EXASPERATION WITH LAWYERS

I am going to talk today about the place of the lawyer in labor relations.

Some people would make very short work of this topic. They would say the lawyer has no place in this field at all. You have undoubtedly heard, as I have many times, some employer or labor representative say that if we could just get the lawyers out of the room it would be a lot easier to work things out and get an agreement. Even more frequently one hears it said that the trouble with such legislative fields as workmen's compensation is that the lawyers have taken over, and that what workmen's compensation really needs is to throw out the lawyers and, for good measure, the courts and judges too.

This sort of exasperation with lawyers and courts has, of course, been going on for centuries, and still plagues the profession. The other day, a well-known judge told me about a widow whose husband had left her a rather substantial fortune in an estate with more than the usual number of legal complications. The poor woman found herself, week after week, going from lawyers' offices to courtrooms, to appellate courtrooms and back to lawyers' offices, and finally, after some months of this, she finally burst out in the courtroom: "You and your lawyers and orders and stays and appeals and whatnots! Sometimes I almost wish my husband hadn't died."

—Arthur Larson

The opening of an address on "The Lawyer and Labor" delivered before the Michigan State Bar Association by Arthur Larson, Under Secretary of Labor, on Sept. 22, 1954.

Chapter Two

The Narrative Opening

It is always easy for an audience to listen to the narrative type of opening. The story method can be used in many speech situations with good results because of the psychological aspects involved. If you get your audience to laugh at a humorous story, pun, or joke during the first three minutes of your appearance, you are on the road to attracting and maintaining the interest of your listeners during the body of your address. Yet it is important that the speaker knows how to pause and get the attention of his listeners whenever a story is related.

MARKED "TOYS"

On April 8th of this year, amid the shrieking of tug boat whistles, the shouting of curt commands, the creaking of huge cables as they were drawn tight, the palatial steamship "Ile de France" came to a stately rest in New York Harbor. At the rails, excited passengers laughed and cried, waved and shouted to friends ashore. Eager to rush down the gangplanks, they milled about the decks. But down in the hold, swiftly and quietly a small group of United States agents were examining three packing cases marked "Toys." Secretly reports had reached these men that here was another consignment in the stream of narcotic drugs ceaselessly smuggled into this country. The crates were broken open. A million dollars' worth of illegal narcotics lay exposed.　　　　　—Joseph Rose

Here is an example of the use of the narrative style by Mr. Rose in introducing the subject of narcotics. This method is effective in securing a favorable audience acceptance of the speaker's point of view.

THE SCARLET LETTER

Long ago, in an old New England town, there was enacted the story which has ever since moved the hearts of men and women. It is a story which has significance for us tonight.

I have in mind the history of Hester Prynne, the heroine of Nathaniel Hawthorne's novel. Hester Prynne, branded for life as a sinner, condemned to wear upon her dress, for the rest of her years, a piece of flaming embroidery, a scarlet letter "A." Who can forget that memorable scene in the market-place, when she stands there upon a wooden platform, her child in her arms, and all eyes fastened upon that mysterious scarlet letter, that glows as from a secret light within, and casts an unholy spell upon the hearts of her persecutors? A voice is heard from the balcony above, pleading with her to deliver up her secret—the voice of the young Reverend Dimmesdale, the man of holiness, the man of God. Nor can we forget the last chapter in that story, how years later those people saw Arthur Dimmesdale mount that self-same platform to confess his guilt with his dying breath, and tearing off his tunic, reveal not a breast of snow-white purity, but one in whose flesh there was corroded and burned, as if by a brand of God, a dull, red, malignant letter "A."

And a shudder of awe ran through those onlookers, for there they saw the purest of them all—a sinner in the eyes of God. And that night every man looked to himself, to see whether God had planted a scarlet letter upon his body—and the man-made brand of Hester Prynne, the outcast, became a badge of pride. Entangled in the coils of a fantastic and stagnant theology, these old Puritans put on the robe of self-righteousness and condemned all who transgressed the moral law —as they conceived it; for all transgressors incurred the wrath of God, and brought down upon a community of sinners the terrible vengeance of the Almighty. Instead of realizing completely the cause of all their hardships—the wilderness, the Indians, the primitive strength of a raw and untamed continent —instead of grasping these realities, they reverted to a "devil" theory of evil, and saw in every misfortune the hand of Satan and his human agents. Thus the tragic story of the witchcraft trials in Salem.

Ah, but you say, this is a tale of dark days that America very likely will never see again. . . . I wonder. . . . Has Hawthorne's story lost its point for us?

—Howard Grossman

The use of the Hawthorne illustration in this introduction by Mr. Grossman is an example of the narrative opening style that may be employed to lead up to the main body of an address. Later Mr. Grossman discusses the implications of congressional investigations.

THE FAILURE OF SUCCESS

In the land that is called the Garden of Allah there once dwelt a powerful Arab sheik. He lived in luxury and plenty. His camels traveled on all the desert trains. His herds were found on a thousand hills. His every wish was quickly granted. His every command was instantly obeyed. His word was law. In truth he was the very personification of power in that oasis of the desert he called his own. For Abdul Khan was the master of thirty human slaves.

Far beyond the desert's rim there is another land where masters are served by many slaves. It is a land of fruit and plenty, a land rich in golden goods. Its toilers are trained to do great tasks. Rapidly with ever increasing speed they carry their masters throughout the land and sky. They tell their lords strange secrets of great power. They build wondrous temples for their owners. Their purpose is to serve; their goal their master's happiness. This is the land that is called America, where dwell more than a hundred million Abdul Khans, each served by his thirty slaves.   —Charles A. Finch

In this introduction Mr. Finch uses an effective comparison of the relationship between human slaves and machine slaves. In this contrast Mr. Finch gives a clear exposition of the great advancement made in America in our technological age.

STRICTLY MY OWN IDEA

(When the speaker changes the subject)

It is characteristic of that pesterous and totally unnecessary breed known as after-dinner speakers that, getting on their feet, they almost invariably are reminded of a story. I am in no way an exception to the run of my kind.

Here and now at the outset of my brief remarks, I recall a story of a colored man in my native state who was hailed before a court on a charge of mayhem. At the same time the victim of his atrocious assault was presented before the jury's eyes as Exhibit A for the case of the prosecution. Now, the unfortunate man's face was but little more than a recent site; his nose was entirely missing, he was shy one ear, and he had only gums where his teeth should be.

The judge, in pronouncing sentence, and pointing meanwhile at the chief complaining witness, said to the convicted man: "That is the most lamentable exhibition of brutality I have ever seen. Surely no human being, unless he was swayed by diabolical influences could deliberately have worked such wreckage on the countenance of a fellow creature. The Devil must have actuated you in what you did; demons from Hell must have inspired your brutality."

After a short pause the convicted man said: "Well, Jedge, in a way of speakin', dat's right. When I was cuttin' his nose loose from his face with a razor it seemed to me like the Devil was right behin' me urgin' me on, an' 'spects it must have been dem demons you mentions dat suggested to me kickin' out his front teeth. But, Jedge, bitin' off his ear was strictly my own idea!"

Now, selecting me to speak on the subject, "Our Country" was a notion which originated with your program committee, but departing from that theme is strictly my own idea.

—Irvin S. Cobb

This opening was used by Mr. Cobb when he decided to speak on another subject instead of the one previously announced by the program committee.

SPEECH BY CANDIDATE TO POLITICAL WORKERS

Ladies and gentlemen: I don't believe that it is necessary for me to tell you about the rigors of this campaign. We are in for a tough one, and I am sure that each and every member of this great political party has full knowledge of this significant fact. I don't believe that you need any urging to get in and fight.

We are all in a similar plight to Rastus Brown from Alabama, who took his wife on a fishing trip way up to Minnesota. Rastus picked out a nice little cabin by the shores of a picturesque lake, which was surrounded on two sides by a dense forest. One day Rastus went out and did a little exploring in the woods. He no sooner became submerged inside the thick trees than he encountered a big black bear. The bear took one look at Rastus and Rastus took one look at the bear. Then Rastus turned and kicked up his heels like heels had never been kicked up in those woods before. And the bear followed suit, blowing a hot breath, which was punctuated with angry growls, upon the soles of Rastus' flying feet.

Momentarily, Rastus broke into the clearing with a leap that would put to shame any such an effort by Pegasus, the flying horse. The bear also leaped, its angry tongue within lapping distance of Rastus' almost supersonic flying feet.

The pair was not exactly traveling faster than sound, which was most fortunate, as the terrible wails, yells and growls reached the ear of Mrs. Rastus Brown, who was sitting in the cabin cleaning fish. Quick as a flash Mandy Brown flew to the door, opened it and beheld the sorry plight of her husband. Holding open the door, she yelled at the top of her lungs: "Run for it, Rastus, run for it! Run for it, man! Run for it! Run likes you never runs before!"

Rastus made one big heroic leap and slid headfirst through the cabin door, escaping destruction by a hair's breath. When Rastus had regained enough energy to utilize his exhausted lungs, he looked up at his wife from his prone position on the floor and said pantingly: "Mandy, you sure done made a fool of yourself, yelling at me to run, run. Youse know'd I'd never lie down in a race like that."   —Sylvester H. McGovern

The story used by this speaker as an opening suggests another style that stresses the humorous side. A funny story is usually effective and examples will be found in the chapter on "Responses."

THE SOVEREIGN ALCHEMIST

You'd have liked my friend, Bill Martin. When I met him he was a military governor in Germany. In his position Bill had a great deal of influence. People were constantly making requests—currying his favor. But when Bill came home it was to a $65.00-a-week job in the bank. Instead of giving orders he took them—no influence, no authority—and Bill resented it. The one time that Bill felt as though he were still somebody was when he could get together with some of his old buddies over a glass of beer. Then once more he seemed to have his old authority and position. You know the story. Bill began to drink oftener until the inevitable—he came to work drunk and lost his job. Already discouraged, he became convinced that the world in general was "down" on him. He drank more and more until even his wife could no longer stand it. From now on Bill was headed downhill and going fast. It was getting so that he couldn't tie his shoelaces—his hands were too shaky. He had to walk upstairs backwards for fear of falling. Many were the nights that he tied one end of a sheet to his leg and the other end to the bed post to keep himself from jumping out the window in a drunken frenzy. His cheeks became slack, he drooled and his face took on that peculiar mottled appearance common to all chronic alcoholics. Not long ago Bill Martin was found floating face down in the river.

—Frederick Tyler

An introduction used by Mr. Frederick Tyler to begin an address on the problems involved in dealing with chronic alcoholism. The narrative style is effective in making graphic the main theme of his talk.

PUNISHMENT?

The authorities of the Massachusetts State School for Girls at Lancaster, Massachusetts, have a problem on their hands. One of the inmates of the school, a fourteen-year-old girl, escaped yesterday. The authorities notified the police, who tracked her down across the country for a distance of sixteen miles. Through hedges and over barbed-wire fences the four-teen-year-old girl had walked and run until she reached the hospital at Worcester, where her mother was in a critical condition. It was worry over her mother that had led the lass to run away. She went to the hospital, because she had heard that her mother needed a blood transfusion, and she asked whether she couldn't be allowed to help.

While the doctors were examining her, the police, who had been chasing her, arrived. The officers waited until the operation was completed. Then they took the youngster back to the state school. And now the authorities are trying to make up their minds whether they ought to punish her.

—Lowell Thomas

This opening used by Mr. Thomas on one of his radio broadcasts illustrates the effective use of the narrative style in winning audience attention immediately.

THE ARM OF THE LAW

One cold February morning in 1930, Sun Wan lay sick abed in Washington, D.C. Suddenly, without warrant or warning, three officers of the law battered their way to his bedside, carried him out to the street, and flung him into their car. Wan was locked up without arrest on the top floor of Hotel Dewey, was told he had murdered three Chinamen, was tortured for eight nights and days by nine men working in eight-hour shifts. In the grey evening of the eighth day he was taken to the scene of the crime, and although painfully sick, was forced for ten hours to walk up and down stairs, made to examine photographs and bloody clothing of the dead men, and compelled by "the arm of the law" to tell again and again that he knew nothing of the murders. The following morning the formality of arrest took place, and Wan was subjected to an even more thorough so-called "shellacking" with leather belts, revolver-butts, blackjacks and a baseball bat.

Still unwilling to confess a crime of which he was innocent, the Chinaman was kept sleepless until the twelfth day, when, after two hundred and eighty-eight hours, he finally succumbed under the very shadow of the United States Capitol, which he heretofore had thought a protecting symbol of justice.

Wan confessed all that was required of him, and lapsed into unconsciousness. A doctor testified under oath that Wan's painful sickness coupled with the suffering from his ruthless treatment would have made him, or any man, confess anything to escape further torture.

This, my friends, is a typical case of the "third degree," based on facts taken directly from the opinion delivered by Justice Louis Brandeis when the United States Supreme Court reversed the life imprisonment sentence imposed upon Wan resulting from his "voluntary" confession.

—John M. Kitchen

The use of a specific illustration by Mr. Kitchen in his introduction to an address on the methods used by police departments in third degree procedures is exceedingly effective in stating the main premise of his arguments which follow. It's an excellent example of the narrative method.

THE VISION OF A SCIENTIST

Forty-two years ago, the leading electrical engineers of the world assembled in New York City. They gathered to find solutions to the problems that faced their infant industry. The most pressing of these problems was to prevent expensive machines from burning out as soon as alternating currents of electricity were sent speeding through them. The use of electrical energy for power seemed to be doomed as impractical. They pondered, talked, argued, and accomplished nothing. If they could only find some way of subjecting the alternating current to their will, shoes, clothes, and scores of other things that men need could be produced by machines driven at practically no cost. Not only were billions of dollars and the future of a great industry at stake, but also the comfort of mankind; and these engineers were baffled—bewildered.

Suddenly, a little hunchback stood up in the rear of the hall, and asked for permission to speak. That ill-clad cripple hobbled to the platform, and commenced to talk in a shrill, high-pitched monotone. To the mediocre in the audience, his address meant nothing, and they walked out. But the experts listened, at first indifferently. Then as they grasped the import of his discussion of the Fundamental Law of Magnetism and the significance of his calculations, they forgot the cripple, they forgot his hunched back, they forgot his twisted body, they forgot his shabby clothes. They realized that they were listening to a mathematical genius who had at last solved their problem. The vagaries of the alternating current were at an end. It had been bent to the uses of man. The name of that sorry jest of nature with the body of a dwarf, but the brain of a titan, was Steinmetz—Charles Proteus Steinmetz, the god of modern electricity.

When Steinmetz addressed that convention, he was a draftsman working for twelve dollars a week. Thirty years later he received no salary whatsoever, but he had an unlimited drawing account against the surplus of the General Electric Company. When Steinmetz addressed that convention, he was unknown. Thirty years later he wielded as much power as any other person in the electrical industry, and when he died in 1923 he received one of the greatest tributes that American business has ever given to any man.　　—Seymour Simon

This narrative style of introduction as used by Mr. Simon is very popular, particularly when the speech is biographical and eulogistic in treatment.

THE AMERICAN WAY

A few years ago I borrowed some money from a bank on good security and went to Scotland to visit my aging father and mother. The first night I was at home, my old Scots-Irish mother said to me: "Son, did I hear you say you have a telephone in your home?" I said, "Sure, Mother, we have a telephone." Her next question was perfectly natural. "Tell me, Son, how much does it cost you?" "Nine shillings a month." (You see, it was a party line which cost us $2.25 a month.)

Then she asked: "Son, how many calls can you make for that?" "Any number of calls, Mother." "Can you call at night?" "Sure, any hour of the day or night." I can still see her eyes open wide as she said to me: "Son, that must be a wonderful country." And I remember my answer: "Yes, Mother, and you'll see it before you die."

She did, too. And the night I parted with her in Montreal I asked her: "Mother, what do you think of it now that you have seen it." Would you like to know her answer? Listen! This was it: "Son, if I were only twenty years younger, Scotland would never see me again. I could make a living in this country." That, ladies and gentlemen, was from a seventy-five-year-old woman. She had seen what America had done under the system of free enterprise.　　—William A. Irwin

In beginning his address on "The American Way," Mr. Irwin uses this personal reference to his experience and this narrative style provides an effective method of introducing his address on the American system of free enterprise.

TO FIGHT IN PEACE

You are a curious people up here. You are never satisfied to eat your dinner in peace and give it a chance to digest. With the fact fully established by medical science that dull, leaden after-dinner speeches stop the process of digestion in those compelled to listen and are the source of most of the dyspepsia, apoplexy and paralysis that affect the country, you still go right along inviting these deadly maladies. Where I live people are allowed to eat their dinners in peace and give them a chance to digest. When I get into such a situation as this, I feel like the Kentuckian.

There is a mountain region in Kentucky where from time immemorial it has been the custom of the people to gather at the county seat of their county each Saturday and have fist-fights. This was an amusement witnessed and applauded by all, including the peace officers.

After the construction of the Cincinnati Southern Road, which ran through one of these counties, one of the old-time fighters concluded he would go out and see something of the world. The first thing he did when he got to Cincinnati was to fill up on Cincinnati whiskey, take a position on the sidewalk and proceed to knock down every passer-by until he had five or six prone on the sidewalk. The minions of the law gathered around him, finally succeeded in overpowering him, and carried him before the police judge, who said: "Sixty days and one hundred dollars." From the police court he was taken to the jail. He immediately sent for a lawyer. When his lawyer came he told him what he had been doing and begged to know what on earth they put him in jail for. The lawyer explained to him that it was for a breach of the peace, that it was for fighting, whereat the Kentuckian was profoundly astonished, and said to the lawyer: "Mr. Lawyer, for God's sake, get me out of here so I can go back to Kentucky, where I can fight in peace."

When I fall into the hands of one of these despots called toastmasters, I feel like the old darkey down in Arkansas who had lost four wives. After he had lost the fourth his pastor called on him and asked him how he felt, to which he responded: "Well, Brother Johnson, I feel like I was in the hands of an all-wise and unscrupulous Providence."

—Judge Henry C. Caldwell

This opening was used by Judge Caldwell who was invited to speak before the New England Society of St. Louis on December 21, 1895. It is an example of the use of the narrative style.

EFFECTIVE KNOW-HOW

Everyone has probably heard the story about the engineer who was called in to fix a balky machine. After a minute's study he picked up a hammer and tapped gently on the affected part of the machine.

"How much?" inquired the pleased owner of the now smoothly running machine.

"Fifteen dollars," said the engineer.

"For the love of mud, fifteen dollars for tapping that machine with a little hammer?"

"Certainly not," said the engineer. "One dollar for coming over and tapping the machine, and fourteen dollars for knowing **where** to tap."

Dangers, obstacles, problems are the very things that enable us to tap our inner powers. Men do not realize their greatness in a secure environment. If they did, our greatest men would come out of our prisons—the most secure environment in the world today.   —York Trade Compositor

This narrative opening may be used as an introduction to the inspirational type of address.

THE POWER OF AN IDEA

In the year 1892 in a small brick garage a few miles from my home in Dearborn, Michigan, a young man was tinkering with—an idea. It was an idea for a gasoline engine suitable for one of "them thar horseless carriages." It was only an idea— but it was an idea that put the whole world on wheels and meant work for six million people in this country alone.

In the year 1924 in the small bleak cell of an old fortress prison, another young man was tinkering with—an idea. It was an idea for a Nationalist Socialist Labor Party to meet the needs of his humiliated country. It was only an idea—but it was an idea that put the whole world in a state of war and meant death and suffering to millions of people everywhere.

These were but two ideas of two men. As illustrations they serve to show us the potential power of a mere idea. One idea conquered the great distances on earth and brought economic prosperity to millions of people, while the other idea brought destruction on earth and poverty to millions of people.

Now what made these ideas so great in their effect that they changed the very face of the earth? I think part of the answer lies in the personality of their authors. For personality, you know, is a powerful thing and an idea is a great force. Sometimes when the two are combined important history is made.

Henry Ford was a common man of common heritage who loved his family, feared God, and believed in simple, quiet living. I think it would be wrong to say that Mr. Ford wasn't motivated by selfish and mercenary interests in his life. I say this in the sense that as a young man he wanted the power of economic success for himself and his family just as you and I do. He didn't build the first automobile—he did, however, build in 1892 an automobile that was practical—and in it he saw his answer to economic success. Henry Ford knew the power of the common people of the middle classes and capitalized on it. He presented to them his humble horseless carriage not only as a better means of transportation but also for their own economic and social prosperity. These common people took to it nicely, didn't they?—and Henry Ford became a rich and respected man.

By the same token, Adolph Hitler was a common man of common heritage. Personally, Hitler was known to have been strict and sincere in his conduct, but he had no family to love, no God to worship, and he believed in living by sheer brute force. Hitler had his desire for power, too. But he wasn't satisfied with man's normal want of economic success—this man wanted political power to the outrageous extent of world domination. He, too, knew the power of the common people and capitalized on it. He presented to them Germany's redemption in social and economic reform through his propagandized theory of moral and physical damnation. His humiliated countrymen took to it nicely, didn't they?—and Adolph Hitler became a dictator.   —Donald Mitchell

This narrative introduction was used by Mr. Donald Mitchell to stir audience response to his argument for the support of the United Nations. By contrasting the basic philosophy of each man, Mr. Mitchell shows how a basic idea determines the future action of people, thus making clear the objective of his speech to the audience.

THE BEST IS YET TO BE

There is an old Arabian fable about the angel Ishmael, who desiring to learn if man ever grew so old that he ceased to desire life, traveled the earth for a thousand years. He looked into the faces of numberless men and women, but found in each a passionate love of life that the years did not dim. Finally, he discovered a man of 150. "What is your greatest wish?" the angel asked him, and the old man answered, "To live."

And so it has been for the ten thousand years of his existence on earth, man has loved life and lived in dread of dying. From the cave man witch doctor, to the alchemist and his Philosopher Stone; from Ponce de Leon and the Fountain of Youth to the modern research laboratory, the human race has been engaged in the never ending search for longer life. Today, we in the United States have come closer than any nation has ever come before to fulfilling that dream—that dream which is as old as the race itself. In the last one hundred years we have stretched the life span of our people from forty-two years to sixty-seven years.

But lest we rejoice in the accomplishment too soon, let us remember that each new achievement brings with it new problems. And today there is a problem of enormous importance to the future of the nation and the world—a problem seldom considered and for which no solution has been attempted or proposed. It is the problem of America's age. For we are growing old. —Milton Weiner

An introduction used by Mr. Milton Weiner in an address, "The Best Is Yet To Be" in which he discusses the problem of old age in America. The use of the Arabian fable is an effective narrative device to lead into the main subject of the talk.

COMPLIMENTS

I am glad that at last a man has been found with justice enough in his heart to pay me the compliment which I have so long deserved, and which has been denied me by so many generations of supposedly intelligent beings. Ranking me with the saints! There is nothing which pleases me more than that, because there is nothing left which I have deserved more than just that. I have ranked myself with St. Andrew for several years, and I really think that this should have been a dinner to the two of us, as St. Andrew was born on the same day in the same year as I was. If St. Andrew had not been born as early as he was on the 30th of November, I should stand now about where he stands. He got in a little ahead of me.

Now it is an interesting thing, St. Andrew here is here as a special guest, and he has heard himself complimented, and complimented, and complimented. You know, it is anybody's experience who has had any large experience in being the chief guest at a banquet, and you must know how entirely under-served that entire proceeding is, for the reason that the chairman begins by filling him up with compliments, and while they are well done, they are not quite high enough to meet the demand.

Now, this man has suffered this evening from hearing compliments poured out on him, apparently with lavishness, but he knows deep down in his heart that if he could overcome his diffidence he could improve those compliments. But he tries to dissemble, as our chief guest always does—look at the expression he has got on now! And the man always thinks he is doing well! Anybody who knows, knows that it is a pretty awkward performance, that diffidence that he is working on his countenance doesn't deceive anybody; but it is always interesting to see what people will find to say about a man. It is not a matter of what Carnegie has done, for I would have done it myself, if I had had to.　　　　　　　　　　　　　　—Mark Twain

This humorous opening was used by Mark Twain at a banquet honoring Andrew Carnegie who had previously referred to Mr. Clemens as St. Mark. This was perhaps the last speech that he made before his death in 1910.

NOT SECURITY — BUT AN OPPORTUNITY

Suppose your birthplace had been a farm near Falsmouth, Virginia. Suppose, when you were eleven years old, as a result of infantile paralysis, you became an invalid. Five years later, when you were still an invalid, suppose your father had died. Thus, a bed-ridden cripple at sixteen, you found yourself stranded with your mother and three other children on a 200-acre farm, heavily mortgaged. If this had happened to you six years ago, what would you have done?

Would you have thrown up your hands in despair? Would you have said, "what's the use?" Would you have decided that you were just one of the twelve and a half million—the "lost" generation, the doomed generation—jobless, without a future?

Would you have taken this attitude? It's a familiar one to you and me.

You and I might have sung this tune. But Hunter Roy Greenlaw did not. He was born twenty-two years ago, near Falsmouth, Virginia. At eleven he was stricken with infantile paralysis. Then his father died, and at sixteen, he found himself a crippled member of a family of five living on a mortgaged farm of two hundred acres. Someone had to take over. Hunter climbed out of bed and began. He farmed so well that, five years later, out of a field of 171,000 young farmers, a national committee of experts picked young Greenlaw for the degree of Star Farmer.

Hunter Greenlaw didn't let himself be called lost. He didn't just sit down and charge the wreckage of the world to his elders. He didn't decide that the world owed him a living. He had enough spunk and sense and stamina to stand up and accept his problems, not as insurmountable barriers, but as challenges. The young man who gives up without a fight, who looks at a situation and decides it's hopeless, that young man is not lost, he's sick. Perhaps not physically sick, as young Greenlaw was, but worse yet, mentally and spiritually sick.

—George I. Meisel

A narrative introduction used by Mr. Meisel to arouse the interest of the audience in the main topic of his address—that there are countless opportunities for young people in this changing, modern world.

AGAINST CHILD MARRIAGES

Yesterday, as the train passed through a city not far away from here, I was reminded of a marriage that took place there a few years ago. Because many other marriages in this state have been just as hasty and disastrous as this one, I am going to begin what I have to say today with some of the details of this individual instance.

It was on December 12 that a high school girl of fifteen in that city met for the first time a junior in a nearby college who had just attained his majority. On December 15, only three days later, they procured a marriage license by swearing that the girl was eighteen and was therefore free from the necessity of procuring parental consent. Leaving the city clerk's office with their license, they applied at once to a priest (the girl was Catholic), but very properly he refused to marry them. In some way, perhaps through this priest, the child's mother received news of the attempted marriage. Before she could find her daughter, however, a justice of the peace had united the pair. The bridegroom then took his bride to a hotel where they spent two days and two nights, at the end of which time he abandoned her and never lived with her again.   —Mary E. Richmond

The speaker used the narrative style of opening with a human interest appeal that always holds the attention of any audience.

THE CAMEL'S NOSE

The title I have chosen for my talk is "The Camel's Nose is Under the Tent." The expression comes from an old Arabian fable, and to an Arab it spells trouble and disaster. The fable of the Arab and his camel goes something like this:

One cold night, as an Arab sat in his tent, a camel gently thrust his nose under the flap and looked in.

"Master," he said, "let me put my nose in your tent, for it is cold and stormy out here."

"By all means, and welcome," said the Arab, and turned over and went to sleep. A little later he awoke and found that the camel had not only put his nose in the tent but his neck and head as well.

The camel, who had been turning his head from side to side, said, "I will take but little more room if I place my forelegs within the tent. It is difficult standing without."

"You may also plant your forelegs within," said the Arab, moving a little to make room, for the tent was small.

Finally the camel said, "May I not stand wholly within? I keep the tent open by standing as I do."

"Yes, yes," said the Arab. "Come wholly inside. Perhaps it will be better for both of us." So the camel came forward and crowded into the tent.

The Arab with difficulty in the crowded quarters again went to sleep. The next time he woke up he was outside in the cold and the camel had the tent to himself.

Independent of how he got there, the important point is that the camel of government control now has his nose under the tent of free competitive industry and is crowding in. We will all have to watch him or he will take over the tent, and we will lose our economic freedom and with it all our other liberties. Of course, if the camel is really successful in taking over the tent, the members of the Society for the Advancement of Management had better be studying how to become government bureaucrats—not how to become more effective members of our marvelous American industrial system.

—Charles E. Wilson

Mr. Wilson used this narrative type of opening very effectively in an address before the Dallas Chapter of the Society for the Advancement of Management. It is an excellent example of how the use of the story style captures an audience's attention at the very outset of a speech. It is significant, too, that this opening keyed itself into the subject of Mr. Wilson's address.

THAT'S HIS PROBLEM

This problem of the age factor in employment is everybody's problem. We are all, in a sense, "aging workers." There are few families that have not had immediate experience with the problem, and there are few individuals who will not, sooner or later, encounter it personally.

They tell a story of a psychiatrist who gave a cocktail party and hired a butler to give the occasion real elegance. The butler, however, as the guests began to arrive, was observed to behave rather oddly. First he deliberately poured a Martini down the neck of one of the guests. Then he pulled a small oriental rug out from under another guest. Finally, as the crowd got thicker, he went about busily dumping trays of drinks on the other doctors and psychiatrists present, tripping them from behind, and generally spreading consternation. Throughout all this the psychiatrist host paid no attention whatever to these unorthodox pleasantries, and maintained an imperturbable calm. Finally, one of his guests came up to him and said, "Really, now, don't you realize this fellow is pouring drinks on us and pulling rugs from under us and behaving very strangely indeed?" With an airy wave of the hand, the host psychiatrist replied, "Well, after all, that's **his** problem."

The recognition that the problem of age in employment is **our** problem — everyone's problem — is implicit in the roster of those attending and addressing this Conference. I was gratified to see that there are, on the panels, representatives of labor, business, insurance companies, State and Federal Government agencies, the University and the Church.

—Arthur Larson

The introduction of an address, "Age Barriers of Our Own Making," delivered by Under Secretary of Labor Arthur Larson at Philadelphia on Oct. 21, 1954.

Chapter Three

The Dramatic Opening

Of all the types of openings that a speaker may use, no doubt the dramatic opening is the most effective. When used effectively it usually attracts and holds the audience's attention. Extreme care must be exercised to develop the ideas to build toward a climax which usually appeals to the emotions of the audience. Every speaker will use his own individual style and the treatment will depend, of course, on the subject matter.

The illustrations given here reveal the variety that characterizes the dramatic opening.

NEW OPPORTUNITIES

It was a little before noon on a hot, dry, dusty day in September of 1893. A restless crowd of people pressed as closely as they could to an imaginary line. Men, from every walk of life, fighting, bargaining, cheating, gambling for a place upon the line. At regular intervals as far as the eye could see soldiers stood to keep them back until the signal had been given. One minute to go—all was still. As the smoke came from the sentry's gun, before the sound could break upon the still air, a mighty uproar broke loose as that maddened mass of humanity rushed across the line and on to become the settlers of another of our great commonwealths—Oklahoma. This was the picturesque passing of our great American frontier—the claiming of the Cherokee strip.   —Edward O'Hare

In this introduction, Mr. O'Hare has used a graphic style to create audience attention to his main discussion of the new frontiers that exist in America today. The action story always fascinates an audience and helps to concentrate attention by its dramatic treatment.

MERELY PLAYERS

Take yourselves back with me to a dank autumn day two years ago in the Northwestern football stadium. The scoreboard tells a catastrophe, not altogether unprecedented; the University of Wisconsin has been defeated. During the excitement of the contest Don Heap was knocked out, and with no one else to put into the game, the coach, in desperation, called upon me. Quaking in my shoes, I stumbled out on the field, and while Jankowski was looking at an airplane I managed to wriggle and crawl to a touchdown. While carrying the ball through a hole about as big as the dancing space at the Junior Prom, I had but one idea; get across that goal line—nothing more! Truly, my perspective of football as a mere player was just about as narrow as the hole I was knifing through.

Not so today! The curtain is now drawn on that act. I take a seat, figuratively, on the goal post. From this position I can see the game as it really is. I see it now as an appealing dramatic spectacle; the frenzied fans, the anxious coaches, the highstrung players. The whole scene rolls before me in a colorful panorama. The band blares out a marching-song as eleven bright-suited warriors take the field. The gold-tinted helmets, the crunching bodies, the clashing of cleats, all give it a fascinating glamour. Something primitive crops out when 60,000 people roar for a touchdown, and as the game tightens there is fear ... anger ... fear again ... amazement ... credulity ... exultation. Every elemental emotion sweeps through their hearts in this Roman holiday.

These gladiatorial combats have spread throughout our modern empire. Think of the "big" games played every year, each a spectacle drawing from 50 to 100,000 people: Southern California versus Notre Dame, Army against the Navy, Harvard's classic with Yale, Minnesota and Michigan. Yes, on a single Saturday 20,000,000 people in the United States watched 1,000,000 youths at play. Football—a mere harmless sport? It may have started so, but it has become one of our great educational problems. Its influence, magnified by our universities, touches every playground, every home, every office. It is written about in every newspaper from the tabloid to the Christian Science Monitor.   —Albert Adelman

In a speech on the merits of college football, Mr. Adelman used this striking observation by personal participation to attract the audience to his point of view. The dramatic movements on the football field re-create the action and excitement to arouse a good audience reaction.

THE DILEMMA OF DEMOCRACY

The time: the night of February 20th, 1939. The place: a great auditorium. Everywhere, flags—Italian flags, German flags. A uniformed band playing. From the back appears a column of storm-troopers. The waltz stiffens into a sharp military march. Stern, trim in their grey shirts and Sam Browne belts, eight abreast, they march down between the massed saluting sections. More and more of them, tightlipped, silent, marching. From above, a blue spotlight plays on the grey of the marching men, on the bloody crimson of the huge floating swastika banners.

Thrilling!—the martial music, the lights and flags, the crowd hysteria, the shouting. It's electric and real—and crushing!

This is not the Nurnberg Nazi Party Congress. This is not Berlin's Sports-Palast, not Vienna, not Rome. It is Madison Square Garden, New York City, the United States of America. These, who are so faithfully giving the Nazi salute, are not Germans; they are Americans, pledging allegiance to the foreign dictatorship of Adolf Hitler.

It can't happen here, we said. It can't happen here. But it has happened.   Abraham L. Schneider

This dramatic narrative was used by Mr. Schneider to stir his audience at the very beginning of his speech to a realization that the Fascist influence was just as prevalent as is the Communist infiltration today.

SHRINKING FREE WORLD

You pay the embattled people of Korea a great honor by inviting me, their servant, to address you here today. These are times of dreadful mental anxiety for all of us—all of us who remain in a shrinking free world.

Thousands of splendid American boys lie buried in the soil of Korea. Tens of thousands of Korean soldiers have suffered the same fate. My country is a vast charnel house with ruins and rubble everywhere. I have termed it a land of the dead and the dying. This it has been for more than two years now.

—Dr. You Chan Yang

An introduction given by Dr. Yang, Korean Ambassador to the United States, in a speech delivered at a convention of the National Women's Republican Clubs. It's a splendid example of the dramatic opening used by a speaker who appeals to the audience's emotions.

THE CREATIVE CITIZEN

Two years ago an Iowa town was awakened in the night by newsboys shouting "Extra." These papers announced that the last bank had closed. But another headline read—"A. C. Kahl to reorganize bank." This brought confidence to the community, for A. C. Kahl was their leading citizen; he always succeeded. Fifty years ago he was driving horses for a construction gang. Now he was head of a steel corporation, owner of a newspaper, and head of an insurance company. Last month these people were again awakened by newsboys shouting "Extra." This time they were startled by the headline—"Kahl commits suicide."

I knew this man well. Shortly before his death I visited him in his office and was shocked to hear him say, "My boy, don't build your life as I have—upon worldly success. It's not substantial enough. If it stays, you're not satisfied. When it goes, you've got nothing left."

A. C. Kahl is but a symbol, typifying a life built on materialism. This basis proved too brittle to uphold him. His failure is the failure of what Bertrand Russell calls the "possessive group" of men. These people look upon living as a process of squeezing as much as possible out of life for themselves. To them the ultimate goal is to satisfy their insatiable thirst to possess, to control, to dominate. —Paul Ziffren

Mr. Ziffren uses a specific example in his introduction which forms the foundation for his address on the ideals of good citizenship. Although the illustration shows a negative side, it shows what the ideal should be by contrast. Nevertheless this dramatic opening secured the immediate attention of the audience.

THE SHADOW OF THE SWASTIKA

In the basement of an old house in Munich, seven men sit about a table. If we were eavesdroppers, we should hear heated discussions on the problems of government, nationalism, and race prejudice. Night after night they have assembled. They have sent out invitations asking people to join them. They have waited hopefully for newcomers, but always, none save the seven original members have come. Now, discouraged and depressed, they are deciding to make one last desperate attempt. They will throw every earthly possession into the project. They will rent a hall and advertise their meeting in the newspapers.

At last, success is achieved; one hundred and eleven people attend. For the first time the man who has been the leader of the group tries his talent for oratory. His instincts have told him that he can speak. Now he actually proves it; and National Socialism has become a force in the life of Germany. This is the humble beginning of Adolf Hitler's phenomenal rise to power.
—Lucile L. Benz

This dramatic introduction was used by Miss Benz in opening her address on the rise of Adolf Hitler to power. The gradual approach to the main subject is effective because the interest of the audience is aroused and complete attention is given when the main body of the address is presented.

THE 49TH STATE

John Adams, "The man of the New England town-meeting," is addressing the members of the Caucus Club in the year 1769. The place of meeting is the garret in the home of Tom Daws, the adjutant general of the Boston regiment. It is a serious moment. The discussion has lasted for more than three hours. John Adams has been called upon to summarize the discussion and to state the cause of the colonists. His words ring out in the smoke-filled garret with sincerity and conviction. "Taxation without representation is tyranny."

The following day found the city of Boston repeating the phrase in every home and inn. The word spread throughout the country. Town hall after town hall echoed its refrain. Patrick Henry, the orator of the South, aroused the southern planters with a speech in which he said "Taxation without representation is tyranny!"

Colonial relations became tense. English statesmen pointed out that the colonies were a "hot-bed of revolt." From New England to the South were heard the cries—"Repeal the Stamp Act," "Throw Out the Tea," "Burn the Ships!" "Remove the Fourteenth and Twenty-Ninth Regiments!" Back of all this violence ran the phrase—"Taxation without representation is tyranny."

Friends, that happened one hundred and seventy years ago. Yet today, my aim is to again draw your attention to that phrase. We in Hawaii can perhaps understand the significance of it more so than the average American.

—Jack Dunn

In his address urging that Hawaii be made the forty-ninth state of the Union, Mr. Dunn uses reference to historical facts in his introduction and uses the theme, "Taxation without representation is tyranny!" This type of introduction is always effective because the main premise of the argument is stated at the very beginning and the audience knows exactly what course the speaker is to follow.

THE VISION OF WAR

The past rises before me like a dream. Again we are in the great struggle for national life. We hear the sounds of preparation; the music of boisterous drums; the silver voices of heroic bugles. We see thousands of assemblages, and hear the appeals of orators. We see the pale cheeks of women, and the flushed faces of men; and in those assemblages we see all the dead whose dust we have covered with flowers. We lose sight of them no more. We are with them when they enlist in the great army of freedom. We see them part with those they love. Some are walking for the last time in quiet, woody places with the maidens they adore. We hear the whisperings and the sweet vows of eternal love as they lingeringly part forever. Others are bending over cradles, kissing babes that are asleep. Some are receiving the blessings of old men. Some are parting with mothers who hold them and press them to their hearts again and again, and say nothing. Kisses and tears, tears and kisses—divine mingling of agony and love! And some are talking with wives, and endeavoring with brave words, spoken in the old tones, to drive from their hearts the awful fear. We see them part. We see the wife standing in the door with the babe in her arms—standing in the sunlight, sobbing. At the turn in the road a hand waves—she answers by holding high in her loving arms the child. He is gone, and forever.   —Robert G. Ingersoll

This dramatic and emotional opening was used by Mr. Ingersoll in his famous address that has been recognized as a model for speech development.

DICTATORS IN AMERICAN POLITICS

Never, Mr. President, have I known or read of an administration which expires with so much agony, and so little composure and resignation, as that which now unfortunately has the control of public affairs in this country. It exhibits a state of mind, feverish, fretful, and fidgety, bounding recklessly from one desperate expedient to another, without any sober or settled purpose. Ever since the dog days of last summer, it has been making a succession of the most extravagant plunges, of which the extraordinary cabinet paper, a sort of appeal from a dissenting cabinet to the people, was the first; and the protest, a direct appeal from the Senate to the people, is the last and the worst.
—Henry Clay

This dramatic opening to his address denouncing Andrew Jackson, delivered in the United States Senate on April 30, 1834, is an excellent example of introducing the theme of his entire address at the outset.

LET MEDICINE WASH ITS HANDS

Behind a desk in a large hospital in the city of Vienna sits a young doctor. Before him stand twenty women, each of whom has come to the hospital with the hope in her heart that she is about to give to the world a child. Nineteen of those women will never leave that hospital—alive. Only one will survive. For it is the year 1845, and the scourge of childbed fever rages unchecked through the hospitals of all Europe. But one man, young Phillip Semmelweiss, has discovered the answer, and he has shouted his discovery to the world, that millions of women need not die—if only doctors will wash their hands. But the world cannot hear the young doctor. The world hears only the pontifical chant of authority. And the world repeats like a parrot the ignorant screeches of Dr. Kline, archpriest of an arrogant aristocracy of medical authority; authority that damns Semmelweiss, damns the "filthy washings"; authority that buried millions of women—rather than pause to wash its hands.

Today we live in a world in which Semmelweiss has been vindicated, a world in which the advances of medical science almost astound the human mind; yet for all practical purposes a large segment of our medical profession still lives in the world of 1845. For there still exists within our own nation a countless number of Dr. Klines, forming an aristocracy of medical authority that denies to a great mass of people the right to life. High on the throne of the medical profession sits the American Medical Association, led by a reactionary and mentally bankrupt oligarchy that refuses, in modern times, "to wash its hands." I am here tonight to indict the American Medical Association as a medieval influence in modern medicine.

—Hershel Sarbin

The introduction of an address, "Let Medicine Wash Its Hands," delivered by Mr. Hershel Sarbin in which he indicts the American Medical Association for its failure to support a liberal and progressive program of medical service. The reference to the historic practice of doctors as stated in the introduction enabled Mr. Sarbin to get an immediate audience response to his argument. You can imagine the audience's irate response to this dramatic opening, especially if the majority of the audience were doctors.

THE CHALLENGE IS ACCEPTED

My Fellow Americans: The sudden criminal attacks perpetrated by the Japanese in the Pacific provide the climax of a decade of international immorality. Powerful and resourceful gangsters have banded together to make war upon the whole human race. Their challenge has been flung at the United States of America. The Japanese have treacherously violated the long-standing peace between us. Many American soldiers and sailors have been killed by enemy action. American ships have been sunk. American airplanes have been destroyed.

The Congress and the people of the United States have accepted that challenge. Together with other free peoples, we are now fighting to maintain our right to live among our world neighbors in freedom and common decency, without fear of assault.   —President Franklin D. Roosevelt

THE CHILDREN'S HOUR

The other afternoon while rather lazily turning the dials of my radio, my ear caught the rat-tat-tat of a machine gun. Amid the confusion that ensued after the gun fire, the cries, and yells, and the leading character barking out orders, I could gather very little in the form of an explanation. But soon the din faded away and the narrator's voice mysteriously whispered, "Will Dick Tracy be able to out-wit the mobster group? Will he win in his race of death?"

Listening to the other programs, some of the key lines were as follows: "Huge spiders running down the wall. . . . If that spider runs up my leg it'll kill me. . . . Put the handcuffs on him, boys. . . . Just looking at that haunted house gives me the creeps. . . . The tunnel seems to be dark and damp. . . . I might have killed you, Ryan. . . . Look, see, he has a hook instead of a right hand. . . . Don't let him get that hook into you. . . . Have you got your gun? . . . It wouldn't be the first time I pulled the trigger to this gun. . . . I'll find him and kill him. . . . They'll never find me in this dark jungle. . . . You aren't going to put the heat on me, are you, boys?"

This is the kind of trash that the sponsors and producers are placing before our youth today. —Alfred Brown

By quoting a variety of statements made in the average children's programs heard on the radio, Mr. Brown succeeds in giving adequate stress to his subject. It's a dramatic method that always attracts the audience's attention.

Chapter Four

Using A Quotation As An Opening

One of the most effective methods of opening a speech is to use a familiar quotation that is apropos and serves to properly introduce the basic subject. It is assumed, of course, that the quotation will be selected with great care; it must relate to the theme of the address. You will note in the examples that follow how well-chosen the quotation is as a means of leading into the main body of the speech.

This word of caution must be given. Never use a quotation unless it supports the main theme of your speech.

NEW BIRTH OF FREEDOM

"We have it in our power to begin the world over again. A situation similar to the present hath not happened since the days of Noah. The birthday of a new world is at hand."

These words are not the prophesy of an immature orator. They were written by Thomas Paine before the American Revolution 160 years ago. We know today that Tom Paine's was a prophetic voice. A new world was born. A new experiment was launched on this continent in those closing years of the eighteenth century, an experiment the immensity and the daring of which has never been equaled. The Minute Men at Lexington and Concord truly "fired the shot heard 'round the world." —Willard Hunter

It is sometimes effective to begin an address with a quotation as Mr. Hunter has done in this instance. However, then it is important the quotation be chosen appropriately.

FITNESS TO SURVIVE

In the current issue of Foreign Affairs the former Secretary of War, Henry L. Stimson, discusses "The Challenge to America." He describes in realistic terms the present grim international scene, and, after refusing to subscribe to the doctrine of an inevitable conflict with the Soviet Union, says, "We must make it wholly evident that a non-aggressive Russia will have nothing to fear from us. We must make it clear, too, that the western non-Communist world is going to survive in growing economic and political stability. If we can do this, then slowly —but perhaps less slowly than we now believe—the Russian leaders may either change their minds or lose their jobs. The problem of Russia is thus reduced to a question of our own fitness to survive."

I have taken the last phase of this quotation from Mr. Stimson's article as the text for my remarks today.

—Dr. James B. Conant

A HOUSE DIVIDED

On the evening of the seventeenth of June, 1858, an angular and homely-clad figure arose by a table in the Hall of the House of Representatives in Springfield, Illinois, and stood before a cheering audience. He was the spokesman of a cause, and great events, still in the future, were to make his words historic. He began his speech, slowly, with frequent emphasis on particular words. "If we could first know where we are, and whither we are tending, we could better judge what to do, and how to do it."

Abraham Lincoln had not proceeded far with his famous address when he uttered the words, "A house divided against itself cannot stand." This old proverb is as true today as when Lincoln quoted it from the Bible before the Civil War. He saw clearly that a nation half slave and half free cannot endure. Today our modern leaders are declaring that, with Labor in a deadlock with Capital, our Industrial House can no longer stand. The keen-edged blade of class hatred has severed the unity in the House of Industry.   —John Roberts

Lincoln's famous words of philosophy are quoted by Mr. Roberts in opening his discussion of the present problems of labor and capital. It is interesting to note that Lincoln's famous statement applies to the subject under treatment.

Chapter Five

The Personal Experience Opening

The most successful professional lecturer is the individual who has passed through some unusual personal experience. He might be a world traveler, a diplomat who has escaped from behind the Iron Curtain, the inventor of an exceptional labor-saving device, or a flier who has traveled around the world faster than sound. The announcement of his appearance will always attract an audience because people are interested in the personal experiences of others. It gives them a certain vicarious thrill.

Moreover, the speaker has more freedom and spontaneity in his delivery which makes it easy for the listeners to follow his trend of thought. No other type of opening is more effective, especially if the speaker is a novice. The audience's attention is diverted from making a cold appraisal of the speaker's personality, his voice, his appearance, and his word choice. In concentrating on following his narrative, they forget to be too analytical. Instead they fasten their attention on the speaker's remarks.

The following openings are examples of the personal experience type which illustrate another method of beginning an address:

THE SCROLL OF DESTINY

When a Negro appears before a white audience, he is usually met with a humorous reception. Everyone smiles. He is expected to dance a jig or cut some capers. He is either a smiling Sambo, a lazy bones, or a razor-toting Rastus—anything but an intelligent, serious-thinking human being. From the black face of the comedian, the darky-skit of the radio, the Rastus-jokes of the speaker, to the Sambo-cartoons of the newspapers, the Negro has become an over-loaded pack-horse for ridicule and humor. But, I assure you that I have no chickens under my coat; watermelon season has long passed; and I will not degenerate this assembly by starting a crap game. It is a strange thing to see a Negro before a white audience playing an intellectual role, for when he assumes a cultural pose, he faces that American philosophy: "Nigger, stay in your place; this is a white man's country."   —William McClain

Here is another example of the use of the personal reference in opening a talk. Mr. McClain does this in a very effective manner. He states commonly accepted facts about members of his race from a negative approach. In the main body of his address he outlines the many contributions that the Negro has made in all fields of endeavor.

SAFETY FIRST

One evening not so long ago I chanced to be on Cleveland's Public Square hurrying to meet a friend. Not thinking of autos, I stepped hastily into the street without stopping to look. I was nearly hit, as a machine whizzed past me. Then I looked about me; and there, where I could almost touch it, was a large sign erected by the Cleveland Safety Council which read, "Jeepers Creepers—Use Your Peepers."

I laughed! But then, I became serious. This sign made me think. It made me think more than the honking of the auto that nearly ran me down. It made me realize, as it has many another Clevelander, that one makes a tremendous mistake in roaming about the streets with little or no regard for life or safety.

The sign itself was humorous, but what it warned me against was tragic. By my carelessness I had just come close to being one of the thirty-six thousand people killed, or one of the million injured in motoring accidents each year.

—Myron C. Hoff

A personal reference to an actual experience was used by Mr. Hoff to introduce the main subject of his address on safety precautions on the highway.

THE COLOR LINE

Eighty-five years ago tonight I would not have been permitted to talk before a white audience. I am the grandson of a slave. Two months from now I will be barred from participation in another intercollegiate oratorical contest on this very campus, because my skin is black and my hair is kinky. Eighty-five years have not been long enough to erase from the minds of many people the fact that Negroes were once a servant class. We are even now hedged in by barriers and restrictions. And the motto reigns supreme, "Nigger, stay in your place."

If a colored citizen of the United States excels in any of the so-called worthwhile fields of endeavor, the white man declares that he can't be an American Negro, because American Negroes are ignorant. The man must be a South American, a Cuban, or even a Filipino. We are darkies who know only the language of the spiritual, "I ain't gwine a-study war no more." We are pictured as running past graveyards, shying at corpses, and believing in "hants." We are expected to carry a rabbit's foot and keep a hoodoo bag. We are happy-go-lucky Sambos who fish and eat watermelons all summer, and dine on possum all winter.

Our history is the history of slave ships, cotton fields, and 245 years of bondage. My grandfather told me that when the Emancipation Proclamation was signed he and his whole family wept. "Uncle Billy," as he was known, had served as advisor and godfather to his master's children and grandchildren. He loved the blood-red cotton fields, the pleasant white houses, and the sluggish yellow rivers. He was used to the jingling harness chains, the careless laughter of Negro voices as the hands came in from the fields, and the plantation melodies in the soft Spring twilights. My grandparents had been among the chosen few who had known a good master.

—Herbert Bracken

This human interest style of treatment as used by Mr. Bracken is an excellent example of an ideal type of introduction whenever the speaker draws upon his own personal experience and observation as has been done in this instance.

SANCTUARY

I have assisted at many functions during recent years, but at none more calculated to touch the hidden springs of the heart than that in which I have participated today. Bewdley, as most of you know, was in distant ages a sanctuary town to which a man, whatever his sins, might flee and be safe from justice. So whenever the rude waves of the outside world buffet me with more than usual vigor, I have only to remember that in Bewdley there is a sanctuary even for a Prime Minister.

—Stanley Baldwin

In opening his speech on "My Native Town" given in his home town on August 8, 1935, Prime Minister Baldwin used a reference to his own personal sentiment and affection for the town and its people.

I AM A DEMOCRAT

I am a Democrat. I have been an active and I can truly say a belligerent Democrat for forty years. I have never been a "fair weather" Democrat, Democratic when the Democrats were in power and something else when they were out. In office and out, I have given to the service of the Democratic party more time and energy than to any other interest in my life except the profession of the law by which I earn my daily bread. In return the Democratic party has honored me beyond my highest hopes and has put upon me a debt of gratitude beyond my power to repay.

It is precisely because of these honors and this debt that I have been driven to conclude that I cannot consult my own distinct preference and remain entirely silent in the present campaign. There are times when it becomes a duty to one's conscience, one's party, and one's country to stand up and be counted. I owe it, as it seems to me, to my fellow Democrats to make my position clear and, if I am led to disagree with any of them, to give my reasons for this disagreement. I am speaking tonight primarily to Democrats, but since I am an American even before I am a Democrat, I must, if I speak at all, speak the truth as I see it without fear and without evasion.

—John W. Davis

In this opening, Mr. Davis gave a declaration of his personal philosophy about his party affiliation and loyalty. It was an excellent method to follow because the audience was attracted to the speaker's informal sincerity.

THE DEN OF YOUTH

Helen was my classmate in high school, a beautiful, vivacious girl, a leader in our school. Helen's father was a successful businessman. She had all the advantages a fine home could offer. She rode horseback, played golf and tennis. Hers was a life that held every promise for the future. But Helen never finished high school. Today her fine features and stunning beauty are permanently marred by ugly scars. For three months she lay unconscious on a hospital bed enclosed in a rigid plaster of Paris cast. Now she moves painfully about in a stooped position, hideously deformed by a permanent injury to her spine. That is Helen's case.

Her boy friend's name was Roger. He was president of his class in college, a halfback on the football team and an "A" student. He was an all-around boy whom everyone liked. Any father would have been proud to have called him his son, but like Helen, Roger could not finish school. Today he wears the drab garb of the reformatory. Dejectedly he stands behind steel bars. Instead of being in college, he is serving time for criminal negligence while driving his father's automobile.

—Barbara Dailey

In this introduction, Miss Dailey uses a graphic personal illustration as a basis for the development of her main subject in which she indicts the use of drugs and strong drink as one of the main causes of automobile accidents.

WHY I FEEL AT HOME

I feel very much at home at an occasion of this kind. Some of my most vivid recollections are just such open-air celebrations as this. We used to have a lot of them when I was on the farm. We'd always have them, of course, on the Fourth of July.

The first such celebration I can remember was when I was five years old. I must explain that, like Calvin Coolidge and George M. Cohan, I was born on the Fourth of July. My mother tells me that my arrival ruined her plans for the best picnic she had ever arranged. Well, when I was five years old, my parents took me to a big outdoor Fourth of July celebration in a grove near my grandfather's farm in Yankton County. My head was full of thoughts about the birthday presents I had just received and about the achievement of the great milestone—my fifth birthday. I looked around at the flags, the bunting, the band on the bandstand, the fireworks going off, the orator on the platform—and finally said to my parents, blushing modestly, "This is wonderful, but they really shouldn't have gone to so much trouble."

And so, it is no mere formality when I tell you that I am glad you asked me to be with you here today. I like the Midwest and I like Midwesterners.   —Arthur Larson

These were the opening remarks used by the Under Secretary of Labor at a Diamond Jubilee Celebration held in Freeman, South Dakota, Aug. 12, 1954.

DOLLARS AND SENSE

Last month I was confronted with a curious financial problem that is perhaps not peculiar to college students. I approached the twentieth of the month with but one of those precious seventy-five dollars left. The more I studied that dollar and the more I wondered how I would spend it, the more impressed I became with its smallness. It was small in the amount it would buy for me. I suppose that, to the average student, a dollar means a cup of coffee, a pack of cigarettes, a malt, and perhaps the Special over in the Union during the noon rush. By the time evening arrives a dollar has diminished to nothing and we have received little in return. Yet there exists within the boundaries of my home state, Minnesota, a place where that dollar will still buy a great deal. It will provide food, clothing, shelter, medical attention—and every physical requirement necessary for life. For that one dollar is the amount spent each day on each patient in a mental institution in the State of Minnesota.   —Don Sikkink

This effective introduction was used by Mr. Don Sikkink in opening his talk on the mental health problem in Minnesota. It's another example of the use of personal narrative.

MUST I DIE?

Ladies and Gentlemen:

I come before you this evening with the sincere hope of impressing upon you a message. To me it is a very important message. Important—for you see—I am going to die. Before I die I may lose my arms, perhaps my legs and even my mind. But before this happens to me—before I die—I feel it is imperative that I tell you not only how I will die, but why I will die.

How will I die you ask? The answer is quite simple. I will undoubtedly die as a result of enemy fire on a battlefield in Europe, Asia, or perhaps even here in the United States. I will die in a third world war which our unnecessarily blind statesmen today are making almost inevitable.

Why will I die you ask? The answer here again is quite simple. I am one of those innocent youths who are going to have to fight and perhaps give their lives to end another world war which may in the end destroy all humanity. I am one of those powerless, politically impotent young men who throughout history have been forced to sit back in silence while their countries' statesmen provided the occasion on which they might give their lives in vain.   —Irvin J. Robinson

An introduction used by Mr. Irvin J. Robinson in address in which he made a plea for an intelligent plan to avert a third world war. The direct personal style of Mr. Robinson is particularly effective.

THE PACIFIC CHARTER

Perhaps I have no right to say the things I shall say to you tonight. I have frequently imposed upon myself the obligation not to criticize the faults of America. I have rather, in the past, undertaken to examine the faults of my own people, the Chinese, and to ask your aid for them.

But today, I am wearied, and confused, and pained. For three years now, I have lived in America, privileged to pursue my studies in one of her greatest institutions of learning. For three crucial years, I have witnessed every step this great nation has taken inevitably toward war. During these years, I have talked intimately with American students, American businessmen, and American factory workers. And in nine cases out of ten, I was disappointed, until I began to believe that what they said represented widespread confused thinking in the great masses of the American people. They extolled my people's fight; they made much of fine phrases about international bills of rights and Atlantic Charters, but they seemed addicted to circumlocution whenever challenged to take their clear and realistic role in defense of right throughout the world. I had expected the deep, clear faith that America had brought into the world in the Declaration of Independence—but it was not there.

That is why I must speak frankly to you today, not in bitterness, but because, having lived in America, I love America. And loving America, and hoping for the common salvation of both America and China, at this dark hour I must speak of you as I would of my own people, without reserve. If I offend, I shall ask your forgiveness. But I shall also be gratified that the offense will have attested to a truth sent home.

—Paul Lim-Yuen

In this introduction Mr. Lim-Yuen states his personal observation of the American people's attitude toward his country as a basis for his argument that China deserves our help.

AN ENGLISH BELL

I remember many years ago standing on the terrace of a beautiful villa near Florence. It was a September evening, and the valley below was transfigured in the long horizontal rays of the declining sun. And I heard a bell, such a bell as never was on land or sea, a bell whose every vibration found an echo in my innermost heart. I said to my hostess, "That is the most beautiful bell I have ever heard." "Yes," she replied, "it is an English bell." And so it was.

For generations its sound had gone out over English fields, giving the hours of work and prayer to English folk from the tower of an English abbey, and then came the Reformation, and some wise Italian bought the bell whose work was at home and sent it to the Valley of the Arno, where after four centuries it stirred the heart of a wandering Englishman and made him sick for home.

Thus the chance word of a Latin inscription, a line in the anthology, a phrase of Horace, or a "chorus ending of Euripides" plucks at the heartstrings and stirs a thousand memories, memories subconscious and ancestral.   —Stanley Baldwin

Here again Mr. Baldwin stirs a distinct audience response with the use of a personal observation with some emotional impact in an address on "The Classics."

DEATH RIDES THE HIGHWAYS

Have you ever thought that you had killed a man? Have you ever felt like a murderer? I have! I can't tell you how I felt—it's a chapter of my heart. But I can tell you how it happened.

My vocation last summer kept me one hundred and twenty miles from home. I decided in a hurry one evening to go home. The enthusiasm of this natural desire seemed to influence even my car; it responded with a leap. The numerals on the speedometer whirled past the conventional limits, 25-

35-45-50. The summer air blew gently through the open windshield. It was cool and pacifying. The red eye of a tail-light faded as my own head lights revealed an automobile ahead. With my foot held firmly on the accelerator, I prepared to pass. Suddenly, without warning, the car ahead of me swerved to the right with the ominous sound of protesting brakes. A dark form staggered directly into the stab of light from my head-lamps. There was a thump, a jolt, a jangle. The form was tossed from my bumper and, with arms and legs dangling, flew grotesquely into the shadows. Instantly, with terrifying rapidity, there was a crash as the other car careened into the ditch.

And now—that unutterable feeling. Did you ever feel that you had killed a man? Did you ever feel like a murderer? I did.

When I started on that trip I thought I was alone, but that grim passenger Death, with his grasping bony hand sat beside me. And so he consorts with many, for Death is busy these days. He rides the highways, walks beside the pedestrian, dances in fiendish glee at the crossroads. Sometimes he kills; other times he betakes his privilege of being erratic, and maims, and crushes and leaves only a small burning ember of life.   —J. Woodrow Magnussen

It is surprising how many addresses are opened with a personal reference to experience or observation. In this introduction Mr. Magnussen succeeds in making the audience realize the seriousness of highway accidents and he prepares the way for acceptance of his main discussion.

STRANGE FRUIT

This is the land of my birth. My father and mother before me were also born in this country. My old-world ancestry can be traced back at least five generations on American soil, and through Indian heritage many more. America is my country, my native land, my home. Yes, I, too, by the grace of God, am an American, old stock as compared with recent immigrants.

And yet, many Americans, some unable to speak the English language so recent is their arrival on these shores, may partake at will of America's manifold freedoms and joys, though I may not. They may freely make use of her hotels and restaurants, her railroads and buses, her hospital and recreational facilities. I, who was born here, may not. They are free to work at occupations for which they are fitted, buy property, build or rent homes. Once naturalized, they may vote, even in Alabama or Mississippi, if they reside there. They may attend the nation's schools, colleges and universities—even Northwestern—with only normal restrictions; they may live in the dormitories and join the fraternities. And yet, I may not. Yes, I am an American; but I am a "colored" American!

There are thirteen million more like me, over ten percent of the total population. Yes, one out of every ten Americans is a Negro. And one out of every ten Americans is restricted, oppressed, looked down upon and kept down, because his skin is darker than that of his Caucasian brother. We are the strange fruit of America, the dark fruit, the "forbidden" fruit.

—William B. Branch

The introduction of an address delivered by William B. Branch on the subject of the race problem in the United States. If the beginning of a speech should be aimed at a direct introduction of the subject, then Mr. Branch accomplishes this purpose in an admirable way.

THE MEANING OF AMERICA

I am glad to have your invitation to come again to this Iowa village where I was born. Here I spent the first ten years of my boyhood. My parents and grandparents came to this village in the covered wagon—pioneers in this community. They lie buried over the hill. They broke the prairie into homes of independent living. They worshipped God; they did their duty to their neighbors. They toiled to bring to their children greater comfort, better education and to open to them wider opportunity than had been theirs.

I am proud to have been born in Iowa. As I have said before, through the eyes of a ten-year-old boy it was a place of adventure and daily discoveries. The wonder of the growing crops, the excitements of the harvest, the journeys to the woods for nuts and hunting, the joys of snowy winters, the comfort of the family fireside, of good food and tender care. And out of the excessive energy of all small boys, the evenings were filled with accounts of defeat and victory over animate and inanimate things—so far as they were permitted in a Quaker community.

Indelible in those recollections was a widowed mother, sitting with her needle, cheerfully supporting three children and at the same time ministering to her neighbors. After that came life with Uncle Allan on his farm near this village, with the joys and sorrows which come to every small boy en route to life's disciplines by way of farm chores. And among them was the unending making of provisions for the next winter. But in those primitive days, social security was had from the cellar, not from the Federal Government.

—President Herbert Hoover

The opening of an address by Mr. Hoover at the homecoming celebration in his honor at West Branch, Iowa, on his seventy-fourth birthday.

WHERE WE COME FROM

Mr. Toastmaster and Gentlemen:

I feel that the least I can do to show my appreciation of your kindness in allowing me to be here tonight would be to have prepared you in some manner for the kind of speech I am going to make.

A long time ago I was a candidate for the Indiana Legislature, and the campaign managers told me that I would have to make speeches. I did; that is, I made two. (Laughter.) Those speeches attracted the attention of William Jennings Bryan in his own newspaper. You may feel that I am speaking too much of my own achievements, but I cannot refrain from reminding you that "The Commoner" referred to me and my orations, devoting several paragraphs which led up to an important place among the editorials. It said: "Mr. Tarkington made two speeches during the recent campaign. On the first occasion he is reported to have suffered so from stage fright that he was unable to uttter a syllable. From what we have read of his second effort we think it is a pity he didn't have it both times." (Laughter.)

Unless it be considered too wide a digression, I might best state that in spite of my oratory I succeeded in being elected, but I hope, however, your committee didn't invite me to address you tonight from the same motive that brought me the solid vote of the farmers in Marion County. Friends of mine were out on election day who asked a group of farmers whom they were for. "We're all for Tarkington out here," they said. "We want him to get in." This puzzled my friends a little, because they couldn't think of anything I had done to arouse any particular enthusiasm among the farmers. So one of my friends asked them why they were so strong for me. "Why," they said, "we want to see what the darned fool will do."

—Booth Tarkington

In the opening of his address, Mr. Tarkington produced a good response from his audience because of the manner in which he related his experiences and gave them a chance to laugh at the speaker.

WHO IS HE?

I was going down Christian Street in Jerusalem one day when I met a man clad in the gorgeous robes of an oriental potentate; and, at his side, hung the curved gold sword worn only by the descendants of the prophet Mohammed. But this man had none of the appearances of an Arab. He had blue eyes; and the Arabs' eyes are always black or brown.

—Lowell Thomas

Mr. Thomas began his lecture on Lawrence of Arabia with this personal experience type of opening that immediately arouses the curiosity of the audience to learn more about the man. It is always a most effective opening.

IF I HAD YOUR CHANCE

Mr. President, Members of the Graduating Class, Guests: It is an inspiration to me to return in this manner to the institution that started me on my life course. I well recall the thrill of my arrival that first Sunday morning. I strolled across the campus here to Billings Hall, along a walk improvised from planks, suitcase in hand. The world seemed to me a wonderful place.

I am sure it is as wonderful to you today. For on this day you deserve to experience that glorious feeling of satisfaction that comes from reaching an important milestone. You have worked hard. You have made sacrifices. You have acquired training and knowledge. You possess new tools you will learn how to use in search of progress. For this is no final goal. It is put preparation for something you want but have not yet achieved.

—Paul Garrett

In this opening of a commencement address delivered by Mr. Garrett at Whitman College in June, 1947, he referred to his own personal experience which attracted the attention of his listeners immediately and illustrates the effective use of this type of opening.

Chapter Six

The Tactful Opening

As has been stated many times before, one of the principal reasons why speakers fail to win their audiences is because they lack the fine attribute of being able to analyze the attitudes of their listeners successfully. It is important that a speaker devote considerable time during his speech preparation to determine what the possible reaction of the audience will be and the best way to win them over to his point of view. The use of tact and diplomacy is almost always advisable in the speaker's opening remarks.

A careful analysis of these samples will illustrate most clearly how a speaker can win an audience to his side during the opening:

THE USE OF TACT

"This is a red-letter day in my life. It is the first time I have ever had the good fortune to meet the representatives of the employees of this great company, its officers and superintendents, together, and I can assure you that I am proud to be here, and that I shall remember this gathering as long as I live. Had this meeting been held two weeks ago, I should have stood here a stranger to most of you, recognizing few faces. Having had the opportunity last week of visiting all the camps in the southern coal fields and of talking individually with practically all the representatives, except those who were away; having visited in your homes, met many of your wives and children, we meet here not as strangers but as friends, and it is in that spirit of mutual friendship that I am glad to have this opportunity to discuss with you our common interests.

"Since this is a meeting of the officers of the company and the representatives of the employees, it is only by your courtesy that I am here, for I am not so fortunate as to be either one or the other; and yet I feel that I am intimately associated with you men, for, in a sense, I represent both the stockholders and the directors."   —John D. Rockefeller, Jr.

This introduction was used by Mr. Rockefeller when he appeared before an audience of striking employees who were bitterly opposed to management. It is an excellent example of how the use of tact and good judgment will win an audience to your side as it did for Mr. Rockefeller.

SHINING CITY

Ladies and gentlemen: In less strenuous times it has been my good fortune to follow the sun to Florida a couple of times on less urgent business. And, as always, I find myself wondering today if you who live in this well-blessed land fully appreciate your fortunate estate. Or is that a minor compensation reserved for us to whom blue sky, bright sea, and white sand are a benediction after a gray Northern winter?

To me, as to most outlanders, Florida has always seemed a very special place. As I have come to know this incredible peninsula of yours since I first came here as a boy more than forty years ago, I have understood why every visitor looks upon Florida with a proprietary interest—feeling a personal sense of discovery as though he alone had found a green land rising from the sea.

Here where we stand you have brought forth a world-famous flowering park from a mangrove swamp. Behind it you have erected your shining city of the sun. Seaward you have raised from the waters that fabulous island, Miami Beach. These things you have added to God's bounty in little more than half a century.   —Adlai Stevenson

This introduction was used by Mr. Stevenson during an address delivered in Miami in which he complimented the audience for the splendid scenic beauty of their city. A commendation of this kind always produces a warm reception for a speaker.

AMONG FRIENDS

I am happy to be in the South again and I am proud to be in South Carolina. It is good to be among friends—and it is particularly good to be welcomed here by my close and long-time friend, your distinguished Governor, Jimmy Byrnes.

You know, going South is becoming a habit with me—and a very pleasant one. From what Governor Byrnes says, I gather the habit is beginning to catch on. I know you will give my distinguished opponent a warm welcome when he comes. But you will forgive me if I say I am glad I got here first. It is my aim to continue to keep ahead of him—right through November 4.   —Dwight D. Eisenhower

An introduction used by President Eisenhower in an address delivered at Columbia, S. C., on Sept. 30, 1952. The references to the South and Gov. Byrnes revealed good tact in winning over his audience.

DISARMING THE OPPOSITION

"Your Excellency, Ladies and Gentlemen, my fellow Americans:

"I am largely indebted to President Lowell for this opportunity to address this great audience. He and I are friends of many years, both Republicans. He is the president of our great university, one of the most important and influential places in the United States. He is also an eminent student and historian of politics and government. He and I may differ as to methods in this great question now before the people, but I am sure that in regard to the security of the peace of the world and the welfare of the United States we do not differ in purposes.

"I am going to say a single word, if you will permit me, as to my own position. I have tried to state it over and over again. I thought I had stated it in plain English. But there are those who find in misrepresentation a convenient weapon for controversy, and there are others, most excellent people, who perhaps have not seen what I have said and who possibly mis-

understood me. It has been said that I am against the League
of Nations. I am not; far from it. I am anxious to have the
nations, the free nations of the world, united in a league, as we
call it, a society, as the French call it, but united, to do all that
can be done to secure the future peace of the world and to
bring about a general disarmament."

—Henry Cabot Lodge, Sr.

*Senator Lodge used excellent tact in opening his argument
in a debate with President Lowell on the League of Nations. The
public had come to identify Lodge with complete opposition
to the League and his remarks in this introduction had the effect of disarming both his opponent and the audience.*

BEATEN PATH

There are two interesting things about the character of this
Businessmen's Organization, its remarkable solidarity on the
one hand, and on the other, the individual concern for honest
and quality service in your merchandising.

There is an interesting and challenging maxim which is
credited to Emerson; it is in no way dated, and I sincerely feel
it bespeaks the honest integrity of your merchandising in this
community.

"If a man can write a better book, preach a better
sermon, or make a better mousetrap than his neighbor
—though he build his house in the woods— the world
will make a beaten path to his door."

The infinite truth of this statement still applies in the world
today. All of us seek better things, better quality, better value,
better service. Because the people of this community recognize
and demand this superior service, they will constantly make a
"beaten path" to your places of business, and you will excel
as individual merchants, and as a businessmen's organization.

—V. Spencer Goodreds

*The speaker assumes the members of his audience ad-
here to the best business practices which may not be altogether
true. But the audience will think of the speaker nevertheless.
It was a tactful way to begin.*

NO TIME FOR CEREMONY

"Mr. President: No man thinks more highly than I do of the patriotism, as well as the abilities, of the very worthy gentlemen who have just addressed the house. But different men often see the same subject in different lights; and, therefore, I hope it will not be thought disrespectful to these gentlemen, if, entertaining as I do opinions of a character very opposite to theirs, I shall speak forth my sentiments freely, and without reserve. This is no time for ceremony. The question before the house is one of awful moment to the country. For my own part, I consider it as nothing less than a question of freedom or slavery. And in proportion to the magnitude of the subject ought to be the freedom of the debate. It is only in this way that we can hope to arrive at truth, and fulfill the great responsibility which we hold to God and our country. Should I keep back my opinions at such a time, through fear of giving offense, I should consider myself as guilty of treason towards my country, and of an act of disloyalty toward the Majesty of Heaven, which I revere above all earthly things.

Mr. President, it is natural to man to indulge in the illusions of hope. We are apt to shut our eyes against a painful truth, and listen to the song of that Siren till she transforms us into beasts. Is this the part of wise men, engaged in a great and arduous struggle for liberty? Are we disposed to be of the number of those who, having eyes see not, and having ears hear not, the things which so nearly concern their temporal salvation? For my part, whatever anguish of spirit it may cost, I am willing to know the whole truth; to know the worst and to provide for it." ——Patrick Henry

Here is a striking example of the use of tact in winning the opposition at the very beginning of a speech. Patrick Henry knew that there was opposition to him, yet he used this psychological approach to weaken their position at the outset of his famous "Give me liberty, or give me death!" speech.

LET US REASON TOGETHER

"Fellow citizens of Southern Illinois, fellow citizens of the State of Kentucky, fellow citizens of Missouri. I am told there are some of you here present who would like to make trouble for me. I don't understand why you should. I am a plain, common man, like the rest of you; and why should I not have as good a right to speak my sentiments as the rest of you? Why, good friends, I am one of you. I am not an interloper here. I was born in Kentucky, and raised in Illinois, just like the most of you, and worked my way along by hard scratching. I know the people of Kentucky, and I know the people of Southern Illinois, and I think I know the Missourians. I am one of them, and therefore ought to know them; and they ought to know me better, and, if they did know me better, they would know that I am not disposed to make them trouble. Then, why should they, or any one of them, want to make trouble for me? Don't do any such foolish thing, fellow citizens. Let us be friends, and treat each other like friends. I am one of the humblest and most peaceful men in the world. I would wrong no man, would interfere with no man's rights. And all I ask is that, having something to say, you give me a decent hearing. And, being Illinoisans, Kentuckians, and Missourians—brave and gallant people—I feel sure that you will do that. And now let us reason together, like the honest fellows we are."

—Abraham Lincoln

The above introduction was used by Mr. Lincoln during his campaign for the U. S. Senate in 1858 in southern Illinois. Information had been given him that there were many anti-slavery men in the audience who had threatened to kill him. Threats were changed to cheers by the tactful use of this clever introduction.

CUTTING A LONG SPEECH
(When the speaker's time has been consumed by other speakers)

I have attended many New England dinners. I have eaten very few. I think I have never attended one in which there has been such good speaking as tonight, and so much of it; and as I remember a sentence from the Book with which I am supposed to be familiar, that "a full soul loatheth a feast," I do not propose to stuff you at this late period with a long speech, for I have been myself a sufferer under like circumstances. It does seem a pity, and would to you if you had ever been speech-makers, to cut out an elaborate speech with weeks of toil in order that it may be extemporized admirably, and then to find yourself drifted so late into the evening that everybody is tired of speeches.

What must a man do under such circumstances? As he abhors novelty, he cannot make a new one, and he goes on to make his old speech, and it falls still-born upon the ears of the listeners. I do not propose, therefore, to give you the benefit of all that eloquence that I have stored up for you tonight. I merely say that if you had only heard the speech that I was going to deliver, you would pity me for the speech that I am now delivering. One of the most precious elements of religious liberty is the right of a sensible man **not** to speak, or even make a poor speech. —Henry Ward Beecher

This response was given by Dr. Beecher when he was introduced by the chairman to deliver the seventh speech of the evening on "Religious Liberty." He prepared the audience for reducing the length of his prepared speech and is an excellent example of tact in an uncomfortable situation.

THE RIGHT CROWD

There is nothing I enjoy more than getting together with a group of workmen's compensation experts and comparing notes. My feelings are somewhat similar to those of a pair of Tennesseeans in a story I heard the other day. These two had been drinking and carousing all one Saturday night and well into Sunday morning. Presently it occurred to them that it might be a good idea to offset some of these activities by going to church. So they staggered down the street until they found an open church door. The sermon was already in progress as they entered, and they heard the preacher intoning these words, ". . . yea, we have looked on the wine when it was red; we are an evil and adulterous generation; we have done those things we ought not to have done, and left undone those things we ought to have done. . . ." At this point the one Tennesseean turned to the other and said, "I guess we're in the right crowd, all right."

Here I know I'm in the right crowd, and can talk shop about workmen's compensation to my heart's content.

—Arthur Larson

The introduction to an address delivered at Orlando, Florida, on Oct. 28, 1954, by Under Secretary of Labor Arthur Larson to the Association of Workmen's Compensation Administrators. It illustrates how tact was used in setting the stage for his address.

HUMAN LIBERTY

Mr. President, Mr. Speaker and distinguished members of the Congress: I stand on this rostrum with a sense of deep humility and great pride—humility in the weight of those great architects of our history who have stood here before me, pride in the reflection that this forum of legislative debate represents human liberty in the purest form yet devised. Here are centered the hopes and aspirations and faith of the entire human race.

I do not stand here as advocate for any partisan cause, for the issues are fundamental and reach quite beyond the realm of partisan consideration. They must be resolved on the highest plane of national interest if our course is to prove sound and our future protected. I trust, therefore, that you will do me the justice of receiving that which I have to say as solely expressing the considered viewpoint of a fellow American. I address you with neither rancor nor bitterness in the fading twilight of life, but with one purpose in mind, to serve my country.

—General Douglas MacArthur

Upon addressing a joint meeting of Congress after his return from Japan, General MacArthur was aware of the public's reactions to his being relieved of his command by President Truman. In this opening he gives a good illustration of the tactful type of opening.

OUR PARTNERSHIP

President Magsaysay, distinguished guests, ladies and gentlemen:

Mrs. Nixon and I are singularly honored in being invited to participate in your celebration of the tenth anniversary of the independence of your courageous nation. It is fitting that we who fought side by side in Bataan and Corregidor should celebrate jointly our days of independence. You are a young nation, but already the wisdom and insight of your counsel is appreciated throughout the entire world. You are known for your devotion to freedom, your courage and integrity in fighting for ideals, your determination to live up to the highest standards of liberty and democracy. We who share your ideals are proud that you have asked us to be here with you on this happy occasion.   —Richard M. Nixon

Vice-president Nixon began his address on the tenth anniversary of the Independence of the Philippines at Manila on July 4, 1956, with this tactful opening in which he stressed the partnership of the two countries during the war.

WHAT CAN I SAY?

In standing before you for the first time in these distinguished robes, which, I take it, embody the appreciation of this University for all those who are trying to promote the cause of peace in the world, I regret very much that I have been unable to accept various other invitations from universities to join them in their membership. But I take it, Mr. President, that those of you who are responsible for the conduct of this distinguished University will allow me to say that I regard you not only as yourselves, but as representatives of the other great educational institutions of the United States.

I have been asked to say something to you. What can I say? I never attended a University, unfortunately. I have been, as I understand so many of you here are, one who has had to acquire his educational attainments in his spare hours, after having undergone the labour that he finds necessary for the earning of his daily bread.　　　　　　—J. Ramsay MacDonald

Chapter Seven

Using A Reference To A Timely News Event As An Opening

One of the most effective methods of catching the audience's attention in an opening is the reference to headline news in the daily newspaper. It may be news about a catastrophe, a political event, the final result of the World Series, or the accomplishment of some prominent individual. By referring to the type of event that has everybody talking and thinking about is sufficient to stir an immediate response from any audience.

Here are examples of this type of opening:

BIGGEST POSSIBLE CIGAR

At a dinner I attended some years ago, the principal speaker began with this story:

Churchill, Truman and Stalin called a meeting, with the object of ensuring peace for all time. During this meeting, which was held behind locked doors, an angel appeared and told these three statesmen that he has been sent upon earth to grant each of them a wish, and that the wish would be granted provided it would help to ensure peace for all time. The angel turned first to Stalin and asked him for his wish.

Stalin stated that he wished for the biggest possible hydrogen bomb—one which, if dropped in the middle of the United States, would be large enough to eliminate that vast country from the face of the earth.

The angel, without comment, turned to Truman and asked him his wish. Truman stated that he wished for an enormous tidal wave, which would sweep right across the U. S. S. R. and eliminate every vestige of life.

Finally, the angel turned to Churchill and asked him his

wish. Churchill, after taking slow and thoughtful puffs at his cigar, said that he wished for the biggest possible (dramatic pause) cigar, but, he said, with a quiet smile, please serve these other gentlemen first.   —A. C. Hazel

Even if this story was fictitious, it was an ideal choice for the speaker to use as an opening because he immediately won the audience to give him their undivided attention.

THE HARD WAY

The scene is the Congress of the United States—with its high-vaulted ceiling and impressive marble pillars. The 600 distinguished members of Congress sit motionless. Every eye is directed to the high marble speaker's stand. There, at the center of attention, is a small, confident figure. Not a sound is heard but the calm, clear voice of the person speaking, to whom every ear is attuned. Madame Chiang Kai-Shek is addressing Congress and the world.

She stands there—a magnificent example of woman emancipated—woman, the helpmate and partner of man. With an American education, she has struggled to free China's 200 million women from the ancient bonds of slavery. She is working at the side of her husband, both of them devoting their lives to a great cause. She is his helpmate. At foreign conferences she acts as his interpreter. Her knowledge of Western civilization, coupled with his experience in Eastern ways, make a perfect political combination. She is not a masculine woman. She does not imitate man's dress or manners. She does not compete with men. As a woman, through the force of her character, she has become the spokesman of her suffering and heroic people.

—Patricia R. Maloney

The specific reference to Madame Chiang Kai-Shek and her appearance before the U. S. Congress was made by Miss Maloney to introduce her main subject—the challenge to American women to take a more active participation in domestic and foreign affairs.

THE UNDERWORLD ON TOP

On the evening of February third, in the city of Cleveland, someone lured a former councilman, William E. Potter, into the stale air of a dusty apartment house. A week later, his body, riddled with bullets, was found cramped in the corner of a davenport. The stench of that crime assailed the nostrils of our community, flooded our newspapers, perverted our thought for a month. "Political grafter!" the people whispered. "Booze war victim!" shouted the prosecutor. When the storm had subsided, an insignificant agent of an unseen power had been sent to the penitentiary. The shadows of the underworld still cloaked our city. The invisible government that pointed a finger at Potter reigned supreme. To itself vice stood vindicated.

—Arthur W. Fiske

In introducing his subject dealing with the subject of vice and underworld activity, Mr. Fiske used a specific case his listeners were familiar with to win the audience's acceptance of the idea that his main premise is true—crime in the underworld does exist.

ADVANCES IN MEDICAL SCIENCE

In an immaculate operating room at the Cleveland Clinic two years ago, Dr. W. James Gardner performed one of the wonders of brain surgery. From the shaved head of a woman he removed the entire right hemisphere of the brain. The patient lived. In a few hours she recognized and talked with her friends. Not long afterwards, although her left arm and leg were stiff she was able to walk.

Here is an excellent example of the advances made during recent years in the fields of medicine and surgery. Scientific medical knowledge has penetrated far into the mysteries of disease. Bacteriologists have invaded the realms of the microbe and germ. In the hands of our doctors have been placed powers heretofore undreamed of. To those who suffer, surgical science has become a Godsend. The end of the age-old conflict between man and disease seems near at hand. We have caught the vision of a day when man, through science, will emerge victorious over all illness. —Cleon Reidinger

In an address outlining the latest advancements in medical science, Mr. Reidinger uses this style of introduction to open his main discussion. The news of this successful operation had been broadcast nationwide.

THE ASSASSIN OF YOUTH

One night last August two young people were parked in an auto on lovers' lane back of the Cleveland Art Museum only a few hundred yards away from this hall. Through the surrounding darkness two figures crept up to the car. There was a shot, a scream; and the young man in the auto slumped over the wheel—dead. The girl, two hours later, weakly staggered into the eleventh precinct police station.

One man killed! A girl criminally assaulted! Here was tragedy enacted very close to us. But its closeness lies not only in the nearness of the place where it occurred, not only in the fact that one of us might have been a victim on that fatal night. Most of all its closeness lies in the fact that any of us might have been the ones to commit that crime.

The two killers were young men. One was twenty-four, the other twenty-six. One had been a student at Columbia University, the other was already known to Cleveland as a successful boxer in the Golden Gloves Tournament. But they were made into killers by a thing that is no respecter of race, age, or position. They were themselves victims—victims of a powerful force that caused them to murder and rape. The real cause of that tragedy was an innocent-looking cigarette that was easy to get in Cleveland—sold openly then, just as openly sold now. This cigarette contains a drug that grows profusely here, as it does in every state in the Union. In a few short years its ever-mounting toll of victims has heaped tragedy upon tragedy.

Already it has been branded by the Director of the Federal Narcotics Bureau as "the assassin of youth."

You and I know it as the reefer cigarette, or marijuana. These are the common names by which we now know a drug that ten years ago was unknown in this country. Replacing morphine, heroin and opium—drugs imported from the orient —the home-grown marijuana now takes front rank among the menaces to the youth of America.

—Norman A. Sugarman

This dramatic introduction by Mr. Sugarman served to lay the basis for his address on the growing danger to American youth of the widespread use of marijuana and other drugs. The reference to headline news that practically everyone in the audience had read was an excellent device to arouse interest in the speaker's topic.

THEN HITLER CAME

As a huge silver monoplane rose into the cold, early morning fog a few months ago, all the world breathed a silent benediction. On board that airliner was a wistful, smiling man clutching a black umbrella and bound for Berchtesgaden, Germany. An anxious world followed that solitary mission, praying for peace, but preparing for war. Today that smile has vanished from that statesman's face; it is a grim Neville Chamberlain who last week issued the call for British mobilization on a war footing. Yes, the umbrella has bowed before the swastika. That contagion has spread to the United States where we feverishly rearm, determined that democracy shall not perish without a fight.

—C. Donald Peterson

In his address on the preservation of American democracy, Mr. Peterson has employed a very terse and concise introduction to his subject. There has been no waste of words in opening up the main discussion of his topic. The opening was based on a mission of failure that everyone in the audience knew about.

WORLD OUTLOOK

Last week American bombers carried the war to the enemy. In Burma, on the island of Timor and in the Philippines we struck at the Japanese supply lines. On top of that we bombed Tokyo. Hitherto we Americans have interested ourselves primarily in our own affairs. We have lived surrounded by protective distances, which automatically kept aggressors from our shores. And we had so much work to do at home that we did not worry much about the rest of the world. But that long comfortable era has come to an end, as the bombing of Tokyo proves. If we can do it to others, they can do it to us.

—Wendell L. Willkie

Attention of the audience was immediately caught by the reference to the bombing of Japanese vulnerable spots which had just occurred. It is an example of the reference to a timely news event.

STARVING CHILDREN

In the entire world, one-half of all the children are in critical need of food. This means about 460 million infants and children under fifteen. When I say these children are hungry, I don't mean that they have the normal hunger of a child who wants a snack before bedtime, or when he comes in from play. These children need more food so desperately that many of them will not live without it.

Much is being done, in familiar and established ways, to help these children. This, however, is not nearly enough. In spite of all the efforts of our governments and private relief agencies, there are—right now—at least 230 million children living on the very border of starvation. They depend totally upon us—and let us never forget that. Each one is an individual, not unlike your own, a child trying for the right to grow up and live.

—Chester Bowles

This opening was used by Mr. Bowles at a time when news bulletins were coming into the United States about the food shortage as an aftermath of war. It is an illustration of catching immediate audience attention by stating the facts of the situation.

Chapter Eight

The Unusual Opening

Some speakers prefer to do or say something unusual, something unexpected, to get a quick audience reaction. Sometimes the chairman will introduce a speaker and, having been prompted by the speaker beforehand, will make an unusual remark about him or even introduce him by the wrong name, so as to give the speaker the opportunity to contradict the chairman's introduction.

I remember an occasion at a sales conference when the chairman introduced a speaker as the vice-president in charge of sales of a corset manufacturing company. The speaker, who stood six feet three in his socks and was equally large in girth, rose ponderously to his feet, smacked himself on his chest, and said, "Gentlemen, I am in the meat-packing business," and one assumes that this particular speaker had found this type of opening was always good for a laugh as, indeed, it was on this occasion. —A. C. Hazel

I am acquainted with a sales manager of a large industrial concern who will use various types of gimmicks at the opening of his talks. Sometimes he will produce small rubber balls from his pockets and throw them over his audience. On other occasions, he will blow a whistle vigorously. After the commotion has subsided, his usual comment is, "I just wanted to be sure you were awake and that you're prepared to listen to me." However crude this method may be, it has produced satisfactory results for this speaker.

However, in more formal situations this type of opening would be unwise. An unusual story, a striking statement, a reference to a personal experience that's different, or a series of pertinent questions, would be preferable. Illustrations of this type of opening are given here:

SPEED HYSTERIA

Children are skating up and down a village street. Their laughter and shouts ring pleasantly in the crisp air. There is the flash of an automobile recklessly driven, the shrill scream of brakes, and the car comes to a stop—too late. The quickly gathered crowd raises the broken body of a child, and as they look at the driver, the murmur goes up, "He was speeding."

—Roxanne Hutchings

Here is another example of the use of a graphic illustration in the introduction to create an audience attention. Miss Hutchings develops the subject of our increasing number of auto accidents in the United States. The brevity of this dramatic opening places it in this category.

THE TRAGEDY OF NINETY-EIGHT CENTS

Enough fat to make seven bars of soap; enough iron to make a nail; enough sugar to fill a shaker; enough lime to whitewash a chickencoop; enough magnesia to settle one stomach—all worth about 98c. Such is the chemical value of a human body.

The human body of Charles Emery withered on a cot. The doctors had given him just three hours to make his peace with God. In one final, feeble gesture, he uttered his last request: "I've never done anything worthwhile before! Reduce my body to its chemical elements—to contribute my little bit!" Charles Emery, a man of splendid promise, an educated gentleman who could have made an invaluable endowment to progress but who had muffed his chances with indifference instead, was able to bequeath to society a puny 98c. The gap between the might have been Charles Emery and the Charles Emery that he really was is the modern tragedy that I wish to speak with you about tonight.

—Jack Turner

This specific example makes clear to the audience the real values of a human being in utilizing his mental capacities. Mr. Turner succeeds in his introduction to establish the main theme of his address.

"THE SILENT MAN"

On a bleak, windswept hillside in Vermont, there is a grass-covered grave. As yet, no large headstone marks the identity of the occupant. I should like to suggest one—an undecorated pillar of stone with no inscription. For the man was silent in life, silent in death, and will remain silent forever.

No words of his will long linger in our memories. We shall retain no colorful stories of his acts as the nation's chief executive. He made no eternal precedents as did Washington; he propounded no new political philosophy as did Jefferson; he lacked the rugged, majestic personality of Lincoln; his public appearances were not filled with the bombastic showmanship of Theodore Roosevelt. He had neither the scholarly mien of Wilson nor the genial simplicity of Harding. Yet we shall remember Calvin Coolidge—remember him for what he was, rather than for what he did.   —Arthur B. Magidson

Mr. Magidson does not disclose the name of the subject of his address. The generalization used in the introduction arouses the curiosity of the audience and prepares the way for the final statement of the subject. The element of suspense characterizes this unusual opening.

THE BARGAIN

I'm discouraged, ladies and gentlemen. I'm deeply discouraged. If any of you have ever been salesmen, I know you'll sympathize with me. Have you ever gone from door to door with something that you know to be a real bargain, only to be constantly turned away with the same old story, "Sure, we'd like to have one, but we can't pay the price"? I'm a salesman and I'm discouraged. I'm selling peace. Look at it, peace—the best product ever put before the public; but I haven't found anyone who can pay the price! Maybe you'd like to hear my story.   —Thornton Shively

The personal treatment in the introduction as used by Mr. Shively is another effective device in catching the audience's attention at the very beginning of an address.

POMP AND CIRCUMSTANCE

I want to talk to you about a racket. It's older than prohibition, but it isn't the slots, or vice houses, or policy slips. There are no sliding peep-holes in steel doors, no passwords, no raids. It's all perfectly legal. It's what men like Al Capone would call a sure thing. The big bosses in this racket don't wear checked suits or loud ties. No, the only outward similarity between our racketeers is that each is identified with a fleet of black, well-kept Cadillacs—that, and their universal, all-powerful craving to handle money. I want to talk to you about the funeral racket.

—William R. Hartman

This unusual introduction used by Mr. Hartman to begin an address on the extravagant practices of morticians in selling their services. The use of the word "racket" immediately arrests the attention of the audience.

YOUR LAST CHANCE!

Have you ever been hit right between the eyes by something you have read or seen? Recently, as I leafed through a magazine I came upon an awesome picture. In the lower left-hand corner, almost too small to be seen, was the tiny figure of a man. He was standing there motionless, a bewildered expression on his face. Before him, rising from his feet like a fan and covering almost the whole scene, was a gigantic, mushrooming column of rolling, seething, black and grey clouds that seemed almost to shout of the terrible power they portrayed. Below the picture in bold-faced type were three short words, "YOUR LAST CHANCE!"   —John Barsness

The introduction of an address, "Your Last Chance" delivered by John Barsness on the effect of the atom and hydrogen bomb on the future of mankind. In this brief paragraph, Mr. Barsness succeeds in introducing his subject in a dramatic unusual way.

MOBILIZATION

All over the country tonight a campaign is starting. We have become accustomed to this campaign, so it does not seem to us to be remarkable. But it is remarkable. It is uniquely American and uniquely democratic. It is given a covering phrase to describe it. It is called a mobilization—a mobilization for human needs. I would call it a mobilization of human decency. That is what makes it peculiar. God knows mobilizations have become commonplace. We have in our times become acquainted with the mobilized nation, with the community constantly and continually prepared for war. Within the last two weeks we have seen whole peoples called to arms, and under the threat of them, we have seen a strange new type of peace—the instigation in the name of peace of a reign of terror. We have seen people mobilized to get something—to get territory—and we have seen them gathered blindly, led blindly. We have seen other peoples mobilized, mobilized blindly—only to discover a few days later that they have been mobilized in order to give something away— something that did not belong to them. We have seen hate mobilized, ambition mobilized, fear mobilized.

But this mobilization, that begins all over America, is different. It does not come from the top, but from the bottom—in every community throughout the nation. It is not animated by ambition, or hatred, or fear, but by love. Its object is not to take something, but to give something. It is not ordered, it is not compelled—it is voluntary. It appeals neither to pride nor to fear, but solely and exclusively to good will. It does not emphasize the State, which is power, but the community, which is cooperation.   —Dorothy Thompson

In this opening Miss Thompson emphasizes the meaning of the word, "Mobilization," in this unusual manner and consequently she wins an immediate acceptance from her audience.

SURPRISED

My feelings on appearing so unexpectedly before you here tonight remind me of a story about two college alumni who met at their twentieth reunion. The first, trying to make conversation after all these years, said to the second: "And how is your wife?" The second replied: "My wife is in heaven." The first alumnus blurted out, "Oh, I'm sorry." Then he realized that this wasn't quite the right thing to say, so he quickly substituted, "I mean, I'm glad." That was even worse, so finally, in desperation, he came out with: "Well, I'm surprised."

In view of the occasion for my being here — the illness of the Secretary — a man for whom I have during our brief acquaintance developed the greatest affection and admiration, I can't say I'm glad to be here tonight; and on the other hand, it would sound churlish for me to announce to your faces that I'm sorry to be with you. The one thing I can safely say is that I am surprised.

I have heard a great deal about this organization, especially since I practiced law for a number of years in a suburb of Chicago-Milwaukee. I have been warned that I would face an overpowering array of **experts** and experience in the field of industrial relations. I almost feel as though I had been asked to give an exposition on the Ten Commandments to an audience made up of Moses, Aaron, and a representative selection of major and minor prophets.

—Arthur Larson

The opening of an address delivered by Arthur Larson, Under Secretary of Labor, before the Economic Club of Chicago on May 18, 1954.

Chapter Nine

When The Speaker Finds Himself
In Unusual Situations

The ability to meet the sudden and unusual situations that occur on many occasions may be a life-saver for the speaker who is alert and quick on the trigger. In this chapter we have assembled a large assortment of responses that may be utilized whenever the unexpected situation arises.

BOTH WERE CRAWLING

(When the speaker comments on the hot weather.)

This is a very fine turnout for a hot night. Speaking of the weather, which certainly is warm, I am reminded of a story about a New Yorker who was complaining about the hot weather to a friend who had just returned from the South.

"Did you say, hot?" said the friend. "You don't know what heat is! Why, when I was down in Alabama last week, I saw a cat chasing a squirrel and they were both crawling!"

—Walter C. Bacon

STALE EGGS

Perhaps I should have prepared a bit more thoroughly before getting onto this platform this evening. Perhaps I should have done what a speaker friend of mine did a few years ago. He was to speak in a small town where public speaking was more or less frowned upon.

He told me a man entered the only grocery in the town and asked the grocer to sell him all the stale eggs he had in stock. The grocer thought it a peculiar request, and asked, "What do you want with all the stale eggs? Are you going to throw them at the speaker tonight?" "Sh-sh!" hissed the buyer. "I'm that speaker."

—Arthur L. Kaser

AN AMBASSADOR TO INTERPRET

Mr. Chairman, I come as a kind of ambassador to interpret you to yourselves, to each other, and to the colleges. The Bishop of Birmingham on one occasion was making a speech to a group of railroad men in England. He said, "You have done a wonderful thing. You have gotten four nationalities to understand each other—the Englishman, who loves his Bible and his beer, the Scotchman, who keeps the Sabbath and anything else he can lay his hands on, the Welshman, who prays on Sunday and on his neighbors the rest of the week, and the Irishman, who doesn't know what he wants but will never be happy until he gets it." They have lived together a long while and yet they seem to have some difficulty in understanding each other.

—Henry M. Wriston

A response used by Dr. Wriston when speaking to a convention of college students.

KEEP YOUR SEAT

(The speaker comments when a guest attempts to leave the room.)

I have been watching with interest a gentleman over on the right side of the room. I notice that he made several attempts to get up out of his chair and leave. I hope that he stays, at least until I have finished with this story:

Elderly and scholarly Mr. Charles Waterbury was riding home on a crowded bus one afternoon, when an attractive young woman entered and stood along side the seat occupied by Mr. Waters, as there was standing room only and that was toe to toe.

Mr. Waterbury made an attempt to rise from his sardine-packed position, but was promptly pushed back into his seat by the attractive young lady, who placed her hands on Mr. Waterbury's shoulders and remarked: "Keep your seat, my dear man."

A few minutes later Mr. Waterbury made another effort to

get up, and the girl again placed her hands on his shoulders, pushed him back and remarked: "I don't want your seat. You keep it."

The bus sped on and finally Mr. Waterbury in desperation squeezed himself to a standing position and very indignantly said to the young lady: "I'M getting off this bus. You have already carried me five blocks beyond my destination."

—Hillary Williams

NO VACANCY

(When a speaker says that, up until this afternoon, he wasn't sure he would be able to appear)

I wasn't sure until late this afternoon that I would be able to make an appearance here this evening. An emergency came up that would have required my presence in an upstate town. Fortunately, I was able to arrive at a solution, as you see that I am here. However, at the time the emergency came up, I called Bill Jones, your chairman of the arrangements committee, and told him about my predicament. Bill said that he was sorry and that they would have to get another speaker to fill my shoes.

I said, "Don't bother about it, Bill, there is nothing to fill."

"What are you talking about?" asked Bill.

"I can best describe it as a story," I said, and then told him this story: Whenever I arrived at the small town of Centerville, I would look up an old friend of mine by the name of Joe Blake, who was a handy man at Peterson's general store. Joe was one of those county bumpkins, not too bright, but Joe was good company. During my visits, I enjoyed hearing him talk about the gossip in Centerville and the surrounding country. On my last trip there, I inquired for Joe and was informed by the owner that Joe didn't work there any more.

"Who took his place?" I asked.

"Nobody," answered the boss. "He didn't leave a vacancy."

—Paul C. Winthrop

BETTER SPEAKERS

(When the speaker belittles his ability.)

I am not sure whether or not the chairman of your arrangements committee made a good choice when he selected me to speak here this evening, which reminds me of a friend of mine who does considerable speaking before the public. My friend was filling an engagement in the southern part of the state, and after he had completed his speech and the audience was disbursing, the chairman came up to him with a check for his services.

The speaker refused the check with a remark that the chairman should give the amount to his favorite charity.

"Then we will put it in our special fund," said the chairman.

"By the way," asked the speaker, "what is your special fund?"

The chairman hesitated for a moment and casually said: "To help us get better speakers next year."

—Horton Smith

NO RETURN TRIP

(When the speaker makes a return appearance)

Ladies and gentlemen, I appreciate your invitation to come back to speak to you for the third time. No doubt this is my farewell appearance because I don't think I'll be coming back again. I am reminded of two years ago when I took a trip to Tennessee for the purpose of looking up some information about a certain hillbilly family through which a link was needed to complete a business deal. The party I was seeking was a fellow by the name of Jed Hawkins who lived back in the hills near a small town called Hillsboro.

When I arrived at the Hawkins shack, after a horrible trip up the rocky mountain roads, there was no one home but young Seth Hawkins, a lad of about twelve years of age.

"Son," I said, "Where's your pappy?" (I called him pappy, for if I had said "father," the lad no doubt would not have known what I was talking about.)

"He's up to the still," said the Hawkins boy.

"Where's your mother?" I then asked.

"She's up to the still, too," replied the mountain lad.

Then I said to the boy, "I'll give you a dollar if you will lead me to them."

The lad looked at me with a questionable air, and no doubt figured that I was a revenue officer. But after a few seconds, the boy said, "All right, gimme the dollar."

"I'll give it to you after we get back," I said.

"No," said the young Hawkins, "give it to me now. You ain't a-comin' back."   —Gus Strauss

MY CORN HURTS

(When rainy weather cuts down an audience)

I want to congratulate your chairman for such a fine turn-out on this rainy and nasty evening. There are always some people who are under the impression that they are made of salt, and likely to melt when exposed to rain. I can see that this audience is made of better stuff.

Speaking of the weather reminds me of an incident that happened in one of our weather bureaus. One weather man was busily looking over his instruments, charts and various other devices used in a weather bureau, and at the same time he was carrying on a continuous conversation with a second weather man, who was doing likewise.

The first weather man said to the second weather man, "It's going to rain today."

"How do you know?" asked the second weather man.

The first weather man continued to work on his graphs, and without looking up from his work casually replied: "My corn hurts."   —Rome Roberts

NOT MY HAPPIEST MOMENT

It would be superfluous for me to say that this is the happiest moment of my life, because it is—not. After-dinner speaking is an effort to appear at ease and happy, though fearful and tumultuous. It is, indeed, an unusual accomplishment. It is the **patti-de-foi-gras** of oratory—a conditional rather than a normal mode of expression. The archetype of the art is the impromptu speech. It is often an unplumed squab for flight, and heavy with "the stuff that dreams are made of"—the art that's long when time is fleeing. It attains its perfection **ex post facto,** or retroactively; that is, after the banquet hall's deserted, and the speaker is homeward bound alone. How pregnant than and cheerful are the words of philosophy: Sweet are the uses of—retrospection.

Upon this occasion I urge no claim to offhand powers of eloquence. I cannot say, and it would be vain for me to assert, that this is an extemporaneous effort. The weight of internal evidence would crush the contention; and the faithful years of laborious preparation would shrink aghast at such wild assertions, and put to shame my base ingratitude. On the contrary, behold in me the sophomoric apostle of the midnight oil.

—F. Charles Hume

NICE PEOPLE

Mr. Toastmaster, ladies and gentlemen: Being at conventions like this might be compared to being a truck driver—in either case one has a chance to run into so many nice people. The smile you see on my face is one of amusement that I should be so audacious as to come before you during the closing minutes of this Delta Sigma Rho convention. I am amused, for I realize the speechmaking powers which all of you seated around these tables possess—you who are here because you are debaters and orators clever and polished enough to become members of this national honorary fraternity of public speakers.

—Kenneth Maxwell

VERY SHALLOW

(When a speaker is substituting for another.)

It is quite an honor to be able to appear here this evening and substitute for the Honorable Martin S. Cook, who I understand was unable to be here, having been called out of town on an urgent matter.

In pinch-hitting tonight for Mr. Cook, I am reminded of an incident that I feel is proper to relate at this time.

Reverend Peter Johnson was suddenly called out of town and consequently he was unable to preach his Easter sermon, which he had so diligently prepared. Reverend John Smith was called in as a substitute. When Reverend Peter Johnson returned home the following day, he asked his wife what she thought of the Reverend Mr. Smith's sermon.

"Very poor," said Mrs. Johnson. "There was absolutely nothing to it. Very shallow," the good wife repeated.

Later on in the week the Reverend Mr. Johnson was passing down the street and he met the Reverend Mr. Smith. "Well, well," said Reverend Johnson, "I want to thank you for taking my place last Sunday. Of course, you got along all right with the sermon?"

"Excellent," said the Reverend Mr. Smith. "The notice was so short that I didn't have time to prepare a sermon of my own, so I delivered one of yours." —Karl Kirsten

GREATER ATTRACTION

(When the speaker comments on the small attendance.)

Ladies and gentlemen, I am rather disappointed at the small attendance here this evening but I can't say that I blame those who were fortunate enough to stay away. As I came into the hall and noticed the vacant chairs, I said to your chairman, "Mr. Brown, do you usually have a larger audience than we have here this evening?"

"Oh, yes," he replied, "When we have a greater attraction."
—Hillary Williams

IT'S A GIFT!

I have been sitting for an hour in such a state of tremulousness and fright, facing this audience I was to address, that the ideas I had carefully gathered together have, I fear, rather taken flight. But I shall give them to you as they come, though they may not be in quite as good order as I should like them.

The gift of after-dinner speaking is one I heard illustrated the other day very well at a dinner at which my friend, Judge Bartlett, and I were present. A gentleman told a story of an English bishop traveling in a railway train with an individual who was swearing most tremendously, originally, and picturesquely, till finally the bishop said to him: "My dear sir, where in the world did you learn to swear in that extraordinary manner?" And he said, " It can't be learned; it is a gift." After-dinner speaking is a gift I have often envied, ladies and gentlemen, and as I do not have it, I can only promise to tell you what I really think on the subject which I am here to speak about tonight.   —Thomas Nelson Page

HE DIDN'T SAY

(The subject of your talk. Making it clear what subject you are talking about)

I noted that the chairman of this meeting, in introducing me, did not mention the subject of my talk to you this evening. So that every one in the room will have some idea of what I am going to say, I have selected the subject of "Birds." I hope that after I have finished my speech, it will be quite clear that I was talking about birds.

I don't want to be classified in the category of a senator from one of our western states. Several years ago this senator was delivering a desk-pounding oration to his constituents at a campaign meeting in a small town. One of the senator's staunchest admirers was late in arriving at the meeting, which was then in progress. Storming into the entrance way, the late arrival bumped into a villager who was making an exit.

"Is Senator Sniffle delivering an oration in there?" asked the late arrival to the exiting villager.

"Yep," answered the villager, proceeding down the steps on his way home.

"What's the senator talking about?" the late arrival called out.

The villager stopped for a moment, turned around, and with one foot on one step, and the other foot on another step, he looked up at the late arrival and said in a slow drawl: "He didn't say."
                                    —Howard C. Wilford

YOU COWARD!

(When a young speaker wishes that he would have turned down the assignment)

When your chairman called me up last week and asked me if I would like to make a short talk at this meeting, I was highly thrilled. Then the next morning, I began to contemplate on what I had gotten myself into, as speechmaking was entirely new to me. For two days I tried to figure a way out, but all of the time my conscience kept saying to me, "you coward." I was somewhat in the position of a certain meek married man, whose wife was a tormentor of the worst kind. Each night as the man returned home from work he was forced to listen to a series of charges from his wife, which continued throughout the night, and until the fellow left for work in the morning.

Finally the nagging and scolding became unendurable, and the meek man sought a way out. Desperately he rushed down to the zoo, entered a tiger's cage and slept peacefully all night long, his head resting on the tiger's neck.

His wife, furious over having lost the target for her nagging, took up the scent and soon discovered her husband in the tiger's cage.

Walking up to the bars of the cage, the nagging wife cried out in rage: "Come out of there, you coward!"
                                    —Paul C. Winthrop

WHO'S CRAZY NOW?

(Response by a speaker who is about to use graphs and charts)

The glowing remarks by your chairman in reference to the elucidity in which I am going to discuss the subject of ———, with the assistance of my graphs and charts, reminds me of a story that came from a school for retarded children in the middle west:

A teacher in sociology was lecturing to a class of retarded children—a group of youngsters in the age range of from twelve to fourteen years, and during the course of his lecture the teacher drew a series of circles, equations, parallelograms, dots, dashes and various other mysterious figures on the blackboard. Throughout this procedure the forty backward youngsters followed the teacher's chalk gyrations with blank stares. (A situation that I personally have been confronted with in some of my own talks.)

When the teacher dropped his piece of chalk and picked up a pointer, one young urchin with snarled matted hair and two buck teeth protruding from the front of his mouth turned to another young urchin with snarled matted hair and two buck teeth protruding from the front of his mouth and whispered behind a cupped hand: "Is that guy nuts?"

(Pause for laughter)

So perhaps tonight we will find out just who is nuts.

—Sylvester H. McGovern

CREDIT GIVEN TO OTHERS

I thought I came here on the condition that I was to do no talking. I get scared to death when called upon to speak, and sometimes I don't say what I want to. So you will excuse me for everything out of the way that I say tonight. I was almost breathless as I listened to your president's speech. The more he spoke the more I thought: "For God's sake, can he mean us?" As he went on and I recognized the name of our beloved chief,

Admiral Dewey, I knew he was simply patting the admiral over our shoulders, and I thought to myself: "He can't do too much of that to suit me." We feel that we may be congratulated on our home-coming, not for what we have done, but for having served under Admiral Dewey. We love him and give him all the credit for what was done by the American fleet at Manila. If we thought it was possible by accepting this kind reception tonight to take away from him one iota of credit, we would feel that we were doing wrong. We were with Dewey from the start to the finish, and on each day we learned to love and respect him. The more we knew him, the more we knew that our country's honor was safe in his hands and that nothing in which he was engaged but would redound to the credit of our country.   —Captain Joseph Bullock Coghlan

This response was given by Captain Coghlan to an introduction given at a banquet in New York City in 1899 where he was the guest of honor together with the crew of "The Raleigh." This is an illustration of a speaker revealing his modesty and showing a willingness to share honors.

HERE I AM

Mr. Chairman and members of the Bond Club: I am deeply sensible of the compliment implied in your invitation to talk with you on this occasion. When I was first approached I was asked to explain what was going on in Washington. That assignment scared me off, and I declined. Then the invitation was modified, and I was asked to come and describe some of the things that are going on in Washington. Well, that is likewise a tough one, even for an intrepid editor. But, here I am.

—Merle Thorpe, editor of "Nation's Business"

SEVERE COLD

(When the speaker has a cold or a hoarse voice)

Unfortunately I had to catch a cold just before making my appearance at this important meeting. Yesterday, while I was going over the material for this talk, I wasn't sure whether I wanted a cold or not. In fact, a severe cold with hoarseness, so hoarse that I would not be able to utter a word, seemed like a welcome way out for me at that time. As I was struggling with my notes and assembling information, and making little headway with it, I felt something like a small boy, who during recess, was running around the schoolyard in his shirt sleeves on a windy and cold March day.

The boy's teacher was sitting at her desk, and upon looking out the window, she spied Johnny in his dangerous predicament. Hurrying to the window, she raised it and cried out: "Johnny, if you don't stop running around in your shirt sleeves, you'll catch such a cold you won't be able to recite 'Lincoln's Gettysburg Address' tomorrow afternoon for the mothers' meeting."

Johnny halted for a moment, and getting the idea, replied: "I don't think I want to be reciting for the mothers." And he took off his shirt and undershirt and resumed his play.

—James Bolden

ONLY GOD KNOWS

(The new or young speaker explains about forgetting what he has to say.)

Gentlemen, I came here tonight for the purpose of making a speech, and when I came there were only two people who knew what I was going to say—God and myself. Now after this very fine dinner, these beautiful surroundings and the general confusion, all that I can say when I look down into your faces is that now there is only One who knows what I am going to say, and it's not me.   —Walter S. Bacon

FAMILY REUNION

I am proud to bring to this Conference the greetings of the President and people of the Republic of the Philippines.

We of the Philippines have a profound sense of the great historic events dramatized by this unique gathering; we were, may I remind you, the first of the new nations to emerge in the great re-arrangement of the world which began after the end of the Second World War. Our Republic came to being, freely and peacefully, on July 4, 1946. Since that time we have watched with proud solidarity and a feeling of oneness the establishment of the other independent nations of a free Asia, so old and yet so new. We have in these nine years taken our stand firmly behind the struggle of every people to become master of its own fate, to enjoy its own identity, to be responsible for its own acts, to join in the immense task of building a new structure of human well-being and free institutions, the task, indeed, of changing the face of the world. To the peoples of Africa, already setting forth on this same path, we pledge our friendship and all the moral and practical support within our power to give as they join us of Asia in the great universal effort to better man's estate.

We come as members of one great family long separated from each other. In this family reunion we are here to talk of **man's estate.** But I do not think it will serve us well to have come here from our many corners of the earth to shroud the truth about man's estate in platitudes, propaganda, or easy self-deception. The world is too harsh a place for this, our problems too great, too perilous, too complicated to allow us this luxury.

—Carlos P. Romulo
Chairman, Philippine Delegation

Mr. Romulo knew that his address at the Asian-African Conference at Bandung in 1955 would throw a bombshell into the conference and his aim was to turn the tide away from domination of the Far East by the Soviets. Wisely he opened his address with an excellent psychological approach to the entire subject.

THE HAPPIEST MOMENT

If this is the happiest moment of my life, it is also the most embarrassing. Words are useless to requite such kindness and generosity, and what would be more becoming than "a great, sweet silence?" But that is denied me. You have sent me forth to the doubtful combats of public life. Sometimes I have returned with my shield, and at least once I returned upon it, but I have always come back. While it is a privilege to hold public office, it is the life beyond the political grave that is the best. In one respect the servant of the people is like that Apostle—he "dies daily." And his paradise of the blest, to which his hope fondly clings, is the old home with the kindred spirits who have not been estranged or deluded by the temporary official accoutrement. It is their welcome and confidence that he prizes most.   —Charles Evans Hughes

This response was given by Mr. Hughes when he was the guest of honor at a banquet in 1925 in answer to tributes given him. It reveals the use of the impersonal style of treatment when a speaker speaks in an unusual situation.

IT IS A PLEASURE

It would be a gross distortion of the truth for me to say, as is customary on these occasions, that it is a pleasure to address you. Pleasure is a totally inadequate word. There is no man living—certainly there is no man who does his living in public—who would not jump at the chance. To have the masters of the American press silenced in front of you for twenty minutes while you tell them is something any public servant would gladly sacrifice his hope of bureaucratic heaven to achieve.

—Archibald MacLeish

Mr. MacLeish, director of the Office of Facts and Figures, used this response to an introduction at an Associated Press Annual Luncheon in which he has an opportunity, as he says, "to talk back to the Associated Press."

THE RIGHT THING TO DO

When I accepted the invitation to address this convention, I was placed in somewhat the same position as one of my fellows who came in all bandaged up the other day. I inquired, "John, what is the matter? Have you been in a fight?"

He said that he hadn't been in a fight. He was rather evasive; he didn't want to tell me. By pinning him down, I found out he had been pretty badly cut up. I asked him how he got so cut up, and he said he had jumped through a plate-glass window.

When I asked him why he had done that, he said that it seemed to be the right thing to do at the time. That is the way I felt in accepting this invitation to address you. It seemed to be the right thing at the time, but I did not know that my subject was going to change so much in the period of time which elapsed between my acceptance of the invitation and today.

—Frederic V. Gardner

THE FUTURE

When Abraham Lincoln was nominated in 1860, and a committee brought the news to him at his home in Springfield, Ill., his reply was two sentences long. Then, while his friends and neighbors waited in the street, and while bonfires lit up the May evening, he said simply, "And now I will not longer defer the pleasure of taking you, and each of you, by the hand."

I wish I could do the same—speak two sentences, and then take each of you by the hand, all of you who are in sound of my voice. If I could do so, I would first thank you individually for your confidence and trust. Then, as I am sure Lincoln did as he moved among his friends in the light of the bonfires, we could pause and talk a while about the questions that are uppermost in your mind.

I am sure one topic would dominate all the rest. That topic is: The future.   —President Dwight Eisenhower

This general opening was used by President Eisenhower to introduce his acceptance speech in August, 1956.

FALSE ECONOMY

(When the speaker considers an economy suggested is a false economy)

Let us be realistic about this, and let us give it more thought. Nobody likes to throw away money, but there is such a thing as a false economy, a foolish economy.

There's the case of Sandy MacDougal. Two friends of his met one day, and one asked: "What happened in the last few weeks to Sandy MacDougal? His hair has turned white."

"Well," said the other. "You know that new scenic railway at the beach that has all the girls screaming?"

"Sure, but what's the connection?"

"It's this. Sandy has been going on that ride quite often— as often as he possibly can."

"He must like riding that thing, then."

"On the contrary. He shakes like a leaf, turns white as a sheet, gets sick at the stomach. When he comes off of it he's in a state of collapse. He has to be helped home and to bed, and he stays in bed several days before he can get up strength and courage to take another ride. Then he goes back there again."

"Heavens," said the other friend. "What's the explanation of that?"

"He found a permanent pass to the thing."

—George A. Posner

Section Three

REPARTEE FOR SPEAKERS

REPARTEE FOR SPEAKERS

"When wit in conversation takes the form of a retort or repartee, it is so rare a weapon, so sudden and unexpected, scatters a man's adversaries with so utter a rout, that the most malicious and spiteful listener cannot restrain his involuntary applause." —William Mathews

The reputation of a speaker can be established on the twist of a phrase or the use of a pun during the first minute or two of his response to an introduction. A clever chairman can take a speaker off guard and unless he is prepared with suitable repartee his opening remarks are likely to "fall flat." It is during this short interval that an audience appraises a speaker and the first impression may become a handicap to him if he lacks the ability to stage an immediate comeback.

Repartee has been described as a snappy comeback that is short and sharp. It is a type of wit and humor that invariably catches the other person offguard. Usually the way has been opened by some remark of the chairman which gives the speaker an opportunity to make his thrust. And he should make it immediately, without any hesitation. The alert reaction of the speaker in taking advantage of an opening always pleases the audience and makes a favorable impression of the speaker's ability as he turns the tables on the other person. Of course, his success will be in proportion to the embarrassment of the victim.

Although repartee may appear to be impromptu and spontaneous, the fact is that the average speaker must be prepared for any eventuality. Even though the comeback should appear to be a spur of the moment remark, it may be drawn out of a reservoir of repartee material that the speaker has stored up in reserve. In this section we have assembled a variety of material that will reinforce the supply of repartee quips and stories for the speaker's use.

THE BEST SPEAKER

There was a boy who walked into a cigar store, and said: "Let me be your salesman. I'm the best salesman in the world."

"All right," said the cigar store owner, "Here's a dozen boxes. Take them out and sell them."

The boy went out and tried hard to make a sale, but couldn't get rid of a single box. Finally he went back to the storekeeper with an apology, "I'm the second best salesman; the man who sold you these cigars is the best."

And so I say, it's the man who introduced me who is the best speaker.

I'm not much of a talker. I've always said: One nice thing about keeping your mouth shut is that you're so seldom wrong.

—George A. Posner

UNLIKELY CONTACT

It has been said that Winston Churchill hated to have heckling stopped in an audience because he knew that he was clever in repartee. Once he got a big laugh when a heckler became so entangled in his attempted abuse that he could only splutter. Churchill quickly subdued him by saying: "My friend should not develop more indignation than he can contain!"

At one time during a political campaign Churchill was cultivating a not very successful mustache. At a meeting one evening a woman rose and shouted: "I don't like your ideas or your mustache!"

To which Churchill replied: "Madam, pray do not distress yourself. You are unlikely to come into contact with either one."   —Walter H. Thompson

Speeches are often like eggs. You don't need to eat the whole of an egg nor hear the whole of a speech to know that it is bad.   —Walter Hines Page

WHEN HE TALKS HE CAN'T THINK

About the year 1857 when Lincoln and Douglas were rival candidates for the United States Senate, they journeyed over the state of Illinois making joint debates from the same platform.

At Bloomington a great throng gathered in the public square. A farm wagon was used as the platform. Mr. Douglas opened and spoke with great force and conviction. During the address Mr. Lincoln sat huddled up on an old kitchen chair, the picture of dispair, and his friends thought it would be impossible for him to meet the strong argument of his opponent and consequently they had great pity for him.

When Douglas had finished, Lincoln arose gradually, stretching himself out on the installment plan, but the following words instantly cleared the deck and changed the whole situation. Lincoln said, "When I was a boy I lived in Sangmon County on the Sangmon River. There plied at that time on that river an old steamboat, the boiler of which was so small that when they blew the whistle the paddle wheel wouldn't go 'round. When the paddle wheel went around, they couldn't blow the whistle. My friend Douglas reminds me of that old steamboat for it is evident from what he has told us this afternoon that when he talks he can't think, and when he thinks he can't talk."   —W. H. Foster

WHAT AN ACCENT!

(First public address for a young speaker)

Gentlemen, this is my first public address. I trembled all day yesterday, thinking about it. And today, I missed my breakfast, lunch and dinner—this dinner, thinking about it. Now that I have begun to talk, it isn't half bad, only my voice sounds so peculiar. In this respect, I feel something like the Brooklyn business man who dictated a letter into a dictating machine. Upon listening to the playback of the recording, he said to himself: "Not bad, but gee, vhat an haccent!"

—Hugh Lincoln

EFFECTIVE REPARTEE

On one occasion when Stephen A. Douglas and Abraham Lincoln were engaged in a debate on the same platform, Douglas referred to the fact that he once saw Lincoln retailing whiskey. "Yes," replied Lincoln, "it is true that the first time I saw Judge Douglas I was selling whiskey by the drink. I was on the inside of the bar and the Judge was on the outside. I was busy selling, he busy buying." This is about as neat a retort as the annals of the stump afford—rich but not malicious. It perhaps had a greater effect on the audience than if Lincoln had spent an hour talking about temperance in general and his own temperance in particular.   —Champ Clark

WRONG CONVENTION

(When several members of the audience leave the room)

Standing up here in full view of this audience, I, of course, noted that several people have left the room during my talk. Three fellows got up over in that end, and walked out. Four fellows over here got up and left. And I believe there were a few more.

I am not inclined to feel that those fellows became bored with my speech. On the contrary, I think they liked my speech, and it was an effort for them to leave the room.

In this respect, I would classify them in the category of the man from Minnesota who went to a convention of implement dealers in Chicago. Upon his return to Minnesota, after a full week at the convention, the partner in the firm said to the implement dealer, "What did you find out at the convention?"

"Nothing," said the implement dealer, "I got into the wrong convention."

(Pause.)

I hope the gentlemen who left will find the right meeting place.   —James Bolden

FENCE - STRADDLING

(When someone at a meeting hesitates about taking a side on a question before the meeting.)

John Brown's refusal to state his position on the important question before this meeting is very disappointing. Time and time again, all evening long we have asked John: "How do you stand?" Every time he has answered, "I haven't decided yet."

This fence-straddling recalls an event that happened in Flatbush last summer, when the city council was arguing whether or not to put up a new flagpole on the volunteer firehouse lawn. The debate was furious, some were for and some were against. One leathernecked old veteran of village politics sat in his chair all afternoon without saying one word while the others wrangled on and on. Finally the president of the council turned to the old veteran and said: "How do you stand on this question, Silas?" Silas took a chew of tobacco, deliberately spat in the gaboon, stroked his beard and replied in slow, drawling words: "I haven't made my mind up yet, but when I do I'm going to be bitter."   —Hugh Lincoln

GIVE ME DIRECTION

(When the speaker is interrupted by the rattling of dishes, squeaking of chairs and other disturbances.)

The falling of that platter out of the agile fingers of the waitress, which no doubt is shattered to small pieces on the floor back of that table, interrupted my chain of thought to the point where I must tell you the story about an elderly lady who had difficulty in orientating herself. This good old lady would make frequent visits to her daughter's house, and when it came time for her to return to her own home, her daughter would start her out in the right direction. One night she left later than usual, and it was a pitch black night, the street lights for some reason or another were not turned on. As the good old lady was slowly feeling her way down the street, having been pointed in the right direction by her daughter, a bustling youth came prancing down the sidewalk and collided with the lady, knocking her as well as himself to the ground.

The youth was immediately full of apologies. "My dear Madam, I am so sorry!" said the youth, "Permit me to help you up on your feet," he added. The elderly lady replied, "I'll accept your apology, young man, if you will tell me the direction I was facing before you knocked me down."

(Pause for laughter.)

I will now try to orient myself back to where I was when the dish fell to the floor.   —Rome Roberts

WITHOUT INTERRUPTION

(When the speaker is confronted with a heckler or persons making rude disturbances.)

The rude disturbances that are taking place in this hall by some person unbeknown to me, appear to be a deliberate attempt to interfere with the delivery of my speech. Therefore, it is quite proper that I now refer to an event that happened at a certain meeting upstate some years ago.

A candidate for public office was making a speech before an unruly audience, and one person in particular seemed to be the author of the disturbances. The speaker sized up the fellow and had him pretty well in mind, when a short recess was called for the purpose of serving refreshments.

As the crowd was milling around the hall, eating doughnuts and drinking coffee, the speaker spied the noisy fellow visiting with a half a dozen other persons in one corner of the room. As the speaker approached this obstreperous chap, he heard the chap remark that his gall bladder was bothering him lately, which afforded an excellent opportunity for the speaker to say: "It ought to. You use it more than any other organ in your body."

I will now proceed with my talk, I hope without interruptions.   —Howard C. Wilford

"NO HITS, NO RUNS, NO ERRORS!"

(When there is a hesitation on the part of the membership to take up a subject.)

Mr. Chairman: I feel that this organization in the past has been negligent in taking an active part in certain civic projects. Time after time a very worthy cause has been presented here for acceptance, and every single time it has been voted down. Everybody seems to be afraid, that should we take on a drive of some nature or another, we will fail. As a result we never start anything. Now take this project before the meeting at this time. It is a worthy cause. It will take some work, and some speculation.

When I mentioned the word, "speculation," I see a great fear flutter across the faces of some of the members. Fear of what? Fear of failure or fear of making a mistake? Yes, gentlemen, some of you are afraid to do anything but sit here and talk and eat. In this respect you remind me of the three old maid sisters who lived chaste lives. They never had a boy friend, and as a result they never had a husband, and as a further result they never had any children, and as a still further result they left no heirs to write the epithets upon the gravestones when they died.

This job fell to a bachelor neighbor of the same age as the old maids, who a half a century before had attempted to kiss each one of them, respectively, and each time he failed, respectively. When told that he was the only person intimate enough with the old maids to write their epithets, he took out his pencil and scribbled: "Here lies Alice, Nellie and Grace." At that point he pondered for a moment and then added: "No hits, no runs, no errors!"

Gentlemen, I move we adopt the project.

—James Bolden

———

Some people have tact—others tell the truth. I am going to use tact and tell the truth. Truth is stranger than fiction and more decent.

I STAND WITH MY FRIENDS

(Taking a stand on an issue when a speaker wants to side-track his position on any issue.)

When the chairman asked me how I stood on the question before this meeting, I feel that I must answer it like the old lawyer up in Pottsville who was running for a seat in the state legislature. The candidate was making a fiery speech before a packed audience in the town hall, and right in the middle of his oration, a farmer jumped to his feet and yelled out: "Mr. Candidate, how do you stand on the 6th amendment to the state constitution?"

Now, that was a burning issue, and sentiment was about equally divided on the subject. The candidate looked down at the farmer for a moment, stroked his chin, and said: "The 6th amendment. Well, let's see. Some of my friends are for it. Some of my friends are against it. I stand with my friends."

—Hugh Lincoln

ON YOUR GLASSES

(When the speaker does not see eye to eye with another)

In my opinion Bill Jones is looking at our proposal with a different viewpoint than the rest of us. He finds this wrong with it. He finds that wrong with it. If I recall correctly, Bill has presented no less than a dozen different objections to it— objections that the rest of us can't detect at all. Now who is right, Bill . . . or the majority of the members at this meeting? Bill reminds me of old Grandpa Snokes, who was out in the backyard of his farm home, polishing the butt of his shotgun. Little Grandson Willie stood eagerly by watching the operation.

"I can't seem to get the darned specks off this gun," exclaimed Grandpa Snokes, polishing and polishing away.

Little Willie looked at the gun and then looked up at his grandpa and said: "Them specks ain't on the gun, Grandpa, they're on your glasses."   —Harold Butterworth

"I'VE GOT THE MEAT!"

(When a speaker is late in arriving)

I want to apologize for being late. I dislike to use that old hackneyed expression that I was unavoidably detained at another pressing engagement. However, I broke away from the other engagement as quickly as I could, and while I was swiftly moving up the street, I was reminded of a story, so I stopped hurrying and took my time.

It seems that a young lad was sent to the store by his mother to bring home some provisions, which is nothing unusual. On the way home he encountered some of his playfellows engaged in a baseball game. He immediately jumped into the pitcher's box and took part in the contest. After the game had passed four or five innings, his big sister walked by the sandlot, on her way home from work. Spying her little brother out on the diamond, she called out to him: "You'd better hurry home, Johnny, you'll be late for supper."

"Oh, no I won't," Johnny replied, winding up for a pitch, adding, "I've got the meat!" (Waves a copy of his speech to emphasize the point, if necessary.)

—James Mitchell

"LOUDER, PLEASE"

(When someone in the audience calls out "louder.")

That cry of "louder" just voiced by a gentleman in the audience brings to my mind a story about Vice-President Marshall. He's the fellow who said, "What this country needs is a good five cents cigar." Well, anyway Marshall was talking to a crowded audience in Buffalo, when he was interrupted by a political opponent, who apparently tried to embarrass Marshall by putting his hand to his ear, and calling out, "Louder." Mr. Marshall then pitched his voice to a higher key; and the only effect upon his tormentor was a repeated yell of "Louder. Louder, please."

When the heckler interrupted the speaker for the fourth

time, Mr. Marshall became indignant, as the fourth interruption came just as the vice-president was swinging into a lofty piece of oratory. Mr. Marshall paused in the middle of a sentence, fixed an angry eye on the heckler, turned and looked over at the chairman, and said: "Mr. Chairman, on the last day, when the angel Gabriel shall have descended from the heavens, and placing one foot upon the sea and the other upon the land, shall lift his lips to the golden trumpet, and proclaim to the living and the resurrected dead that time shall be no more, I have no doubt, sir, that some infernal fool in Buffalo will start up and cry out, 'Louder, please, louder!' "

Note: An opportunity to tell this story can be effected by arranging with a friend in the audience to call out, "louder."

—Sylvester McGovern

GETTING SMART

(When a speaker changes his position or goes along with someone he opposed in the past.)

I must admit that I was strenuously opposed last year to any projects advocated by Bill Jones. I know that Bill and I have had some serious differences at many of our meetings, and some of them have been pretty bitter. But tonight I am going along with Bill. I am going to vote with him for the resolution before the house.

In this respect I feel something like the sixteen-year-old boy, who laughed at every suggestion his father made. Everything the old man said was wrong. In fact, in the lad's mind, the old man was just plain dumb. When the boy reached the age of eighteen, his viewpoint towards his father changed. But one thing perplexed him. He couldn't figure out how his father had learned so much in two years.

(Pause.)

I'm not admitting that I'm trying to figure out how Bill got so smart in a year, but I'm going along with him on the resolution.

—Hugh Lincoln

TALL TALES

(When a speaker challenges a statement in debate before the meeting)

Mr. Chairman: For the past half hour we have listened to Jack Horner speak in behalf of the motion before the house. What he has said should be taken with a grain of salt. His facts are distorted. His logic is not clear. Time and time again during his talk he has brought out half-truths. In fact, Mr. Chairman, Jack Horner is going to have to retract a number of accusations levelled at this body. He is going to have to retract some of his tall tales—tall tales like the story about a fellow who went up in the northern Minnesota woods. The hunter had spent a strenuous day in the woods, and that evening he returned to camp without a bag.

"What happened today?" asked a comrade.

"What happened!" replied the hunter. "I got the scare of my life. I was deep in the woods in pursuit of a big buck, when unfortunately I lost my gun in a thicket, which I was unable to find. For over an hour I wandered and wandered through the forest, unarmed. When lo and behold I saw a big buck with horns six feet wide charging directly at me. For a moment I was stupefied. I didn't know how to make a get away, as the trees were so close together, I could hardly squeeze through. Then all of a sudden I devised a way out. I ran sideways, sandwiching myself between the trees, with the big buck hot on my trail. He chased me all the way to the clearing, where I reached the safety of this cabin."

"Just a minute!" said one of the hunter's comrades. "If the trees were so close together that you had to run sideways, how did the big horned buck get through?"

The hunter contemplated for a moment, and then turned to his comrade and said: "He pulled in his horns."

Mr. Chairman, before this issue is settled, Jack Horner will pull in his horns.   —Paul C. Winthrop

CONFIDENTIAL

(When the speaker asks that what he is going to say must be kept in confidence.)

Gentlemen: What you will hear this afternoon is of a very confidential nature. You must bear that in mind at all times, for we are going to reveal to you information which, should it get into the hands of our competitors, it would be disastrous.

You will see the new designs. You will hear about our plans. You will become acquainted with the great things that are in store for you as an employee of this firm. I ask that you pledge your secrecy, and I hope that there will be no slips of the tongue, such as happened to a certain lady who boasted that she never would tell her age. One day while bragging that she had never told her age since she was twenty-two years old, a gentleman friend said to her: "I'll bet some day you'll tell it."

"Never," said the lady, adding, "When a lady can keep a secret for twenty years, she can keep it forever."

So, gentlemen, no slips!   —Howard C. Wilford

CORRECTED

(When the speaker is corrected by the chairman or by some member of the audience.)

I sincerely appreciate the kindly interruption by your chairman, correcting my last statement. It was an important correction, and I am thankful it was made. However, the pause did more or less upset the delivery of my speech, sort of sidetracking me for the moment.

In this respect, I am somewhat in the same situation as the girl elevator operator who, upon stopping her car at the fifth floor, stepped out of it to wave at a handsome young man, who was sitting at the desk in one of the offices. After a minute or so of hand-waving, winking at each other and the exchange of other facial expressions, the girl returned to her elevator, grabbed the throttle of the car, and then thoughtfully asked herself: "Was I going up or down?"   —Hugh Lincoln

WHEN I GET THERE

(When the speaker emphasizes that his talk will be short.)

Gentlemen, I am going to give a very short talk this evening. I have sat through some of those long-winded, parrot-like affairs that drive an audience to distraction, and I know what a bore a speaker can be.

Last week I heard just such a talk at one of our service clubs. The speaker went on and on, which brought to my mind the story of the slow-moving woodtick that on one cold and bleak day in February started to climb a peach tree. As the woodtick moved almost imperceptibly up the trunk of the tree, an ant, perched on a piece of bark, yelled to the woodtick: "Tickey, you're wasting your time, there ain't any peaches up there this time of year."

The woodtick moved up the tree another one-thousandths of an inch and turned to the ant and quietly said: "There will be when I get there!"   —Howard C. Wilford

WHAT'S YOUR NAME?

(When favoritism is shown to a certain group or individual, or when a clique in an organization is attempting to pass some resolution.)

Mr. Chairman: It would seem to me that the arguments in behalf of the resolution before this meeting are of a decidedly biased nature, and without foundation or fact. The group that is trying to railroad this resolution listens to one side only, and refuses to weigh the significant points of the opposition. Should we adopt this resolution, we would be doing so without due consideration of all of the facts in the argument.

It would simply be a vote of prejudice, something like the decision made by an Irish traffic cop at Forty-second street and Broadway in New York City. One day last week Patrolman Patrick O'Flannigan was standing at the busy street intersection, when two automobiles collided with each other. Rushing over with the authority that is possessed by all traffic cops, Patrolman O'Flannigan said to one of the drivers: "What's your name?"

"Ole Swanson," answered the driver, mournfully surveying the front of his Buick car, which was caved in and crumbled to rubble.

"And what's your name?" said the cop to the driver of the other car, which had only one small dent in its bumper. "Dennis Hennesey!" said the driver with a decided Irish brogue.

Patrolman O'Flannigan put his hands on his hips, and with fire gleaming out of his eyes, walked up to driver Ole Swanson and yelled out: "Swanson, what do you mean by bumping into Hennesey's car?"

Gentlemen, I oppose the amendment.

—James Bolden

AN OPEN MIND

(When a skeptic interrupts a speaker and questions a statement.)

I am perfectly certain that everyone in this audience came to this meeting in an unbiased state of mind, and that every one of you would listen to what I had to say before you would offer an opinion. However, I am afraid that the gentleman who put the last question to me is more or less like a certain Democratic Ward Heeler in Chicago who went to a Republican meeting.

"What are you doing here, Mr. McGillicudy?" asked a Republican leader who spotted the Democratic boss. "You of all persons showing up at a Republican gathering!" he added.

"Well, it's like this," said McGillicudy. "I was a walking down the street, when I spied the sign announcing the Republican rally. So I thought I would go in. But I said to myself, 'I must be fair about it. I will go in there with a completely open mind and hear what I know will be nothing but damn malarkey.'"   —Howard C. Wilford

EARLY APPOINTMENT

**(When the speaker is disturbed by late arrivals or when
someone gets up and leaves during a speech.)**

I don't know whether or not the disturbance out there in the
hall is caused by persons coming or going. I am somewhat in
the same position as a certain Mrs. Jones. One morning at the
early hour of four o'clock, her husband, William, who had a
heavy evening at his club, returned home, cautiously and quietly, so as not to awaken the sleeping Mrs. Jones. Carefully, Mr.
Jones removed his shoes; then his shirt and tie; and at the time
he had his trousers half way off, Mrs. Jones woke up.

Looking at the clock on her dressing table, she said to her
husband, "William, where are you going so early in the morning?"

"I have an early appointment at the office," replied Mr.
Jones, and then he proceeded to pull up his half-removed trousers, put on his shirt, tie and shoes, and walked out, perplex-
ingly, into the early morning air.   —Rome Roberts

THE LAST CHANCE

**(When a speaker had difficulty in finding the
right meeting room.)**

There are so many meetings going on right now in this
hotel that I had difficulty in finding the right place. When I
first stepped off the elevator, a good looking young lady pinned
a badge on my lapel and ushered me up to the speaker's table.
I was leisurely looking over the menu, when a fellow sitting
beside me, turned and said: "What do you think of Dr. Borum's new hog serum, Doctor?" "Doctor Borum's hog serum!"
I exclaimed in astonishment, and rushed out of the room.

Then I wandered around until I found what I thought was
the proper place. I hurriedly entered to find a lecture going
on about the intricate details of a milking machine. I began to
feel like the fellow who traveled from Montana to New York

to attend a convention, and didn't find out he was participating in the wrong convention until the last day.

I tried a half dozen more, with the same result. When I came to the door of this room I said to myself, "This is my last chance," and I thought of the story about the fellow who had a bad habit of staying out nights, which resulted in some bitter nagging on the part of his wife when he returned home.

The situation became so serious that the fellow's wife sought advice from a lady friend. "Be nice to him when he comes home late. Try different tactics," advised the lady friend. So the wife accepted the advice, and the next time the husband made an early morning appearance, the door was locked. The husband pounded on the door, which immediately was opened by his wife.

"Come in, dearie," she said.

"I might as well," he replied, "I'll get hell when I get home anyway."   —Rome Roberts

ALLERGIC TO BALONEY

(When someone in the audience coughs or sneezes.)

I notice considerable coughing and sneezing going on among members of the audience this evening. For my sake I hope that these sniffles are genuine, as I once received a very severe lesson in this respect. This happened several years ago in a downstate city.

I was wound up that night and was soaring away in clouds of oratory. Right at the point that my eloquence was what I believed to be reaching its height, a series of coughs and sneezes, together with some facial grimaces burst forth from a person in the audience. These coughs and sneezes were so consistent and so vociferous that I stopped abruptly right in the middle of an allegory, and said to the poor afflicted person: "My good man, you have a severe cold. You had better go home and tuck yourself in bed."

"Cold!" yelled the fellow. "I have no cold! I'm allergic to baloney!"   —Rome Roberts

CUT PRETTY THIN

(When the speaker points out that someone's arguments are flimsy)

I have been listening very attentively to the arguments that Bill Wright has presented to us in behalf of the motion before the meeting. I will say without fear of contradiction that Bill's arguments are cut pretty thin, and that he has presented a flimsy case. In that respect he reminds me of the old fellow who dropped into a lunch counter for a ham sandwich. When the short order man pushed the sandwich across the counter, the old fellow pulled the bread slices apart, and examined the ham in between.

"Did you slice this ham?" asked the customer indignantly.

"Certainly, I sliced the ham," said the short order man. "Anything wrong with it?"

The old fellow picked up the sandwich, and scrutinizing the sliver-like pieces of meat, replied rather dryly: "Well, you almost missed it." —Anton C. Wade

MARRIED LIFE

(When a speaker questions the knowledge of another speaker on a subject)

We have had a lot of talk this evening on the matter that we are debating, but the question that comes up in my mind is, "How much do you fellows know about the subject?" I realize that we have not asked you to present qualifications as an expert witness, but I for one would like to know what is your foundation for some of the statements made at this meeting.

This peculiar situation brings to my mind a story that I heard some time ago. It's about two Irish ladies who attended mass, officiated by the archbishop who gave a lengthy sermon on married life.

"'Tis a fine sermon His Reverence was givin' us on married life this mornin'," said one of the Irish ladies to the other as they were walking home.

"'Twas fine, indeed, Maggie, but I wish I knew as little about the matter as His Reverence."

—Douglas Everett

TIME TO THROW DIRT

(When the speaker comments about members who make an appearance at meetings only once a year)

I am pleased to see that Jack Peterson is here at the meeting tonight as Jack hasn't been very regular in attendance at our gatherings. I believe that he came to one meeting last year, and I think that he showed up at another one about four years ago. There are other members, too, who follow Jack's example. If these people happen to be in the mood, they show up here; if not, they stay away. What this organization needs is a full regular attendance of enthusiastic persons, who will pitch in and put over our program. These irregular fellows remind me of a story:

One sunny afternoon the pastor of the church met a should-be parishioner strolling lazily down the street. "Good afternoon, John," said the minister.

"Good afternoon, Pastor," John replied.

"I haven't noticed you in church lately," the minister remarked.

"No," said John, "the first time I went to church, water was thrown in my face, and the second time I was harnessed to a woman that I have had to support ever since."

"I thought that I had seen you in church between those two solemn occasions," said the minister.

"No, you haven't," said John.

"Well," said the minister, "I was mistaken." And then he casually remarked as he walked away: "We'll see you again, John, when it's time to throw the dirt."

—Dale Farnsworth

BEWARE OF ORGANIZATION

(The speaker talks about a resolution of protest)

Gentlemen: I feel that when we issue a protest against this proposal, the draft of the resolution should be in mild form. I notice that some of you here tonight want to go all out and issue a protest of general condemnation. I believe that would be a mistake. I am of the opinion that we should proceed cautiously, which recalls the incident of the colored boy who enjoyed demonstrating his ability to use a fly swatter.

"See that?" said the colored fellow to a little girl standing by his side. "That's a butterfly. Watch me swat him." And he swatted the little butterfly which fluttered to the ground.

"Goody, goody!" said the little girl.

"See that?" said the colored fellow. "That's a fly. Watch me swat 'em." And he swatted the fly, which dropped to the ground.

"Goody, goody!" said the little girl.

Then the little girl pointed up at a tree and said:

"See that? Swat it!"

The colored boy looked up at the tree and said to the little girl: "A butterfly am a butterfly. A fly am a fly—but a hornet's nest, man, that am an organization."

(Pause for laughter)

We should be certain that we won't bring an organization down on us.   —Rome Roberts

WHEN THE CHAIRMAN IS TACTLESS

(After a good-natured dig or "ribbing" by the emcee)

There's a man after my own heart—with a knife.

———

That guy could make some girl a lucky widow. G-r-r-r!

———

He always disagrees with me. That's his way. He loves to disagree. He won't even eat **food** that agrees with him.

WHEN I WAKE UP

**(When the speaker attempts to smooth over a bitter argument
that is going on between two factions at the meeting)**

The discussion that is taking place at our meeting this
evening has reached the state of an argument, and the argument has reached the state of bitterness. I sincerely hope that
the words spoken here tonight will be forgotten, and that when
we next assemble, we will do so on friendly terms, and that
this regrettable situation will pass over.

Which reminds me of a story: The fashionable Mrs. Jones
was attending a dinner party of quite some social distinction.
When the time came to seat the guests, Mrs. Jones unluckily
drew the chair alongside of a tipsy gentleman. Throughout the
course of the dinner, the tipsy fellow pestered Mrs. Jones with
a reiteration of questions and suggestions that nearly drove
her to distraction. Obviously, Mrs. Jones ignored the tipsy
man's questions and assumed a demeanor of intense indifference.

After a prolonged period, the tipsy person stared at Mrs.
Jones through bleary eyes and blubbered out: "You are the
ugliest woman that these orbs of mine have ever gazed upon."

"Well!" exclaimed Mrs. Jones, astonished at the tipsy fellow's audacity. But in a moment she regained her composure
and measuring up to the fellow she very pointedly stated:
"And you're the drunkest man that my orbs have ever gazed
upon."

"That's correct, Madam," he said. "But I'll get over that
when I wake up in the morning."   —Anton C. Wade

———

Many speakers begin their talks with a promise that they
are going to speak with an open mind. I have always been
somewhat wary of this approach because many listeners find
it difficult to distinguish between an open mind and one that
is merely vacant.

TAKE THE HARNESS UP

(When the speaker comments on the dinner.)

I want to take this opportunity to compliment the chairman of the arrangements committee on the very fine dinner that was served here tonight. There have been times, I have found in my various speaking engagements, when the dinner has not been up to standards.

A short time ago I was attending a gathering of this nature in the northern part of one of our adjoining states. The dinner was very disappointing. The soup tasted like dishwater, the olives were wrinkled and bitter, and the steak might have been compared with a piece of shoe leather. While I was desperately trying to carve off a piece of the beef and was making as much headway as if I had been slicing away at a rubber tire with a butter knife, I noted that my neighbor was having the same kind of difficulty.

"Tough!" I said to him, sawing away furiously.

"Tough's no word for it!" he said. "Dense would be better!"

Then after several more attempts with the knife, my neighbor gave up, turned to me and said: "When they advertise beef and give me horse, that's bad. But when they fail to take the harness off, that's going too far!"

(Pause for laughter.)

Just so there's no misunderstanding. I want to repeat. The dinner this evening was delicious.   —James Bolden

PASS THE HAT

(When a speaker urges donations for a cause)

Gentlemen: We are going to call upon your generosity this evening in behalf of our organization's assessment to the very worthy cause that you have heard discussed here. I want everyone to contribute liberally. We want to make a good showing. Before I figuratively pass my hat among you, I am going to tell you a story.

Reverend Andy Beacon, pastor of a church in the deep

south, had great difficulty in raising funds, as his congregation was very parsimonious (quite unlike you people here, I am sure). On one particular Sunday the Reverend Mr. Beacon preached long and eloquently on the necessity of supporting the church. When he had concluded his sermon, the good minister handed his hat to a deacon who proceded to take up the collection.

When the deacon returned, he handed Reverend Beacon his hat, which was empty.

The minister took the hat, looked in it, turned it upside down and shook it. Then he said to the congregation: "Ah sho is fortunate Ah got my hat back from a congregation like this."

(Pause)

I not only want my hat back, but I want it filled up.

—Hugh Lincoln

I DON'T LIVE HERE

(When the speaker comments on some member who got peeved over something or other and left the meeting)

It is regrettable that Jack has taken this argument so seriously. I was under the impression that the discussion going on here was a constructive debate, and that personalities were not a part of it. But evidently Jack thought otherwise, or he wouldn't have left the meeting.

This unfortunate incident reminds me of little four-year-old Mary, who one day became obstreperous and unmanageable, upsetting her mother to the breaking point. In addition, Mary put to use some naughty words that she had picked up from the older boys next door. That was too much for Mary's mother. She ordered the child out of the house in a shrill voice, the tone of which only an upset mother can attain.

"Out in the street!" cried the mother, "and if you don't stop using those naughty words, you need never come back home!"

The child wandered out the door and then sat down on

the front steps. At that moment Mrs. Smith, a neighbor lady, came up the walk and approached Mary. "Is your mother home?" inquired Mrs. Smith.

Little Mary looked up at Mrs. Smith with tear-filled eyes, and in a sobbing voice replied: "How the hell should I know! I don't live here any more!"

(Pause)

I hope that Jack hasn't got the idea that he doesn't live here any more.   —Dale Farnsworth

BUSY ANTS

(When the speaker has been put on the spot by someone in the audience.)

The last three questions put to me by the membership reminds me of a story about an artist who was searching throughout the South for something unusual in pastoral scenes. After wandering through half of Georgia, he came across a magnificent setting of pine trees which framed an old white cottage. This was just what he had been looking for, only he desired a personality of some sort to give life to the scene. At that moment an elderly colored lady came out of the cabin door, and the artist immediately hailed her.

"Sit right down there on the grass," the artist said, "while I paint you." The old lady responded and the artist set up shop and began to paint. After about fifteen minutes had elapsed, the old lady shouted out: "How much longer dis goin' to take?"

"Just a few minutes," the artist replied, and continued with his work.

Ten minutes later the woman became impatient and cried out again, "Mister, how much longer dis goin' to take?"

"Just a few minutes," the artist answered. "But why do you ask? Have you something to do?"

The old woman puckered up her face and said: "I ain't got nuttin' to do, but dese ants have. I'se sittin' right on der hill."   —Horton Smith

NIGHTSHIRTS PREFERRED

**(When something a speaker said is misunderstood
by the audience.)**

I don't know whether it's the public address system, my poor articulation or perhaps my inability to express myself clearly, but the membership seems to have misunderstood my last statement, judging from the comments we are now getting from the floor.

In this connection I am reminded of the hard-of-hearing professor who attended a banquet of some pretensions. Along side of the old gentleman sat a very lovely lady, dressed in the height of fashion, and who was of a conversational mood. Throughout the course of the dinner she attempted to carry on a conversation with the professor, but of no avail since the professor heard little of what she said, and furthermore the professor was busy enjoying his soup and the other delicious courses served at the table. By the time the dessert was ready for serving, the professor still maintained silence. But the lady decided that she would make one more attempt to get the professor to speak.

"Do you like bananas?" she asked the professor.

"What was that?" the professor replied, cupping his ear.

"Do you like bananas?" the lady yelled so loudly that the other guests dropped their silverware and stared in amazement.

The last outburst had somewhat punctured the professor's eardrum. He turned to the lady and said: "My dear lady, what a ridiculous question to ask of an old man like myself. You might know that I prefer the old-fashioned nightshirt."

—Hillary Williams

———

Every time I start to speak I cannot help but recall an excerpt from a mediocre politician of some few years back. He said, "It is only a snake in the grass who will attempt to knife a man in the back with such lying insinuations."

—Arthur L. Kaser

THEY'RE ANIMALS

(When the speaker denies that a movement adopted by the organization is his)

I am charged here this evening as being the father of the subject of discussion before the house. At least three persons have risen to their feet, and pointing to the failure of the movement, have cited me as the father of it. I had no more to do with it than any other member. It was brought up to a vote last year and accepted by this group. But I certainly deny that I am the father of it.

These repetitious accusations against me recall the story about the fellow who was traveling on the local train between Jonesville and Brownstown one day last fall.

The traveler was reading his newspaper. Two pigeons were perched on the crown of his hat. The conductor of the train stepped up to him and said: "Mister, it's against the rules to carry animals on this train."

"They're not animals," said the traveler. "They're a species of ornithology."

"I don't give a damn what you call 'em," retorted the conductor. "In my language they're still animals and they can't ride on this train!"

"And further," said the traveler, "they're not mine. They got on at Smithville." —Anton C. Wade

TOO LAZY TO HOLD BACK

(When the speaker attempts to block something that is being railroaded through the meeting)

It seems to me that we are acting too hastily on this important issue. I feel that we should very carefully weigh all of the facts pertaining to it, and then deliberate very thoroughly before acting. It is also apparent to me, that there is a conspiracy to railroad this measure through. When I use the word "railroad" I, of course am not referring to everyone who is talking in behalf of the issue. A few of you are trying to railroad it through, others are just joining it for the sole reason of being through with it. In that respect those persons remind me of Lester Blunt, who lived on top of a mountain down in Kentucky.

One day word reached Lester that a letter was waiting for him at the postoffice, in the village at the foot of the mountain. Upon receiving the news, Lester started down the mountain side at a slow walk. Part way down, the path sheered into a steep descent, which forced Lester into a run.

While trotting down the path, Lester passed two hillbillies on the way up. "Just look at Lester," said one hillbilly to the other, "Too lazy to hold back."

Yes, gentlemen, there are persons in this audience who are too lazy to deliberate this important question.

—Anton C. Wade

NOT TACTFUL

It reminds me of those political opponents, Gladstone and Disraeli, who never forgot their differences of opinion whether the occasion was public or private. They loved to argue, it often seemed, just for the thrill of verbal combat.

One day, at a reception, there arose a question as to the difference between an accident and a disaster.

Disraeli, noticing Gladstone standing nearby, was on his feet in an instant, and drily observed, pointing a finger at his opponent: "Now if our Right Honorable friend here was to fall into the Thames and drown, it might be an accident; but if anybody pulled him out, there would be a disaster!"

———

Yes, the worthy chairman was not very tactful, I might say. Like a couple of women I overheard at my wife's Saturday afternoon tea. One said: "Why, Matilda, you look positively beautiful today!"

The other answered: "Oh, you flatterer!"

And the first said: "No, it's true. I had to look twice before I recognized you."

SELF STARTERS FOR SPEAKERS

As an after-dinner speaker, I'm in an occupation monopolized by men. Women can't wait that long.

I'm supposed to be a lecturer—one with his hand in your pocket, his tongue in your ear and his faith in your patience.

Public speaking is the art of diluting a two-minute idea with a two-hour vocabulary.

The world's best after-dinner speech is, "Waiter, give me both checks."

When Daniel got into the lions' den and looked around he said to himself: "Whoever's got to do the after-dinner speaking, it won't be me."

There are three things to aim at in public speaking—first to get into your subject, then to get your subject into yourself, and lastly, to get your subject into your hearers.   —Gregg

---

To be a convincing talker, I should be able to show my son just wherein algebra is essential to his future success.

My friends, when I came here tonight only God and myself knew what I was about to say to you. Now only God knows!

A newspaper points out that the Government prints and distributes the speeches made by Congressmen without the slightest profit. It might also be added they are read the same way.

There's a man who pats you on the back, to find a soft place to put the knife. Then he'd put the knife in, and have you arrested for carrying concealed weapons.

—George A. Posner

As a speaker, I admit I'm sort of an amateur. Standing before you now I feel like the absent-minded professor in a revolving door. He couldn't remember whether he was going in or coming out.

_____

I hope you will not treat me as did a group of collegians years ago that assembled to hear me play the piano. When I sat down at the piano I turned to them and said, "Well, fellows, what'll I play?" In chorus they yelled, "Dead!"

_____

As I stand here ready to address you it reminds me of a political speaker who was endeavoring to explain that our tariff on imports was too high. He said, "My friends, if you don't stop shearing the wool off the sheep that lays the golden egg, you'll pump it dry."

_____

My friends, I am not new to politics. For a number of years I was dog catcher in my home town, and through my honest efforts I lost my job. I finally caught the dog.

_____

On my way here I was accosted by a middle-aged, stern-faced lady. She said, "Mr. Speaker, I'm not one bit prejudiced. I'm going to listen to your speech with a perfectly open and unbiased mind to what I'm convinced is pure rubbish."

_____

✓   Friends—I'm not going to begin my speech with Ladies and Gentlemen. I know you too well for that.

_____

It's good to be back among you again. This being my first visit to your beautiful city, I look forward to renewing old acquaintances, including those I have never met.

_____

During my many years in politics I have often been called a self-made man. But lately I've thought it over and have decided that if I had to do it over **again**, I'd call in an architect.

When I arrived in town this afternoon I remarked to a man in front of the hotel, "My, my, when I was here a number of years ago this town was just a flyspeck on the map? Now it has a prominent place on the map. How do you account for it?" He said, "Bigger flies."

___

If, during my speech, any of you wish to leave the hall, please do so quietly so you will not awaken the others.

___

I have no ghost writers. I write my own speeches. You know, something like the carpenter who never uses a blueprint. He can build a house out of his head and have enough wood left over to build a garage.

___

I am speaking to the men only, so you ladies may keep right on talking to one another.

___

Some listeners are like blotters—they soak it all in and get it all backwards.

___

It is good to be a guest in such a hustling and thriving city as you have here. It is quite a contrast to the last place I visited. It was what is known as a poke-and-plumb town. You **poke** your head out of the car window and you're plumb out of town.

___

The first time I addressed the public I was standing before thousands of people in Madison Square Garden. My first words rang loud and clear, "Peanuts, popcorn, hot dogs!"

___

I refuse to vouch for this, but I've heard it said that if all the people who sit through after-dinner speeches were lined up three feet apart, they would stretch.

___

I remember the first time I spoke before a large audience. I began my speech with, "Ladies and gentlemen, lend me your ears . . ." I was interrupted by an elderly man who piped, "You can borrow mine, and thank heaven I can't hear without them."

'Tis said after-dinner speaking is monopolized by men—women can't wait that long.

_____

When I have finished you will all know where I stand when I have taken my seat.

_____

I hope you will not find in me a speaker that goes back and forth over one little idea like a stocking darner.

_____

My message this evening is so vital to this great nation that if George Washington were alive today and heard it he would turn over in his grave.

_____

I was told before I came here that you were an up and going people. Please don't up and go while I'm speaking.

_____

Speaking before an audience is something new to me. I have the same feeling I had the first time I ever rode a horse. I told the man I had never ridden a horse before, so he gave me a horse that had never been ridden before. Right then I would have given fifty dollars for a nice comfortable chair. I feel that way now—I could use a nice comfortable chair. My knees feel like worn out folding rules. Did you ever feel as restless as a mad cat's tail?

_____

Last night in Denver I began my speech with, "I always speak straight from the shoulder." Someone in the audience said in a very loud whisper, "Too bad some of these talks don't originate a little higher up."

_____

The fountain pen writes, and having writ, blots. The wise speaker, having speaked, stops.

_____

A short time ago I spoke in one of your neighboring cities. When I had finished my speech and had left the stage they called and called for me to come back. They finally dared me to come back.   —Arthur L. Kaser

You can't usually tell whether a man is a finished speaker until he sits down.

———

Speakers can learn a lesson from the horse and buggy days —the longer the **spoke** the bigger the **bore**.

———

It is said that public speakers should speak up so they can be heard, stand up so they can be seen, and shut up so they can be enjoyed.

———

I have been talking to your chairman during dinner and we exchanged ideas. Now my mind is a blank.

———

My speech will be like the latest fashion. It will be long enough to cover the subject and short enough to be interesting.

———

My problem is that when I begin to talk on this subject, I don't know where to stop.

———

The speaker who fails to strike oil in ten minutes should stop boring.

———

I know now how a pancake feels when it is covered with a lot of sweet maple sirup.

———

The reason there are so few good talkers in public is that there are so few good thinkers in private.
—Arthur L. Kaser

———

The functions of a chairman are the same as the piece of parsley that is placed on top of a fish.
—The Wall Street Journal

———

It takes a great man to make a good listener.
—Sir Arthur Helps

———

The more you say, the less people remember.
—Francois Fenelon

"Freedom of speech" does not give a person the right to shout "Fire" in a crowded theatre.

—Justice Oliver Wendell Holmes

———

All of us here tonight are in the metallic age—gold in our teeth silver in our hair, and lead in our pants.

———

It is when a man gets as tight as a drum that he makes the most noise.

———

Talk is cheap because the supply always exceeds the demand.

———

It was Benjamin Franklin who said that great talkers are little doers.   —Arthur L. Kaser

Many speakers begin their talks with a promise that they are going to speak with an open mind. I have always been somewhat wary of this approach because many listeners find it difficult to distinguish between an open mind and one that is merely vacant.

*   *   *

Some people have tact—others tell the truth. I am going to use tact and tell the truth. Truth is stranger than fiction and more decent.

*   *   *

The fountain pen writes, and having writ, blots. The wise speaker, having speaked, stops.   —Arthur L. Kaser

THE PIPING COSTS MONEY

The preacher, after talking to his congregation about free salvation, asked Brother Smith to take up the collection. A parishioner got to his feet and protested: "Parson, I thought you said salvation was free—free as the water we drink."

"Salvation is free, Brother," replied the minister. "It's free and the water is free, but when we pipe it to you, you have to pay for the piping."   —The Wall Street Journal

CHLOROFORM

It was an interminable speech, but finally he wound up, "I want land reform. I want housing reform, I want educational reform, I want . . ." Just then a bored voice in the audience interrupted: "Chloroform."   —Readers Digest

TELL THEM ALL

Speaking at a large political gathering, the late Alfred E. Smith ignored a particularly cantankerous heckler. Finally the man yelled, "Go ahead, Al—tell 'em all you know! It won't take long!"

Smiling amiably, Smith replied: "I'll tell them all we both know. It won't take any longer."

—Donald E. Burrows, in **The Saturday Evening Post**

WHAT BECAME OF THE ASS?

One day when I was making a political address before a rather large audience, a heckler yelled at me, "Wait a minute, Mr. George. Isn't it true your grandfather used to peddle tinware around here in an oxcart hauled by a donkey?"

To this question I replied, "I digress just a moment and thank the gentleman for calling that to my attention. It is true, my dear old grandfather used to peddle tinware around with an old cart and a donkey. As a matter of fact, after this meeting is over, if my friend will come with me, I will show him that old cart, but I never knew until this minute what became of the ass."   —Lloyd George

MAY I HAVE YOUR SUPPORT?

Once when I had finished a speech by requesting my audience to vote for me, a man jumped up and shouted angrily: "I'd rather vote for the devil!"

To which I replied: "Quite so, but in case your friend declines to run, may I not then count upon your support?"

—John Morley

THINGS THAT DEFY EXPLANATION

Here is an effective story that may be used when an embarrassing question is asked by the audience. It will help the speaker spar for time or evade a direct answer.

"I am reminded of an Arkansas preacher who was telling the story of Genesis in his own way. He told his rural congregation that once there was no life on earth. But the good Lord didn't like it that way, so He came down to earth, scooped up a handful of dust, mixed it with water and produced a man whom He hung upon a fence.

"Then, deciding that the man would be lonesome, He reached down again, picked up a handful of dust, and in the same way produced a woman whom He also hung on the fence.

"'And that, brethren and sisters, is the way the human race got started,' the preacher said.

"A member of the congregation immediately popped up and challenged, 'Not so fast, reverend, if that's the way the human race got started, how come that fence was there?'

"The preacher paused a moment and then turned a disapproving eye on the parishioner.

"'Brother,' he said, 'it's questions like that that is ruinin' religion'."   —Philadelphia Inquirer

WHEN HECKLED

That big boo coming from the rear of the room is nothing new to me. Last week in Pointsville a fellow did the very same thing. He let out a guffaw at one of my statements. So I thought I would fix him good and plenty. "Young fellow," I said, "every dog has his day."

"Yes," he cried out, "and those with stubbed tails have their weak ends!"   —Rome Roberts

Section Four

CONCLUSIONS FOR SPEAKERS

Chapter One

How To Make Successful Conclusions

The final success of your speech is determined by the type of conclusion you use. It is here that you reveal your inexperience or your real ability; it is here that a lasting impression will be made upon your audience. The majority of speakers devote their main attention to the main body of their speeches and neglect to give adequate preparation to a well-planned and effective conclusion.

Common mistakes made by speakers are these:

1—The speaker who says: "Well, I guess I've touched on the important things that you want to know. It's about time for me to stop." This is ineffectual and proves that you are a novice and an inexperienced speaker.

2—The speaker who says: "Before I close, I have one more thought that I wish to leave with you." In fact, he is admitting that he doesn't really know when and where to stop. He rambles on and on and is unlikely to notice the restlessness and yawning in his audience. He fails to observe audience reactions and becomes a bore.

3—The speaker who never reaches the end, but stops abruptly for no apparent reason.

The final impression of the speaker is made during the two or three minutes of the address. The audience will either be pleased or disappointed during the time of the conclusion. Therefore, it becomes important that there be careful and detailed planning.

It is not the purpose of this book to give instructions in the best methods to observe, but the examples that follow are aimed to assist speakers in determining the type of conclusion that will be most effective. Every speech and every occasion requires individual and personalized treatment. It is hoped that these examples will help to emphasize the importance of a well-planned conclusion.

COMPLETE YOUR TASK

"The conclusion, too, has definite work to perform. It rounds out the talk; it holds the audience's earnest attention for a brief moment on the speech as a whole. It draws the thread of thought together; it binds and finishes the fabric of the speech. Definitely plan and word your conclusion. Never break off your speech awkwardly and hurriedly with a mumbled: 'I guess that's all I have to say.' Complete your task and let the audience know it is complete."

—George Rowland Collins in **Platform Speaking**

WATCH THE HANDS

"The clock has nothing to do with the length of a sermon. Nothing whatever! A long sermon is a sermon that seems long. And the short sermon is the one that ends while people are still wishing for more. It may have lasted only twenty minutes or it may have lasted for an hour and a half. If it leaves the people wishing for more, they do not know nor care what the clock said about the length of it. You cannot tell, therefore, how long a sermon is by watching the hands of a clock—watch the people. See where their hands are. If the hands of the men are for the most part in their vest pockets, pulling out their watches to note again how long you have been at it, this is ominous. See where their eyes are! See where their minds are, then you will know exactly what time of day it is for that particular sermon. It may be high time for it to come to an end."

—Charles R. Brown in **The Art of Preaching**

ABRAHAM LINCOLN

I have come today, not to utter a eulogy on Lincoln; he stands in need of none, but to endeavor to interpret the meaning of this gift to the nation of the place of his birth and origin. Is not this an altar upon which we may forever keep alive the vestal fire of democracy as upon a shrine at which some of the deepest and most sacred hopes of mankind may from age to age be rekindled? For these hopes must constantly be rekindled, and only those who live can rekindle them. The only stuff that can retain the life-giving heat is the stuff of living hearts. And the hopes of mankind cannot be kept alive by words merely, by constitutions and doctrines of right and codes of liberty. The object of democracy is to transmute these into the life and action of society, the self-denial and self-sacrifice of heroic men and women willing to make their lives an embodiment of right and service and enlightened purpose. The commands of democracy are as imperative as its privileges and opportunities are wide and generous. Its compulsion is upon us. It will be great and life a great light for the guidance of the nations only if we are great and carry that light high for the guidance of our own feet. We are not worthy to stand here unless we ourselves be in deed and truth real democrats and servants of mankind, ready to give our very lives for the freedom and justice and spiritual exaltation of the great nation which shelters and nurtures us. —Woodrow Wilson

This conclusion was used in an address delivered by Woodrow Wilson on the occasion of the gift to the nation of the Lincoln birthplace farm at Hodgenville, Kentucky, on September 4, 1916.

WITH MALICE TOWARD NONE

"Fondly do we hope, fervently do we pray, that this mighty scourge of war may speedily pass away. Yet if God wills that it continue until all the wealth piled up by the bondsman's two hundred and fifty years of unrequited toil shall be sunk, and until every drop of blood drawn with the lash shall be paid by another drawn with the sword, as was said three thousand years ago, so still it must be said that 'the judgments of the Lord are true and righteous altogether.'

"With malice toward none, with charity for all; with firmness in the right, as God gives us to see the right, let us strive on to finish the work we are in; to bind up the nation's wounds; to care for him who shall have borne the battle, and for his widow and his orphan—to do all which may achieve and cherish a just and lasting peace among ourselves, and with all nations." —Abraham Lincoln, Second Inaugural Address

Of this inspirational ending, Carl Schurz has written: "This was like a sacred poem. No American President had ever spoken words like these to the American people. America had never had a President who had found such words in the depths of his heart."

William E. Barton in his "Life of Abraham Lincoln" writes: "It is the greatest of the addresses of Abraham Lincoln and registers his intellectual and spiritual power at their highest altitude."

It is the type of conclusion that all speakers can strive to emulate as the most dramatic speech ending ever delivered.

Chapter Two

General Conclusions

The common type of conclusion is the general ending simply because many addresses require a summary of facts, an appeal for general action, or to produce a changed mental attitude toward the subject.

There follows an assortment of general conclusions in this chapter that we hope will serve as patterns. Some of these illustrations may be adapted to actual use by rewriting and adjusting to the speaker's own individual style and phrasing.

There is nothing unusual or different about the general type of conclusion. In fact, we suggest that speakers try to eliminate this type as far as is possible and substitute a more interesting style as shown in subsequent chapters.

JUSTICE FOR ALL

On a hill in ancient Brussels, overlooking a city full of memorials for dead soldiers, stands the world's greatest monument—the Palace of Justice. Today it is unused, and the whole main entrance is blocked by a solid row of billboards advertising various commercial interests. Through the infrequent cracks one can see a few workmen methodically repairing the steps to aid any capricious wanderer. But, as our guide told us, a man once alone there can easily become lost. This is symbolic of the whole world horizon today. America must strive toward the removal of the barriers of uncontrolled nationalism, must energetically prepare for the time when it may make justice safe for all, must change this bleak structure from a sorrowful reminder of human futility into a sanctuary where all may find what has long been denied them. We must have a plan of peace for congenial souls.   —Harold Margulies

This is an example of a general type of conclusion used by Mr. Margulies in which he appeals to reason and sound logic.

SOUTH AMERICAN BROTHERS

America, in her continued role of friend, will receive the friend's reward. If we implant in the hearts of our South American brothers passions and prejudices, they will bide their time, and when opportunity comes and strength permits, they will turn upon their oppressor. In all history hate has never failed to breed war. I plead against any policy or program that tends to rewrite on the palimpsest of these virgin continents an epilogue to Europe's history of hate. On these two vast continents, "furrowed by mighty rivers and dotted with inland seas," three thousand miles away from that saturnalia of hate . . . here . . . on this magnificent domain . . . where God has given us the means to start anew and work out in peace the great problems of mankind . . . here . . . let us reveal to the world that "Whom God has made neighbors, justice can make friends."   —Herbert N. Johnson

In this general conclusion, Mr. Johnson uses the appeal method for a changed point of view toward our South American neighbors.

ASSASSIN OF YOUTH

My further purpose in exposing the dangers of marijuana is to give at least a partial answer to the question, "What shall we do about it?" Legislation can be made more effective. The Federal Narcotics Bureau can be aroused to more vigorous action. We can expect the police to do something—occasionally. But the final answer rests with the intended victims, with you and me. Now that we know the facts, let us see to it that others know, to the end that this drug shall not engulf our generation. In the name of the assaulted and murdered, who cried out in vain for protection; in the name of the youthful addicts, who must be freed from this drug; in the name of the unsuspecting, who are seeking a thrill—may all of us help to sound the warning that will free America from the assassin of youth.   —Norman A. Sugarman

Here again Mr. Sugarman makes an appeal for audience reactions. Although the style is general, there is an emotional climax.

THE ROAD BACK

We must return to those concepts of world co-operation, understanding and compromise which we advocated only four short years ago. We must accept the challenge issued by Franklin Roosevelt in an undelivered speech written the day before his death. "More than an end to the war," he said, "we want an end to the beginnings of all wars—yes, an end to this brutal, inhuman and thoroughly impractical method of settling the differences between governments."

Out of the First World War we evolved the League of Nations. The United Nations came as a result of the second world conflagration. Will it take a third "lost generation" of American veterans to prove to us that we cannot afford another war? What good will it do to go to war against Communism or any other "ism," if, in the process, the spiritual stamina of our future generation of American manhood is lost in the twists and the turns of the road back?   —George W. McBurney

The conclusion used by Mr. McBurney in an address he delivered on "The Road Back" dealing with the problems involved in averting another world war.

A HOUSE DIVIDED

Lincoln, speaking to the Republican state convention in 1858, began with the biblical quotation: "A house divided against itself cannot stand."

Today the world is a house divided.

But—as is sometimes forgotten—Lincoln followed this quotation with a note of hope for his troubled country:

"I do not expect the house to fall—but I do expect it will cease to be divided."

A century later, we too must have the vision, the fighting spirit, and the deep religious faith in our Creator's destiny for us, to sound similar note of promise for our divided world; that out of our time there can, with incessant work and with God's help, emerge a new era of good life, good will and good hope for all men.

One American put it this way: "Every tomorrow has two handles. We can take hold of it with the handle of anxiety or the handle of faith."

In firm faith, and in the conviction that Republican purposes and principles are "in league" with this kind of future, the nomination that you have tendered me for the presidency of the United States I now—humbly but confidently—accept.

The conclusion used by President Dwight D. Eisenhower in his address accepting the Republican nomination for a second term as president of the United States.

FREE ENTERPRISE

Free enterprise and its essential elements can be compared to an automobile engine and its parts. Savings and credit are the flywheel, banks and financial institutions are the crankshaft balancers and the lubrication system. Confidence is the self starter. The hope of a profit is the spark plug and ignition system and the fuel used is the productive effort of all of us who work. The octane number of the fuel is raised through education, initiative and attitude toward work. At present some people feel that the fuel has a pretty low octane number which cuts down the power of the engine and makes it knock a bit.

As efficient and useful as this free enterprise engine is, I still believe that it can and will be improved just as I believed twenty-five years ago that the rough and at that time somewhat inefficient four-cylinder motor car engines, that we thought were so marvelous, could be improved. But I am certainly against discarding this proven efficient engine that gave the American people the highest standard of living in the world and replacing it with some imported type from east of the Rhine or even from England—like for example the jet engine—which has only one spark plug, the state, and depends for its power on a blast of hot air.

—C. W. Wilson, former president
of General Motors

OUTWARD BOUND

Twenty-five years ago we lost the spirit of democratic existence through the blind acceptance of abstract ideals and passive living. When those ideals fell, our lives were thrown into chaos. This time we shall not fail. Our future must not be born out of an age of dead apathy. We simply cannot afford to be negatively cynical again. Come! Let us build together. If our ideals be without meaning, let us give them new life and flexibility. If the spirit of our technology be cold, let us direct it with a warm and clear-headed intelligence. If our leaders be confused, let us point the way ourselves. A new spirit is arising in the youth of America. Let us nurture it, care for it deeply, for it is the very substance of democracy. Let us launch out with the poetic fervor of Walt Whitman, "For **we are bound** where mariner has not yet dared to go, and **we will** risk the ship, ourselves, and all." —William Rodiger

In this conclusion, Mr. Rodiger sums up the general purpose of his address and makes a plea for courageous action by the audience.

THIS TRASH MUST GO

We can do something about this if we will. We can voice to the vendors of filth our disgust instead of joking with them as they pass it over their counters. Just as the man in Buffalo was able to purge his city, each of us can be a moving spirit in a campaign that will raise our home community to a new level of decency. Most of us belong to clubs, lodges, church groups, or business organizations that will do this if somebody will only open their eyes to the filth that lies about them.

—Raymond S. Beard

The conclusion of a talk, "This Trash Must Go," dealing with the sale of objectionable magazines and literature illustrates a rather weak type of ending.

A TIME FOR GREATNESS

Finally, as American citizens, like you and I, face these intricate and involved problems of the world we must at all times bear in mind that for every question there are two sides —and that the philosophy "my country, right or wrong," does not fit into a pattern of postwar peace. Instead, to form constructive and wholesome attitudes toward world problems we must at all times think and talk with restraint, suspend judgment, and distrust all forms of propaganda.

This is a minimum program for strengthening our foreign policy. Never in all history has any one nation been given such a glorious opportunity for leadership in the paths of peace. This is our time for greatness. The war weary peoples of the world look to us at this crucial hour. Let us hope that this nation shall rise and respond to this call for vigorous world leadership. —Gunnar E. Hoglund

Mr. Hoglund uses this conclusion after discussing the world situation and the leadership that the United States is obliged to assume in the future. This general type of closing is usually effective.

STILL BELIEVES IN GOD

I am reminded of a little incident much earlier in my career which forms an almost exact parallel. I must explain that I once had some ambition to be a preacher, but never quite brought myself to it. But one day my chance came when a minister I knew fell ill and asked me if I would take his pulpit on the following Sunday. I did so, and for forty-five minutes I delivered a passionate sermon denouncing atheism. I refuted atheism, I disproved atheism, I ridiculed atheism, I trampled all over atheism. When the service was over, a prim little old lady came up to me and said, "Young man, you're a mighty convincing talker; but I still believe in God."

Well, I hope I have done a better job than that of getting my message across tonight, and of convincing you that it is the most natural and logical thing in the world to be, at one and the same time, a Republican, a rugged individualist, a private enterpriser, and an emphatic advocate of an expanded and perfected social insurance system for our beloved country.

—Arthur Larson

The conclusion of an address delivered before the Capital Press Club at Washington, D. C., on May 22, 1954 by Arthur Larson, Under Secretary of Labor.

HIGH PLACE

We face important decisions. We have got to understand ourselves, our country, and the world around us. We have got to be right about our ideals and objectives, and we have got to be imaginative and courageous about our techniques and methods. Above all, we have got to understand that the cornerstone of our American tradition is the freedom and worth of the individual human person, and that this ideal of free individuals and free government, is absolutely meaningless except as the product of a deep and abiding faith in a Creator who made us all in his own image.

And if you are accused of approaching your responsibilities with diffidence and reluctance, remember the words of Plato:

"High place is best in the hands of those who are reluctant to assume it."

For the place of responsibility you are now being asked to assume is indeed the highest that any generation has ever assumed in the long history of mankind.

—Arthur Larson

The conclusion of a Commencement address delivered at the University of Pittsburgh on Aug. 25, 1954 by Arthur Larson, Under Secretary of Labor.

THE LAWYER AND LABOR

And so, my friends, the next time someone says that the trouble with labor relations or workmen's compensation or labor legislation is that there is too much participation by lawyers and courts, and that the solution is to "kill all the lawyers," remember that he is indirectly by this quotation paying the legal profession a high compliment. He is unwittingly recognizing, by this reference, the well-known fact that the lawyers have always stood and still stand against violence and arbitrary power and all the things that communism preaches, and have always stood and still stand as the guardians of individual freedom, individual rights of person and property, and the fundamental right of all men peacefully to work out their common destinies as equals before the law.

—Arthur Larson

The conclusion of an address on "The Lawyer and Labor" delivered before the Michigan State Bar Association by Arthur Larson, Under Secretary of Labor, on Sept. 22, 1954.

RECOGNITION WHILE LIVING

It is a gratifying thing to see a man achieve what will bless the world and in his young manhood receive recognition for it, because it so often happens that the benefactors of the world can do their work and wait for a monument to be erected after they are dead instead of receiving flowers while they live. Emerson has told us that if a man write a better book, if he can preach a better sermon, if he can make a better candlestick than anyone else, though he may make his home in the woods the world will beat a trodden path to his door. Tonight we stand and the world will stand beating a path to the door of our distinguished friend whom this club honors and, honoring him, honors itself.

—Josephus Daniels

The conclusion of an address given by Mr. Daniels at a dinner honoring John J. Carty, the perfecter of the wireless telephone system.

MESSAGE OF CONFIDENCE

And so I come back to you from the men at the front, from the French people, from the British people, with a message not only of determination, but of confidence. One cannot tell what in the final sifting may come from this war. The events through which we are moving are so wonderful, so tremendous, so world-compelling, that we hardly realize their significance. One of my colleagues said to me a year ago that this war seemed to him as the suicide of civilization. Let us hope rather that it may prove to be the death of much that marred and hindered the progress and development of civilization and democracy. Shall we not hope and indeed believe, that this war may prove to be the birth-pang attending the nativity of a truer and nobler civilization, in which this country, as one of the great free nations of the Empire, will have no inconsiderable place and play no unworthy part?   —Sir Robert Laird Borden

The concluding statement made by the Prime Minister of Canada upon his return from a visit to the front during the first year of World War I.

TEN MILLION HOMES

We must place ten million families in homes. Thus we will strike a mighty blow against crime; against disease and epidemics; against those by-products of the slums, gangdom, vice, and corruption; against the very roots of the depression itself, the breakdown in manhood and womanhood. We will raise our fellow humans out of the hopelessness, despair, and degradation of their surroundings and place them in a life worthy to be called American.   —Walter F. Probst, Jr.

Here is an example of summing up the main objectives as stated in the main body of the address.

YOUTH'S CHALLENGE

My friends, you are the representatives of these institutions of the best in American life. I welcome you therefore to a noble task—yours is the heritage of leadership. Will you guide youth of your community, your state, your nation in their experiments with life? Will you as educated men and women assume the responsibility of directing the youth of the nation in experimenting with government?

Yours is the task to perform in payment for the privileges of education which have been yours. May you meet the challenge and in so doing you will keep American youth from knowing the horrors of communism, the stifling mental torture of Nazism, and the crushing ruthlessness of fascism.

—Phyllis Roberts

In an address on the "Challenge to Educators," Miss Roberts gives an effective conclusion by emphasizing the listeners' personal responsibility.

ONE HUMAN FAMILY

Gentlemen, you are confronted with something here tonight that does more than merely transmit the human voice to the uttermost parts of the earth, and it has raised great questions of a political nature, questions as to whether we are ever going to be one human family. We have a conductor; we have medium; it has been demonstrated to you tonight. There is a medium joining together all created things that will transmit the tones of the human voice and that will transmit music, the grandest anthem that can be composed, transmit it to the uttermost ends of the earth. If we are ever going to be joined together in one great peaceful family, may it not be through this wonderful mysterious medium which in my judgment permeates all creation? Sometimes I wonder what is going to come out of it. We are at work on something that is bigger than any of us; we can't understand it; but we must do what we may, and I have a strong feeling that we are building up while elsewhere they are tearing down, and that sometime, at some Christmas or Easter there will be heard a great voice that will say: "On earth peace, good will toward men."

—John J. Carty

The conclusion of an address given by Mr. Carty on the occasion of the establishment of wireless telephone connections across the continent to San Francisco in November, 1915.

SEARCH FOR PEACE

On a hill in ancient Brussels, overlooking a city full of memorials for dead soldiers, stands the world's greatest monument —the Palace of Justice. Today it is unused, and the whole main entrance is blocked by a solid row of billboards advertising various commercial interests. Through the infrequent cracks one can see a few workmen methodically repairing the steps to aid any capricious wanderer. But, as our little guide told us, a man once alone there can easily become lost. This is symbolic of the whole world horizon today. America must strive toward the removal of the barriers of uncontrolled nationalism, must energetically prepare for the time when it may make justice safe for all, must change this bleak structure from a sorrowful reminder of human futility into a sanctuary where all may find what has long been denied them. We must have a plan of peace for congenial souls.

—Harold Margulies

This conclusion was used by Mr. Margulies to end an address on the way to find a solution to world misunderstanding. It illustrates the general type of conclusion.

NOT ENEMIES, BUT FRIENDS

"I am loth to close. We are not enemies but friends. We must not be enemies. Though passion may have strained, it must not break our bonds of affection. The mystic chords of memory, stretching from every battlefield and patriot's grave to every living heart and hearthstone all over this broad land, will swell the chorus of the Union when again touched, as surely they will be, by the better angel of our nature."

—Abraham Lincoln, First Inaugural Address

TORCH OF FREEDOM

Democracy in America is in great danger, not from outside forces alone but also from an inner decay. You have only to give a real democratic education to keep that treasure which is ours. My friends, won't you educate your young people fairly, won't you give democracy a fair chance and yourself the satisfaction of knowing that in New York harbor there will always be a Goddess of Liberty holding aloft her torch of freedom for the down-trodden countries of the world to see and follow?   —Dorothy Schrader

This is an example of the general type of appeal for action. It can be used when the treatment of the subject has been general in itself.

MAJESTY OF THE LAW

If this we do, our relentless, unwavering determination to restore the majesty of the law to its rightful place in the hearts of American citizens will have its effects upon all charged with the enactment and enforcement of our laws. Legislators will know that the people are watching their doings with a new interest in the lessening of crime. Enforcement officials will feel the spur of an aroused public conscience. Both will feel an assurance that they are backed with a public opinion which tolerates no lawlessness.

I would not speak in vague and general terms. May each of us in this audience tonight go out resolved hereafter to take his firm stand against lawlessness. May we radiate our influence to all those about us. May we, as Americans, be proud of our land and her achievements! May there ever be within her people a deep and abiding reverence for the majesty of the Law!   —Durward E. Balch

This is an example of the general conclusion in which the speaker appeals for action.

THE ROAD BACK

We must return to those concepts of world co-operation, understanding and compromise which we advocated only four short years ago. We must accept the challenge issued by Franklin Roosevelt in an undelivered speech written the day before his death. "More than an end to war," he said, "we want an end to the beginnings of all wars—yes, and end to this brutal, inhuman and thoroughly impractical method of settling the differences between governments."

Out of the First World War we evolved the League of Nations. The United Nations came as a result of the second world conflagration. Will it take a third "lost generation" of American veterans to prove to us that we cannot afford another war? What good will it do to go to war against Communism or any other "ism," if, in the process, the spiritual stamina of our future generation of American manhood is lost in the twists and the turns of the road back?   —George W. McBurney

This conclusion by Mr. McBurney to his address on the problems involved in winning the peace after World War II illustrates how the use of restatement of the main theme is effective.

WORTHY OF TRUST

"I am afraid, gentlemen, that I have departed from my reserve, and talked about myself a good deal too much. But I wanted to tell you, as the largest audience that I have been privileged to address in Canada, what I feel about my position and the responsibility which it entails. I can only assure you that I shall always endeavor to live up to that great responsibility and to be worthy of your trust."

—Duke of Windsor, former King of England

INTELLECTUALS ON TRIAL

Perhaps we can turn out hatred of brutality and our aversion of war into a heightened energy and enthusiasm in support of those ideals that make for life amid a world of death. Education with its interpretation of human life is one of those ideals. Those who hate war can be busy making the case against war still stronger. As they see old ideals crumble, they will be busy forging new ones. As they see other minds harden, they will beware mental atrophy in themselves. They will try to see that this era is not, like the one before it, spiritually futile. If these things can be done, or even gloriously attempted, intellectuals can justify their faith and themselves. If these things are not attempted, society may rightly question the right of intellectuals, and of their universities, to survive. In these terms are intellectuals on trial.   Dr. Alan Valentine

In his speech on "Intellectuals on Trial," Dr. Valentine uses a conclusion aimed to summarize the main purpose of his address. His closing remarks give the basis for audience action.

NOMINATING ALFRED E. SMITH

America needs not only an administrator but a leader—a pathfinder, a blazer of the trail to the high road that will avoid the bottomless morass of crass materialism that has engulfed so many of the great civilizations of the past. It is the privilege of Democracy not only to offer such a man but to offer him as the surest leaders to victory. To stand upon the ramparts and die for our principles is heroic. To sally forth to battle and win for our principles is something more than heroic. We offer one who has the will to win—who not only deserves success but commands it. Victory is his habit—the happy warrior, Alfred E. Smith.   —Franklin D. Roosevelt

In this conclusion, President Roosevelt climaxes his nominating speech with this summary and emotional appeal.

TIMELESS NIAGARA

It calls up the indefinite past. When Columbus first sought this continent—when Christ suffered on the cross—when Moses led Israel through the Red Sea—nay, even when Adam first came from the hands of his Maker; then, as now, Niagara was roaring here. The eyes of that species of extinct giants whose bones fill the mounds of America have gazed on Niagara, as ours do now. Contemporary with the first race of men, and older than the first man, Niagara is as strong and fresh today as ten thousand years ago. The Mammoth and Mastodan, so long dead that fragments of their monstrous bones alone testify that they ever lived, have gazed on Niagara—in that long, long time never still for a moment, never dried, never frozen, never slept, never rested.   —Abraham Lincoln

This climatic effect was used by Mr. Lincoln in an address on Niagara Falls. This type of conclusion always retains the audience's attention to the last word.

YOUTH'S RESPONSIBILITY

America is one of the few countries left in which individual thinking is still permissable. We are still able to live like human beings, not like cattle. Let the young American take advantage of this unique privilege before it is too late. Guided by his immutable principles of conduct, let him adopt a policy of thinking, analyzing, questioning, doubting, investigating. Let him beware the unctious bleatings of propagandists and panacea vendors, who would coax him toward the "easy way out." Let him divest all Youth Movements of their aura of emotionalism, and see what lies beneath, before he agrees to champion them. Let him be sobered by the realization that in his hands lies the responsibility of moulding the nation's future. He must exercise that responsibility with care.

—Ramon Irwin

In this conclusion Mr. Irwin makes an appeal to young people to be motivated by high ideals. Although it is a cumulative development toward the end, much will depend upon the delivery of the speaker to make it effective.

LOVE AND AFFECTION

"And when you get back home, some of you send me a postcard. I will send you one if you do not send me one. You will easily know it is from me because there will be no stamp on it. But I will have some writing on it, and the writing will be this:

Seasons may come and seasons may go,
Everything withers in due course, you know,
But there is one thing still blooms as fresh as the dew,
That is the love and affection I still have for you."

—Sir Harry Lauder, addressing American
delegates to a convention in Scotland.

Chapter Three

Narrative Conclusions

One of the most effective types of conclusions is the narrative or story ending. It is always easy for an audience to give its undivided attention to the story-type of conclusion. Then, too, a speaker can plan for the timing of his narrative conclusion and time its delivery with less effort than with almost any other type of conclusion.

The examples that follow in this chapter have actually been used in real situations and have been tested for good audience responses.

OUR LAST CHANCE

Long ago I saw another picture that I have never forgotten. It was of two poorly dressed boys. One was much larger and heavier than the other but his legs were shriveled and encased in the braces of a cripple. He couldn't walk. The other, tow-headed and whole, was smaller, much smaller, yet he was carrying the heavier boy on his back. It was hard work, but he was managing a smile on his freckled face while he trudged along. And the caption of the picture read, "He's not heavy; he's my brother." Does the responsibility which we, as individuals, owe to our country and to the world weigh too heavily on our shoulders, or can we too smile and say, "It's not heavy; it's **my** country, and **my** world." If we can do that, the man who was such an insignificant element in that first picture will no longer be a slave to a pillar of fire and smoke, but he can stand there confident and strong, with an expression of satisfaction and accomplishment on his face, and he can hold in his hand the towering column of clouds as the symbol of his newest and greatest triumph. —John Barsness

This is another type of conclusion that is effective. Mr. Barsness uses the narrative style in direct attention to his final appeal for a continuation of U. S. participation in world affairs.

287

DON'T LOSE YOUR TEMPER

If I seem to have left you with more questions than answers, even in the comparatively narrow field which I have discussed, I can only take refuge behind the well-known saying of Socrates that if you can ask the right question your problem is mostly solved. I hope I have indicated one or two questions that will need far more attention than they have been getting up until now. As to the answers, may I refer to the fable of the Lion who went about in the jungle asking all the beasts: "And who is King of the Jungle?" Each one, with due deference, would reply, "You, Oh Lion." Finally, the Lion came to the Elephant and asked, "Who is King of the Jungle?" The Elephant merely picked the Lion up with his trunk and threw him over a tree into some bushes. Whereupon the Lion said: "Just because you don't know the answer, you don't have to lose your temper."

So, if we don't know all the answers, let's not become disconcerted. Let us redouble our efforts, public and private, through just such activities as this Conference, in the full confidence that, when labor, management, church, school and state all bend their efforts toward a common goal, success can surely not be far away.

—Arthur Larson

The narrative conclusion of an address "Age Barriers of Our Own Making," delivered by Under Secretary of Labor Arthur Larson at Philadelphia on October 21, 1954.

HIGH ACHIEVEMENT

Yours is a great opportunity—and it is a great challenge. The lazy of mind and body may tell you there are no more opportunities—that success is a matter of luck or pull—that there are no more trails to blaze—but that is a disgraceful refuge for indolent and indifferent persons.

A generation ago the books of Horatio Alger were read by almost all youngsters, but I find my sons never heard of Horatio Alger. His books were many, and each was a simple example of how to achieve success. Each was a consuming inspiration and for many youngsters pointed the way to great personal achievement. We might well ask "Who killed Horatio Alger?" What was wrong with his idea of "work and win"—or the story of "rags to riches." Since when can we afford not to exalt the simple virtues of honesty, patience, reliability, energy, ambition, and above all personal sacrifice? These virtues are the only sure way to success. Why do fond and well meaning parents struggle to educate their children and explain their sacrifices with the statement "I don't want my children to work as hard as I do for so little?" What is wrong with hard work?

Perhaps you have heard the story of Christopher Wren, one of the greatest architects, who walked one day unrecognized among the men who were at work upon the building of St. Paul's cathedral in London which he had designed. "What are you doing?" he inquired of one of the workmen, and the man replied, "I am cutting a piece of stone." As he went on he put the same question to another man, and the man replied, "I am earning five shillings two pence a day." And to a third man he addressed the same inquiry and the man answered, "I am helping Sir Christopher Wren build a beautiful cathedral." That man had vision. He could see beyond the cutting of the stone, beyond the earning of his daily wage, to the creation of a work of art—the building of a great cathedral. In your life it is important for you to strive to attain a vision of the larger whole. Not only should you bring ardor and diligence to your work, you should also have the vision to see beyond the daily routine of your tasks and to see your work in relation to the larger whole, for you have your contribution to make, however small it may seem, towards the dignity and worth of your profession or your position. The English philosopher, Herbert Spencer, stated this thought when he wrote—"I am constantly impressed with how infinitesimal is anything that I can do; yet I am even more impressed with how important it is that I do it."

Vision, faith, integrity, the ability to make wise choices,

the desire to grow—these are some of the attributes of those who will find a deep and abiding joy in their work and whose life will be crowned with high achievement. My best wishes to you!   —Henry T. Maschal

This narrative type of conclusion was used by Mr. Maschal in his address on Business Educators Day at Santa Rosa Junior College on May 3, 1955. It illustrates a most effective method in achieving a total audience response to the address.

AN ADMINISTRATIVE PROBLEM

Well, since this is a Research Association, I have no hesitation in leaving all these questions hanging in the air. I do this even more cheerfully, because I know that I am about to be followed by several men who, whatever their other differences have in common the fact that they are all men of uncommon brilliance.

This leaves matters somewhat where they were in the conversation between the discontented grasshopper and the ant. The Grasshopper, in a mood of despair, called upon the Ant, and poured out the story of his unhappy lot. There was no food; a drought had spoiled the grain; what's more, farmers were always spraying poison on things, and a grasshopper just didn't have a chance nowadays; people were always stepping on you, birds were always dive-bombing you, snakes lurked around every stump waiting for you. How much better it would be to be an Ant. "Not so," said the Ant. "All day long dragging heavy hunks of sand or dead beetles; lousy accommodations; stuffy and frightfully overcrowded in the anthill; hundreds of relatives; cold in winter, hot in summer, whenever it rains the whole doggone place flooded. Tell you what," continued the Ant, "if you want to be something else, why don't you be a lark? Boy, there's the life. Soaring about up in the fresh air and sunshine. Sing all day. Go south for the winter. See the whole country. No fears, no worries." "That's for me!" exclaimed the grasshopper. "That's exactly what I want. How do I get to be a lark?" "I'm terribly sorry," said the Ant. "This is the research and information department. That's an administrative question."

And so, having provided a little information and quite a few questions for research, I will now yield to the gentlemen of the panel, all of whom, I believe, have had a wealth of administrative experience and will, I trust, supply some much-needed answers.

This narrative conclusion was used effectively by Arthur Larson, Under Secretary of Labor, in an address delivered before the Industrial Relations Research Association on Dec. 29, 1954.

YOU AIN'T SEEN NOTHING YET

May I close, as I began, with a story which I think will sum up perhaps the way we might feel about this program for the coming year.

One of the participants in this conference told me that as he was coming down Pennsylvania Avenue from the Station, he went by the National Archives Building. He saw carved on the front there, as you may have seen many times, the phrase: "What is past is prologue." He said to the cab driver who was one of these intellectual cab drivers that we have in Washington who is supposed to know about quotations and such, "What exactly does that mean?"

The cab driver said, "That is just another example of this government jargon that you hear about. What it really means is: you ain't seen nothing yet."

Arthur Larson, Under Secretary of Labor.

THE WHITEST MAN OF ALL

I would like this opportunity to tell something that I have never been allowed to tell by Mr. Rogers, either by my mouth or in print, and if I don't look at him I can tell it now.

In 1893, when the publishing company of Charles L. Webster, of which I was financial agent, failed, it left me heavily in debt. If you will remember what commerce was at that time you will recall that you could not sell anything, and could not buy anything, and I was on my back; my books were not worth anything at all, and I could not give away my copyrights. Mr. Rogers had long enough vision ahead to say, "Your books have supported you before, and after the panic is over they will support you again," and that was a correct proposition. He saved my copyrights, and saved me from financial ruin. He it was who arranged with my creditors to allow me to roam the face of the earth for four years and persecute the nations thereof with lectures, promising that at the end of four years I would pay dollar for dollar. That arrangement was made; otherwise I would now be living out-of-doors under an umbrella, and a borrowed one at that.

You see his white mustache and his head trying to get white (he is always trying to look like me—I don't blame him for that) These are only emblematic of his character, and that is all. I say, without exception, hair and all, he is the whitest man I have ever known.   —Mark Twain

Chapter Four

Humorous Conclusions

The humorous treatment always is a most successful way to win a pronounced audience reaction. In this chapter we have included many items that can be used by speakers in actual situations, with very little change or adaptation.

It is important that each speaker utilize his own personality and versatility in relating the humorous conclusion. Not all speakers can give a humorous twist to their remarks so it is necessary that a careful analysis be made to determine the best natural style to use. It is far better not to use the comedy ending unless you can do it exceedingly well.

THREE CHEERS FOR INDIA

(When the speaker is raising funds for a cause.)

Gentlemen, I have presented this case as clearly as is my power to do so. I feel that you will all agree with me that the cause is worthy, and that this organization, both collectively and individually, will support it liberally. We need the cash, gentlemen, and we are banking on you.

I hope that I will not have to face a situation such as did a friend of mine in one of our southern cities last summer. This friend was traveling the country, meeting with fine groups of people such as you, in the interest of India relief. At this particular meeting his speech was eloquent. He carried his audience into the remotest parts of India and portrayed with powerful words the plight of those unfortunate people. His talk was heartrending, so much so that when he asked for a generous contribution, which at the time he was most certain would be forthcoming, one of the listeners arose to his feet and said:

"Gentlemen, I am overcome by what the speaker was saying. He has told us what is wrong over there in India. It certainly is terrible. We should do something about it. Yes, gentlemen, we should. I move that we give three cheers for India."

—Adolph Hintz

Always leave the audience laughing when you say goodbye.   George M. Cohan

AS I SEE YOU NOW

Before closing, I want to thank your arrangements committee, your chairman, and all of the members of this very fine audience for the privilege of standing here this evening and addressing you. I certainly will always remember you as a group of distinguished gentlemen; and I certainly don't want to take leave from you in the manner of a certain speaker of my acquaintance.

This speaker was a big game hunter, and in this respect made numerous forays into the unexplored wilds in search of dangerous game. As he concluded his speech on a particular evening he said: "Gentlemen: I want to thank you for the honor of speaking before you tonight. You have been a marvelous and attentive audience. I shall never forget you. Tomorrow I depart on another expedition into the distant jungles, and when I get there and look upon the warlike and distorted faces of the savage tribes, I will think of you all sitting out here before me, just as I see you now."

—Rome Roberts

DRAWING NEAR

And now, my friends I will borrow a phrase from Lady Godiva. Concluding her historic ride, she said, "I am drawing near my clothes."   —William Smith

HE'S MY HUSBAND

There is always a time in this task of speaking before the public, when a conclusion should be reached before something is said that shouldn't be said. Up to this moment I feel that I have been very fortunate in this respect; quite unlike the fellow who sat in a barber chair, getting a hair cut and a manicure. While the barber was snipping away at the fellow's hair, a beautiful blonde manicurist was picking away at his cuticle.

Now the manicurist was one of those heavenly little creatures that would attract the eye of most any man—blonde, shapely and petite, with a sense of touch that made the customer tingle with delight every time she pressed the implement under his finger nail. For some time while this process was going on, the customer was contemplating a method of approach. Finally, he said to the girl, "Gee, you're cute! How about a date tonight?"

The girl pecked away a few more times at the cuticle and then looked up at the customer and rather indifferently said: "Why don't you ask the guy who's cutting your hair? He's my husband!"   —Rome Roberts

INVADING ETERNITY

I note that several people have been glancing at their watches occasionally. In this respect I am not sure whether I am talking too long, or whether those gentlemen have to catch a train. If a person has to catch a train, he is at perfect liberty to look at his watch during a speech. However, I don't want to put myself in the position of the long-winded lawyer, who after making a plea for two hours, turned to the judge and said, "Your Honor, I sincerely hope that I am not infringing upon the time of the court."

The judge looked down over his glasses and in a matter-of-fact judicial voice said: "There is a difference between infringing on time and invading eternity."

—Rome Roberts

NOT COVERING THE WHOLE SUBJECT

I don't suppose it was intended that I should exhaust all the ramifications of my subject in all its magnitude. I have been foolish enough to believe that it was only expected that I touch only part of the subject—not in the spirit of that small boy in the country who came in and told his mother that he had set the old hen on two dozen eggs. "Why," she said, "you don't expect the old hen to hatch two dozen, do you?" He said: No; but I just wanted to see the darned old thing spread herself."   —Horace Porter

BABY CRIES

The oldest story in the lecture business is still the best. Concerns the crying baby and the lecturer. Baby cries. Lecturer tries to lecture. Baby cries more loudly. Finally, the mother picks up the bawling infant, starts for the door.

"Oh, that's all right, madam," says the lecturer, a fixed amiability on his face. "The baby doesn't bother me at all."

The mother stops, looks down the aisle at the speaker, and fires back, "I know . . . but you're bothering the daylights out of the baby!"   —George Grim, News Commentator

TOO MUCH TALK

Some years ago in Hartford, we all went to church one hot, sweltering night to hear the annual report of Mr. Hawley, a city missionary who went around finding people who need help and didn't want to ask for it. He told of the life in cellars, where poverty resided; he gave instances of heroism and devotion of the poor. When a man with millions gives, he said, we make a great deal of noise. It's noise in the wrong place, for it's the widow's mite that counts.

Well, Hawley worked me up to a great pitch. I could hardly wait for him to get through. I had $400 in my pocket. I wanted to give that and borrow more to give. You could see the greenbacks in every eye. But instead of passing the plate to the crowd then, he kept on talking and talking and talking, and as he talked it grew hotter and hotter and hotter, and we grew sleepier and sleepier and sleepier. My enthusiasm went down, down, down—$100 at a clip—until finally, when the plate did come around, I stole ten cents out of it. It all goes to show how a little thing like this can lead to crime.   —Mark Twain

MY TIME IS UP

Mr. Chairman, I have consumed my allotted time and I will conclude my remarks with the following story:

The attorneys for the two sides of a case in court had been allowed fifteen minutes each to argue. The attorney for the defense began his argument with a reference to the old swimming hole of his boyhood days. He related in flowery oratory about the balmy air, the singing birds, the joy of youth, the delights of the cool water.

In the midst of his eloquence, he was interrupted by the drawling voice of the judge:

"Come out, Chauncey," he said, "and put on your clothes. Your fifteen minutes are up."

—Lawrence M. Brings

NEARLY DONE

Well, I've talked long enough. It is advisable for me to stop now before you make a comment similar to the one made by a stranger who came into a church in the middle of a sermon and seated himself in a back pew. After a few moments he began to fidget. Leaning over to an elderly man who was evidently an old member of the congregation, he whispered: "How long has he been preaching?"

"Thirty or forty years, I think," the old man answered.

"I'll stay then. He must be nearly done."

—James Frohman

ANY PUPS AVAILABLE?

I apologize for speaking beyond your customary time limit. I will conclude my talk, therefore, with an appropriate story. It is told that on one occasion the minister delivered a sermon of only ten minutes' length—a most unusual practice for him.

Upon concluding his remarks he added: "I regret to inform you, friends, that my dog, who appears to be peculiarly fond of paper, this morning ate that portion of my sermon that I have not delivered. Let us pray."

After the service the pastor was met at the door by a man from another parish. Shaking the minister by the hand, he asked: "Doctor, I should like to know whether that dog of yours has any pups. If so, I want to get one to give to my minister."

—James Frohman

I DID MY BEST

When you come to judge our handiwork, then, with all its undoubted flaws and omissions, I ask only that you recall the story of Mary the cook, whose mistress confronted her in the kitchen one morning and said, "Mary, you were entertaining a man in the kitchen last night." Mary replied, "Well, it's not for me to say, Ma'am, but I did my best."

Arthur Larson, Under Secretary of Labor, concluding an address before the Industrial Hygiene Foundation, November 17, 1955.

UNCONVENTIONAL ENDING

At a dinner concluding a long and boring convention in Chicago a parade of reluctant speakers had been pried from their chairs to "say a few words." As the 16th orator took his seat, a sigh of expectation filled the room. Deliverance was in sight. But no! The chairman was on his feet again. "I'm sure this meeting does not want to break up without hearing from our good friend, Ken Roe."

Mr. Roe stood up. "Gentlemen," he said, "I am reminded of the story of two skeletons. For days they had been imprisoned in the mustiest closet imaginable. Finally, one skeleton said to the other, 'What are we doing here, anyhow?' Whereupon, the other skeleton replied, 'I'll be darned if I know. But if we had any guts, we'd get the hell out of here'."

—Matt Roberts in The Saturday Evening Post

CHLOROFORM

It was an interminable speech, but finally he wound up, "I want land reform, I want housing reform, I want educational reform, I want—" Just then a bored voice in the audience interrupted: "Chloroform."

So before someone in this audience shouts, "Chloroform," I'm going to wind up my remarks and sit down.

—Balance Sheet

WHAT TIME IS IT?

A speaker talked loud and long, then asked brightly, "Are there any questions?" A hand shot up. The speaker nodded. "What time is it?" the listener inquired.

—Kenny Nichols

WHEN THEY SHAKE WATCHES

One of the major embarrassments to which lecturers are submitted is the audience's looking at their watches. I once asked John Erskine if, in his lectures, he found the ordeal particularly trying.

"No," he replied, "not until they start shaking them!"

—Frank Crowninshield in Vogue

WHAT'S YOUR POINT?

I am uncertain if I have been able to make clear to you the intricacies of this involved scientific subject. I am reminded of one of those after-dinner speakers who had great lung capacity but slight consideration for the poor sufferers at the table. He wound up his lengthy oration by saying, "Now, if I failed to prove my point to everyone's satisfaction, I'll be glad to answer any questions."

One man raised his hand.

"Did I fail to prove my point with you, sir?" asked the speaker.

"No," replied the bored one, "what I'm interested in finding out is, what **was** your point?"

—John Caster

GOOD PLACE TO STOP

Any old place in a speech is a good place to stop. If, as far as you have gone, you have made a good speech it is a good place to stop; and if, as far as you have gone, you have made a bad speech it is a hell of a good place to stop."

—Max D. Steuer

PASSING THE END

I notice that I have passed my time limit and that there are several listeners in my audience who are beginning to squirm which is a pretty good signal to me that I should bring this talk to an immediate close. I am reminded of a story.

In a midwestern town on a bright June afternoon parents and grandparents assembled in the school auditorium to see their offspring participate in the eighth-grade commencement. The girls, their hair curled as tight as screen-door springs, wore crisp new dresses. The boys, their hair parted in the middle and plastered down, made their speeches with their legs shaking under the knife-sharp creases in their trousers.

The program went off smoothly until a boy launched into an interminable zither solo. At first folks listened attentively, then began to wriggle in their seats. Finally, when everyone was at the breaking point, the principal walked to the edge of the platform and asked in a stage whisper: "Aren't you almost to the end?"

"I've **passed** the end!" the boy groaned.

—A. P. Savage in The Christian Science Monitor

OPPORTUNITIES TO SIT DOWN

When William J. Bryan made one of his earliest speeches, his mother was present. He was particularly eloquent for this occasion and when he finished he asked: "Well, Mother, what did you think of it?"

"William," she said quietly, "it seemed to me you didn't improve all your opportunities."

"How do you mean?"

"Why," said his mother, "you had several opportunities to sit down before you did." —The Christian Science Monitor

DIME ON THE PLATE

Mark Twain, according to Milton Dickens, speech teacher at the University of Southern California, is credited with a story about an overlong sermon. At the end of twenty minutes he was so favorably impressed he decided to put in five dollars when the offering was taken. Twenty minutes later, he decided that two dollars would suffice. After another twenty minutes the considered contribution shrank to one dollar. When eventually the sermon ended, Mark Twain awoke from a doze and placed a dime on the plate.

The chairman may wisely remark, "I shall keep my remarks brief as I should like to be worth at least $5.00. I have a feeling, however, that you would be willing to pay me more if I would sit down right now."   —V. Spencer Goodreds.

TIME TO SIT DOWN

Well, ladies and gentlemen, it's time for me to conclude this speech.

At a dinner where William Collier, the humorist, was to make a speech, he listened patiently while a general and an admiral, who preceded him, each spoke for an hour. When Collier was introduced, he rose and said: "Now I know what they mean by the Army and Navy Forever."

Then he sat down.

And so will I.

—Bugs Baer

NEXT!

The after-dinner speaker droned on and on, his prosaic words slowly emptying the hall until only a solitary figure remained. Finally finishing, he rushed over to this one last hearer and grasped his hand, exclaiming: "My friend, if only you took in my message, I am satisfied. My labors are not in vain if one listener is convinced!"

The other looked at him blankly and stammered: "Who was listening? I'm the next speaker."

—S. J. Goldstein

ON TOO LONG

Irvin S. Cobb once spoke with great prolixity at a dinner presided over by Will Rogers. When he finally sat down, Will said: "Ladies and gentlemen, you have just been listening to the ancient Chinese sage, On Too Long."

—Frank Crowninshield in Vogue

CALENDAR ON THE WALL

I have talked too long. It reminds me of a campaign speech that I delivered long ago in Frenchburg, Kentucky.

I was going along pretty well and had forgotten what time I started speaking. So I picked up my watch, looked at it, then absent-mindedly put it to my ear to see if it was running. Back in the audience some man shouted to me, "Barkley, if your watch has stopped running, there's a calendar on the wall behind you!"   —Alben W. Barkley

WHO INVENTED MONEY?

Clarence Darrow once addressed a woman's club on the civilization of the ancient Phoenicians. When he had run down, the beaming chairlady said: "Oh, how **can** we thank Mr. Darrow for the **fascinating** lecture he has given us tonight?" Darrow returned to the lectern and added the following postscriptum: "I entirely forgot to tell you that it was the Phoenicians who first invented money."

—Frank Crowninshield in Vogue

NEVER MIND THE BABY

While I was editor of **Southern Agriculturist,** I spoke at many meetings. At a country church in Arkansas, after I got well into my speech and began talking loudly and waving my arms freely, a baby started to fret and fuss. When the embarrassed mother got up to take it out, I halted and said, "Never mind the baby, lady. It's not bothering me one bit."

"The baby may not be bothering you," the mother retorted, "but you sure are bothering the baby!"

—J. E. Stanford in Farm and Ranch-Southern Agriculturist

ONLY ON FIRE

"Not long ago, in the middle of a lecture I was giving at a club in Cleveland, I was horrified to see the occupants of the back rows marching out of the hall with almost military precision. You can imagine my intense relief on learning that the matter was not really serious. They were leaving, not because they found me lacking in charm, but merely because the house was on fire."   —Christopher Morley

PUBLIC CONVEYANCE

Now that I have reached the end of my talk, I am reminded of the dapper young man who lost his footing on the long and slippery hill and was tobogganing toward the bottom when he collided with a stout lady, tripped her, and proceeded on his way, with the lady seated on his back.

As they came to a halt at the foot of the hill, the lady seemed slightly dazed by events, and he remarked gently:

"Beg your pardon, madam, but you'll have to get off here; this is as far as I go."   —Ladies' Home Journal

ALWAYS POPULAR

"The speaker certainly made a hit tonight," remarked a club member.

"What did he talk about?" asked an absent one.

"About five minutes."   —V. Spencer Goodreds.

TO BE APPRECIATED

"To be seen one must stand up—to be heard one must speak clearly—but to be appreciated, one must sit down."
                                        —Helen Wills Moody

TOO MUCH TALK

Pat hired a car, and invited his best girl out for a drive. After driving for half an hour in complete silence, Pat turned to his companion, and said, "Maggie, will ye marry me?" Maggie replied, "Sure, Pat." Pat drove another half hour without speaking. Maggie finally said: "Pat, say something." Pat replied: "I won't. I've said too much already."

—Jules S. Bache

*   *   *

THE SUN STOOD STILL

There is one virtue, I am sure, in after-dinner oratory, and that is brevity; and as to that I am reminded of a story. The Lord Chief Justice has told you what are the ingredients of after-dinner oratory. They are the joke, the quotation, and the platitude; and the successful platitude, in my judgment, requires a very high order of genius. I believe that I have not given you a quotation, but I am reminded of something which I heard when very young—the story of a clergyman in America. He was preaching at a camp meeting, and he was preaching on the miracle of Joshua, and he began his sermon with this sentence: "My hearers, there are three motions of the sun. The first is the straightforward or direct motion of the sun; the second is the retrograde or backward motion of the sun; and the third is the motion mentioned in our text—'the sun stood still.'"

Now, gentlemen, I don't know whether you see the application of this story. I hope you do. The after-dinner orator at first begins and goes straight ahead—that is the straightforward motion of the sun. Next he goes back and begins to repeat himself—that is the backward motion of the sun. At least he has the good sense to bring himself to the end, and that is the motion mentioned in our text, as the sun stood still.

—James Russell Lowell

MY FIRST DATE

When I was seventeen I was very bashful, and a sixteen-year-old girl came to stay a week with us. She was a peach, and I was seized with a happiness not of this world.

One evening my mother suggested that, to entertain her, I take her to the theatre. I didn't really like it, because I was seventeen and sensitive about appearing in the streets with a girl. I couldn't see my way to enjoying my delight in public. But we went.

I didn't feel very happy. I couldn't seem to keep my mind on the play. I became conscious, after awhile, that that was due less to my lovely company than my boots. They were sweet to look upon, as smooth as skin, but fitted ten times as close. I got oblivious to the play and the girl and the other people and everything but my boots until—I hitched one partly off. The sensation was sensuously perfect. I couldn't help it. I had to get the other off, partly. Then I was obliged to get them off altogether, except that I kept my feet in the legs so they couldn't get away.

From that time on I enjoyed the play. But the first thing I knew the curtain came down, like that, without my notice, and I hadn't any boots on. What's more, they wouldn't go on. I tugged strenuously. And the people in our row got up and fussed and said things until the peach and I simply had to move on.

We moved—the girl on one arm and the boots under the other. We walked home that way, sixteen blocks, with a retinue a mile long. Every time we passed a lamppost death gripped me at the throat. But we got home—and I had on white socks.

If I live to be nine hundred and ninety-nine years old I don't suppose I could ever forget that walk.

And I tell you one thing, young ladies: I've had a better time with you today than with that peach fifty-three years ago.

—Mark Twain

This conclusion was given by Mr. Clemens when he addressed the young ladies at Barnard College in 1906.

Chapter Five

Inspirational Conclusions

It is only rarely that we find a speaker so well trained and so experienced that he can use the inspirational type of conclusion effectively. However, for the purpose of illustration and study we have included examples in this chapter to serve as models.

It should be the aim of every speaker to develop proficiency in phrasing and thought design. To strive for perfection in delivering the inspirational type of conclusion should be a constant objective of every speaker.

THE NEXT ONE!

A great painter whose hand produced many a work of art was asked "Which is your greatest painting?" The artist paused a moment. "My greatest painting? The next one!"

The people of our state, in this Centennial year, look back upon a record of achievement. A century of struggle and growth, a century of toil and sacrifice, a century in which a wilderness has been transformed into a great progressive commonwealth.

The temptation of any anniversary observance is to glorify the past at the expense of the future. We honor the past, without it there would be no great present, but our eyes are fixed upon the future. The people of Minnesota, like the famous painter, are being asked to name their greatest century. Their reply must be "The next one!"   —Luther W. Youngdahl

The conclusion of the inaugural address delivered by Governor Youngdahl on Jan. 6, 1949, illustrates the use of the inspirational type of ending which stirs an emotional response in the audience.

A MAN'S REACH

Is it not paradoxical that this rich land of ours should be so poor in opportunity? Certainly democracy in a rich land can do as well for its sons as dictatorship in a poor land. It must justify the faith and hope of youth by solving the human problems it has too long neglected. I am confident that youth will gladly do its part in the reconstruction, for we will welcome the coming of a new day with new opportunities. We only want a chance—a chance to participate in the progress of America instead of being a relief burden on the nation. We want to contribute rather than receive. But before we can run a good race we must see the mark—the goal for which to strive. Perhaps we can't grasp the prize today or tomorrow, but if we have something to reach for, an objective, a cause, we can finally succeed; for it has always been true that "A man's reach should exceed his grasp." And so I ask America to "give back the upward looking and the light," and rebuild in youth "the spirit and the dream."   —Norman L. Krause

The conclusion of a speech on "A Man's Reach," dealing with the need for opportunities for young people in the United States. The use of an inspirational appeal is always a good way to conclude a speech.

TAKE THE HIGH ROAD

Over the grave of an American colonel in Italy, who fell in battle, a chaplain put as an epitaph words that had been familiar on the colonel's lips. "Always take the high ground and the enemy will flee." If we take the high ground of consecration to public service, no situation can discourage and no disappointment defeat us in reaching our goal.

—Luther W. Youngdahl

The conclusion of the inaugural address delivered by Governor Youngdahl on Jan. 8, 1947.

GOOD-BYE!

"Farewell," gentlemen, is a word often lightly uttered and readily forgotten. But when it marks the rounding-off and completion of a chapter in life, the severance of ties many and cherished, of the parting with many friends at once—especially when it is spoken among the lengthening shadows of the western light—it sticks somewhat in the throat. It becomes, indeed, "the word that makes us linger."

But it does not prompt many other words. It is best expressed in few. What goes without saying is better than what is said. Not much can be added to the old English word "Goodbye." You are not sending me away empty-handed or alone. I go freighted and laden with happy memories—inexhaustible and malloyed—of England, its warm-hearted people, and their measureless kindness. Spirits more than twain will cross with me, messengers of your good-will. Happy the nation that can thus speed its parting guest! Fortunate the guest who has found his welcome almost an adoption, and whose farewell leaves half his heart behind!   —Edward John Phelps

The conclusion of an address given by Mr. Phelps, Minister to England, on the occasion of a farewell banquet given him by the Lord Mayor of London.

BORN RICH

Between the universes over my head and the universes under my feet, I stand as a child of good fortune. In the mind of the Almighty there is an ambitious plan for me. Greater than any mountain, dearer in His sight than any oil deposit or ledge of gold ore, as eternal as time, I am an immortal soul. I represent the crown of creation, the finest and highest fruitage of the ages of evolution. I am a living soul. The sky can reflect the glory of God, but I can appreciate the glory. The mountains can show the handiwork of God, but I can think the thoughts of God. The river can flow unto the sea, but I run into eternity. The violet drinks the dew that He sends, but "in Him I live and move and have my being." As I find God's plan for me, I find life. Surely, I was born rich!

—Dr. Roy L. Smith

LINCOLN'S FAREWELL ADDRESS

My Friends: No one not in my situation can appreciate my feeling of sadness at this parting. To this place, and the kindness of these people, I owe everything. Here I have lived a quarter of a century, and have passed from a young to an old man. Here my children have been born, and one is buried. I now leave, not knowing when or whether ever I may return, with a task before me greater than that which rested upon Washington. Without the assistance of that Divine Being who ever attended him, I cannot succeed. With that assistance, I cannot fail. Trusting in Him who can go with me, and remain with you, and be everywhere for good, let us confidently hope that all will yet be well. To His care commending you, as I hope in your prayers you will commend me, I bid you an affectionate farewell.

Delivered by Abraham Lincoln at Springfield, Illinois, on Feb. 11, 1861. Here in a few words Mr. Lincoln revealed his remarkable ability to leave a lasting impression with his listeners.

WE WANT TO BE MEN

Take away the flaccid and the flabby and give us men upon whom we can rely; take away the comfort seekers and give us burden bearers; take away the frail and the weak and restore the strong and efficient. Oh, God, take away our comforts and our ease and our enjoyment and our petty satisfaction, and give us tasks that are hard, assignments that are fatiguing, toil that is exacting, and drudgery that is wearying. We want to be men; prove us. Don't let this nation crumble.

—Dr. George Barton Cutten

DAWN OF A NEW DAY

A wealthy man took a poor boy from the slums of a great city to his lodge high in the mountains. The boy awakened in the morning. The sky was illuminated with the red and gold of the rising sun reflecting on the ice and stone of the rocky pinnacles and blazoned across the sky. The boy rubbed his eyes in wonder and a great fear filled him. Looking at the flaming splendor, he remembered the lurid tenement fires in which people he knew had burned to death. Terrified, he screamed, "Please, sir, wake up! Something awful has happened, the whole world is on fire." His wealthy friend opened his eyes and, seeing the flame pictures of the Great Artist on the tapestried skies, replied, "Don't be afraid, my boy, everything is all right. The world is not burning up. It is just the dawn of a new day."

The world is on fire, but it need not be the holocaust of destruction. It can be and it must be the flaming dawn of a new day.   Luther W. Youngdahl

The conclusion used by Governor Youngdahl in his inaugural address on January 3, 1951, is an effective example of the use of the inspirational type of conclusion.

WE HAVE JUST BEGUN TO FIGHT

We have need of that devotion today. It is that which makes it possible for government to persuade those who are mentally prepared to fight each other to go on instead, to work for and to sacrifice for each other. That is why we need to say with the Prophet, "What doth the Lord require of thee—but to do justly, to love mercy, and to walk humbly with thy God."

—Franklin D. Roosevelt

In his speech on "We Have Just Begun to Fight," Franklin D. Roosevelt used a quotation to conclude this speech which in many cases is an effective type of conclusion.

MEN OF FREE SPIRIT

There are today fuzzy-minded people in our country who would compromise in these fundamental concepts. They scoff at these tested qualities in men. They never have understood and never will understand what the word America means. They explain that these qualities were good while there was a continent to conquer, and a nation to build. They say that time has passed. No doubt the land frontier has passed. But the frontiers of science are barely opening. This new land with all its high promise cannot and will not be conquered except by men inspired from the concepts of free spirit.

It is those moral and spiritual qualities in free men which fulfill the meaning of the word American. And with them will come centuries of further greatness to our country.

—Herbert Hoover

A COSTLY CONQUEST

Though outward circumstances are utterly changed, we need to emulate, as we face our next century, the courage, the vision, and the spirit of sacrifice which animated the founders of our state. The road before us today, as it was one hundred years ago, is rocky and fraught with peril.

Too many of us fail to appreciate the hazards and are like the young American who arrived in Zermatt, Switzerland, and seeing the towering peak of the Matterhorn, asked, "What's the name of that big rock?" When told it was one of the most famous of the Alpine summits he said, "Do you think I could get up there this afternoon?"

Little did he know of the story of the peak's costly conquest, of the lives it had taken, of the hazards still involved in the ascent. So is liberty, a decent society, a lasting peace, each a majestic mountain peak. How much do we really want them? Do we appreciate their cost? Are we willing to pay the price for them and sacrifice for them?

The pioneers of a hundred years ago did not hesitate to pay

the price for a strong society. They did not allow their spiritual values to be smothered beneath the false riches of material possessions. May the high idealism, the courage, the selflessness, and the implicit faith in God which characterized the founders of Minnesota inspire us. In the same spirit of consecration may we also move ahead to our next and even greater century of advancement, building together a nobler Minnesota.

—Luther W. Youngdahl

The conclusion used by Governor Youngdahl in his inaugural address on January 6, 1949, the Centennial year of Minnesota. It shows how an apt illustration is the basis for the final inspirational appeal of his address.

THE GREAT BOY MOVEMENT

Well, that's my sales story on Boy Scouting—the great boy movement that serves not only the boy but the man, the community and the nation as well. Some of you sales executives here are probably saying, "He hasn't asked for the order." I intend to do that now.

I ask you leaders of Kansas City to give more support to Boy Scouting than you have ever done in the past. Those of you who have been too busy for Scouting, I ask you to find some time for it. Get into it actively. See that more troops are organized so that more boys may come to know and benefit by the adventure of Scouting. If you cannot serve as Scoutmasters or in some other capacity, see that men in your company are encouraged to do so and that they are given the time and encouragement so they can do the job well. Finally, see that the coffers of the Kansas City Council are never so light that this movement cannot operate at top effectiveness.

Do these things and I will assure you this: Years hence when you are resting from your life's labors, you will look back with pride and satisfaction on the part you played to make this great boy movement greater.

—William H. Fetridge

KEEP THE AIM SHINING

On Bataan the Filipinos and Americans, fighting side by side, learned the real meaning of equality. We know now, in a way that we could never have known before, the real equality between races. We know, too, that in a way that we could never have known before, the real equality between races. We know, too, that in that idea of equality lies the hope, and the only sure hope, of the future. The day is gone when men and women, of whatever color or creed, can consider themselves the superiors of other creeds or colors. The day of vast empire is past. The day of equal peoples is at hand.

Let us keep that aim shining before us like a light—a light for the people of Europe, for the people of Africa, for the people of Asia, for the people of South America and for the people of our own beloved land.   —Wendell L. Willkie

DO UNTO OTHERS

Ah, my friends, if I could have my way, I would bound the United States on the North by that good will which tolerates no fort or defense of any kind between Canada and this country. I would bound her on the West by "Forgive thine enemies," on the East by "Love thine enemies as thyself," and I would bound her on the South by the Golden Rule, "Do unto others as you would they should do unto you." When we have adopted such a policy, my friends, we will then have made another great contribution to the progress of civilization. We will then have reached a time when the peoples of all lands and tongues, awakened to hope by the inspiration of our example, will follow with the years the luminous pathway that leads to a destiny beyond the reach of vision but within the providence of God!   —J. Leslie Goddard

This conclusion includes an emotional appeal for acceptance of the speaker's philosophy.

Chapter Six

Dramatic Conclusions

The dramatic ending is always climatic in treatment. It is an excellent way to conclude a speech. Of course, it cannot be used for all subjects and will fit into certain situations. In its development it usually works up to a climax step by step as is illustrated by the examples that follow in this chapter.

TOUSSAINT L'OUVERTURE

I would call him Napoleon, but Napoleon made his way to empire over broken oaths and through a sea of blood. This man never broke his word. "No retaliation," was his great motto and the rule of his life; and the last words uttered to his son in France were these: "My boy, you will some day go back to St. Domingo; forget that France murdered your father."

I would call him Cromwell, but Cromwell was only a soldier, and the state he founded went down with him into his grave. I would call him Washington, but the great Virginian held slaves. This man risked his empire rather than permit the slave trade in the humblest village of his dominions.

You think me a fanatic tonight for you read history not with your eyes, but with your prejudices. But fifty years hence, when truth gets a hearing, the Muse of History will put Phocion for the Greek, and Brutus for the Roman, Hampden for England, Fayette for France, choose Washington as the bright, consummate flower of our earlier civilization, then dipping her pen in the sunlight, will write in the clear blue, above them all, the name of the soldier, the statesman, the martyr, Toussaint L'Ouverture.   —Wendell Phillips

The conclusion of one of the best-known of American lyceum lectures delivered by Wendell Phillips in hundreds of American cities during his lifetime. It illustrates the use of the dramatic form as a most effective type of conclusion.

OLD SOLDIERS NEVER DIE

The world has turned over many times since I took the oath at West Point, and the hopes and dreams have all since vanished, but I still remember the refrain of one of the most popular barracks ballads of that day which proclaimed most proudly that old soldiers never die; they just fade away.

And like the old soldier of that ballad, I now close my military career and just fade away, an old soldier who tried to do his duty as God gave him the light to see that duty. Goodbye.

—General Douglas MacArthur

This effective conclusion to his address before the joint sessions of Congress on April 19, 1951, by General MacArthur will be one of the most remembered portions of his speech. It indicates that basing a conclusion on some well-known story or narrative gives it dramatic effect.

BLACK MAN'S DESTINY

Will black men go on through the ages crucified upon a cross of race prejudice? Will we forever consider blackness a badge of shame, an emblem of evil, and a standard of inferiority? Will worth of character and the power of personality be cast aside and men be judged solely on a color basis? If so, let us scorn our education, scoff at our morals. If so, then let us take God's Holy Bible and tear it to shreds. If this be so, let us throw our American constitution on the funeral pyre of a dead civilization.

But, the Negro believes in the American Constitution, for it embodies the principles of liberty, equality, and justice. I believe in the American white man, for his civilization has eclipsed that of the ages. I believe in a greater humanity that transcends race, color, and creed. Therefore, I believe in the Black Man's Destiny . . . that somewhere, sometime in this land of ours, though black-skinned and kinky-haired, he shall climb the mountains of life and emerge above the clouds of blackness into the sunlight of freedom and social justice.

—William McClain

This dramatic conclusion has a climatic effect, particularly since the speaker is a Negro himself.

I IMPEACH HIM

Therefore it is with confidence that, ordered by the Commons,

I impeach Warren Hastings, Esquire, of high crimes and misdemeanors.

I impeach him in the name of the Commons, in Parliament assembled, whose parliamentary trust he has betrayed.

I impeach him in the name of all the Commons of Great Britain, whose national character he has dishonored.

I impeach him in the name of the people of India, whose laws, rights, and liberties he has subverted; whose properties he has destroyed; whose country he has laid waste and desolate.

I impeach him in the name and by virtue of those eternal laws of justice which he has violated.

I impeach him in the name of human nature itself, which he has cruelly outraged, injured, and oppressed, in both sexes, in every age, rank, situation, and condition of life.

—Edmund Burke

In his "Impeachment of Warren Hastings," Edmund Burke has given us a classic example of a conclusion that utilizes a recapitulation of the main points of his main address and the cumulative repetition of the phrasing gives a dramatic flavor to the ending.

WE DON'T HAVE TO COME BACK

It is related that off the New England coast a ship was hurled mercilessly against the rocks. The Coast Guard arrived, under the command of an experienced captain. There were some inexperienced fellows on board who lacked vision and courage. One of them said to the captain, "Captain, with that tide against us and the terrific gale, we will be able to get out there all right, but we will never be able to get back." To this the captain responded, "Prepare the boat. We have got to get out; we don't have to come back."

And so it is with us. Despite the difficulties, we have got to find the means to conduct research in the field of human engineering. If we did not shirk in financing a war, bringing unfathomable destruction, we dare not shirk the much lighter task of financing construction.

Today, no less than in wartime, there is a premium on fortitude. In the face of tides of apathy, pessimism and timidity, endangered by the jagged rocks of practical difficulties and amid the cross winds of selfish interests, our duty is still clear. The words of the New England Coast Guard captain still ring true, and they are spoken to us: "We have got to go out; we don't have to come back." —Luther W. Youngdahl

The conclusion used by Governor Youngdahl in his inaugural address delivered on January 8, 1947. It is a clear example of using a graphic story to give dramatic effect to the main theme of his address.

GUNS OVER BUTTER

Nearly three years ago I clipped an item from a newspaper which seems ominously prophetic today. It told of a boast made by a Soviet general. This general boasted that the Western Democracies were bound to be defeated by the Soviet Union because they would not make the sacrifices necessary to arm themselves. They prized their standards of living too highly. They would not be willing to accept the disciplines to put "guns" over "butter." In Russia, though, this general boasted, the people were inured to hardship. The Soviet government would force the sacrifices to mobilize. A lean, hungry, but mobilized Russia would over-run a Western world which couldn't bring itself to mobilize—in time.

This is the test which confronts us—not only this country

but all of the free peoples of the world. It is the choice of "peace" or "butter," of mobilizing our strength now, while peace can still be saved, or of clinging to petty wants and petty profits, imperiling our freedom and our civilization.

No outside enemy can defeat us. We can defeat ourselves. Gentlemen, yours is the decision. Which shall it be—discomfort or defeat?   —Bernard Baruch

Here is another illustration of the use of a dramatic conclusion.

SAFEGUARDS OF FREE MEN

I have faith that there are principles which neither communism nor socialism, nor neutralism, nor other evil ideas, nor even the march of time can defeat. These truths came into the universe along with the shooting stars of which worlds are made. They are as inevitable as the existence of the Supreme Being, the forces of gravitation, and the ceaseless struggle of mankind to be free.

I have lived a long life. I have witnessed and even taken part in many great and threatening crises. With each time they have been surmounted, the American dream has become more real.

My faith arises from the genius of our people, their devotion to personal liberty and their sustaining religious beliefs. If the American people are guided aright, there will be no decline and fall in American civilization.

I wish for the guidance of the Almighty Providence in your task. And with deepest sincerity may God bless you.

                                    —Herbert Hoover

The dramatic impact of this conclusion was the realization by the audience that would no doubt be the last appearance of Mr. Hoover as one of the main speakers on the program of a national Republican convention.

THE DEMOCRATIC WAY OF LIFE

No, my friends, I don't think we have come to where we are, only to surrender blindly to a new super-barbarism, a new super-imperialism, a new super-power. We do not want leaderships in our countries subservient to foreign rulers, be they in London, or Paris, The Hague or Washington, or, we must add, Moscow. I think our peoples want to worship the Almighty and live in accordance with His laws, to better their lot, to educate themselves and their children, raise themselves from the degradation of want and disease and misery, by holding up their own heads and acting freely to achieve these great and difficult aims by their own free means in partnership with similarly dedicated people everywhere in the world.

That is the freedom of the democratic way of life. That is the freedom we want all the people of Asia and Africa to enjoy. That is the freedom that President Ramon Magsaysay of the Philippines had in mind when he authored the Pacific Charter which enshrines the dignity of man, his well-being, his security, his progress, his nation's right to self-determination. The Philippine Delegation is here not only to reiterate the ideals of that Charter but to underscore in this Conference that it is the sense of the Filipino people that such right of self-determination includes the right of nations to decide exclusively by themselves their ability to assume the responsibilities inherent in an independent political status. This is the time for Asia and Africa to reassert this principle and serve notice to the world that only by its unqualified acceptance by everyone can there be peace and justice for all mankind.

—Carlos P. Romulo, Chairman, Philippine Delegation

In his address before the Asian-African Conference at Bandung in 1955, Mr. Romulo used this very dramatic conclusion in which he summed up the essence of democracy and no doubt influenced the final decision of many delegates to this Conference.

Section Five

STORIES FOR SPEAKERS

STORIES FOR SPEAKERS

IT PAYS TO ADVERTISE

Coming one day to a crossroads town, our friend found that there was only one store. The proprietor did not receive him enthusiastically. "Why should I advertise?" he demanded. "I have been here for twenty years. There isn't a man, woman, or child around these parts that doesn't know where I am and what I sell."

The advertising man answered very promptly—because in our business if we hesitate we are lost—and he said to the proprietor, pointing across the street, "What is that building over there?" The proprietor answered, "That is the Methodist Episcopal Church."

The advertising man said, "How long has that been there?"

The proprietor said, "Oh, I don't know; seventy-five years probably."

"And yet," exclaimed the advertising man, "they ring the church bell every Sunday morning."   —Bruce Barton

GO TO BED

An old hillbilly and his wife went to the city on business. Since they had never stayed over-night in a hotel, they decided on the most swanky one in the city. They were shown to their room.

A television set was turned on when they entered, so they sat down and enjoyed the show very much for a while. Then the old man became angry and shouted to his wife: "Maw, tell those show people to get away from our window so I can undress and go to bed."   —Bindery Talk

THE PARROT CONVERTED THEM

As you are aware, ladies and gentlemen, we have on our program tonight a mind reader. So if any of you are telling your neighbor in the next seat how much money you have in the bank or how much A and Z stock you own, be careful. It might get around to our mind-reading friend and you'll be caught with a little white lie.

However, if you are in business or are a politician a little untruth is permissible. I am thinking of Sam who ran a pet show. A little old lady entered Sam's shop and said: "I'd like to buy a parrot to keep me company, but mind you, I want a parrot that doesn't use foul language." "Lady," said Sam, "a cow uses bovine language; a dog uses canine language, and a parrot uses fowl language." "What I want," said the lady, "is a parrot that doesn't swear." "I have the parrot that you really want," beamed Sam. "Now this parrot right here is a practical missionary. We have five other parrots that swore like — well, they swore. We had to sell them at a loss because this parrot converted them."

—Arthur L. Kaser

YOU PUT HIM TO SLEEP

The speaker stopped abruptly and pointed to a man in the audience. "Wake up that man seated next to you," he said. The man shook his head. "You do it," he said. "You put him to sleep."

—Arthur L. Kaser

SELF-CENTERED SPEAKER

A self-centered speaker was addressing a very small audience in a very large auditorium. He started out by eulogizing himself highly. He said: "I am a man of many talents. I am a musician. I write plays and novels. I am an expert at golf. I even find time to specialize in flower culture." A listener spoke up. "How unfortunate that there are so many of you and so few of us."

—Arthur L. Kaser

HOME TOWN PRIDE

Ladies and gentlemen, I wonder if all of you are as proud of your home town as I am. I consider this town a perfect example of real American democracy, and no doubt there is the same feeling in every city in this land concerning home towns like ours.

Do you realize that this is the only country in the world where a man can ride in his own car to the courthouse or city hall to collect his unemployment compensation check?

In our humble town you can rub elbows with other men without being afraid he will report you to the commissar. Yes, my friends, you can rub elbows without fear. It is different when it comes to rubbing fenders. In this country we can think as we please, and people seldom think alike until it comes to buying wedding presents.

—Arthur L. Kaser

IT PAYS TO BE PREPARED

I have found from my experience as a speaker that it always pays to be prepared by analyzing the prospective audience situation and by adapting my ideas to the needs of the occasion.

I am reminded of the frontier town in which the big boys resolved that no school teacher should remain at the school longer than a week, and successfully drove out half-a-dozen until the trustees feared that they wouldn't be able to secure any one to teach their children.

The place was vacant for some weeks until at last a young Easterner drifted out to the West without intending it, heard of the vacancy and made application to be principal of the school. And the chairman of the board looked at him and said: "Those roughs play pretty mean there, and it is a hard job. Every teacher they have had they have driven away. But you can have the job if you want it."

The youth accepted, and the first morning he went into the school, the scholars beheld him carrying a card to the back part of the room, and he tacked it up there over their heads, returned to his desk, drew a revolver and hit the bull's eye seven times. Then he reloaded his weapon, laid it down, took out two derringers and laid them on the desk. All this time there was not a sound. And then the young Eastern teacher looked up and said, "This school will open with prayer!"

—Josephus Daniels

HARMLESS DELUSION

A woman went to a doctor to complain about her husband's delusion. "It's terrible, Doctor," she said. "All the time he thinks he's a refrigerator."

"Well," consoled the medical man, "that isn't too bad. Quite a harmless delusion, I'd say."

"The delusion I don't mind, Doctor. But when he sleeps with his mouth open, the little light keeps me awake!"

—George A. Posner

REGARDING COOPERATION

A Negro who had been transferred to Heaven, called his friend in another region, far below, by means of a spiritual seance—and here was a real spiritual seance—and he asked: "Well, how goes everything down there with you, Rastus, old boy?"

His erstwhile crony answered: "Oh, I'se havin' a fine time. Don't have to work much; just shovel in some coal now and then. How you-all?"

"I'se workin' purty hard. We have to sweep up de clouds, turn de rain on an' off, blow de wind, keep de sun a-going and keep him warm; polish all de halos and de golden sidewalks, keep de harps tuned up, and give de planets a shove every mornin'."

"How come you all hev so much work to do?"

"Well, Rastus, to tell de truth, we're kinda short o' help up heah."

————

A woman who had just completed a First Aid course saw a man lying flat on his face in the street and was shocked that passers-by paid no attention to him. So she rushed up and began giving him artificial respiration.

Finally the man raised his head with an effort, and said: "Lady, I don't know what you're trying to do, but I'm trying to get a wire down this manhole!"

Cooperation is a fine thing, and so are good intentions, but they can often be mis-directed.   —George A. Posner

HE'S READY

The football team had done nothing but fumble all afternoon. So when a substitute, warming up in front of the bench, dropped a ball someone flipped to him, it was too much for a leather-lunged fan. "Send him in, coach," he yelled from the stands. "He's ready!"   —Harold Helfer

SHORT WORDS THAT SELL

It is an admirable practice for every speaker to express his ideas in short words and phrases. Listeners can always understand what the speaker means regardless of their age or educational background—they will understand exactly what you mean. This fact is graphically illustrated by the following quotation:

"There is strength and force in short words; words that blast and boom, throb and thump, clank and chime, hiss and buzz and zoom. There is grace and charm in short words too, in words like lull and lush and purr. There are short lush words like dank and drench; and short dry ones like crisp, parch, and husk. There are words that work hard at their job, that pry and push, that slash and hack, that cut and clip, that chip and saw.

"Scan the best ads in print and you'll find them rich in short words that tease the taste, make glad the eye, whet the nose and please the ear. There's nip, twang, bite, and tan in short sales words. They're sweet, sour, tart, or dry as the need be. There are words you can hear like the swish of silk; soft words with the feel of swan's down; words with a smell like musk, smoke, cheese, mint, and rose—all of them good sales tools. Yet oft as not in talk or script we'll force the use of some long hard word, and with it blunt the keen edge and dull the sharp point of what we want to say."

—H. Phelps Gates in Christian Science Monitor

SPEAK WORDS THAT WILL BE UNDERSTOOD

A child of ten was asked to write an essay on a bird and a beast and here is the vivid picture that he painted—a phrasing that could be understood by anyone:

"The bird that I am going to write about is the owl. The owl cannot see at all by day and at night is as blind as a bat.

"I do not know much about the owl, so I will go on to the beast which I am going to choose. It is the cow. The cow is a mammal. It has six sides—right, left, an upper and below. At the back it has a tail on which hangs a brush. With this it sends the flies away so that they do not fall into the milk. The head is for the purpose of growing horns and so that the mouth can be somewhere. The horns are to butt with, and the mouth is to moo with. Under the cow hangs the milk. It is arranged for milking. When people milk, the milk comes and there is never an end to the supply. How the cow does it I have not yet realized, but it makes more and more. The cow has a fine sense of smell; one can smell it far away. This is the reason for the fresh air in the country.

"The man cow is called an ox. It is not a mammal. The cow does not eat much, but what it eats it eats twice, so that it gets enough. When it is hungry it moos, and when it says nothing it is because its inside is all full up with grass."

THE WOMAN I LOVE

A fellow—already feeling his liquor—returned to the bar-room for another drink but couldn't remember the name of it. "All I can remember," he told the bartender, "is that it's tall, cold and full of gin."

Another fellow leaning over the bar turned to him and snarled: "Sir, you are speaking of the woman I love!"

—Alben Barkley

NICE CLOCK

The hill-billy's clock had suddenly ceased to function. So he and his wife went to town to get a new one. There were a lot to pick from, but the cuckoo clock fascinated the hill-billy. That's the clock he wanted. He thought it was fun to watch the bird pop out and tell the hour. But his wife was reluctant to buy it.

"What's wrong with it?" demanded the hill-billy.

"It's a nice clock," admitted the wife, "but what would we feed the bird?"

LOOK AT THOSE FURS

I tried out the notion that it helps a speaker to pick out one person in an audience to whom to address his remarks. In the second row I spotted a most gorgeously furred-up woman. I thought, "That's my audience. Look at those furs! She fairly drips furs."

Through the whole talk I never let my eyes off her. She didn't budge an inch and I felt pretty set up. If a woman like that had remained as intent as she had, all my points had gone over.

After the talk, a friend of mine said: "We thought your talk was splendid, Morley, but why did you keep staring so at the second row?" When I explained how I'd picked my woman, my friend nearly died. I suffer from near-sightedness, and the person I'd picked out was the chair on which half the women in the audience had piled up their coats.

—Christopher Morley

FOR BETTER

A much-married movie star met one of the women who had enjoyed the dubious distinction of having been a wife of his during one of the early rounds of his bouts with matrimony.

"I hardly knew you, dear," said he. "You changed so much."

"For better or worse, do you think?" she asked him archly.

"For better, of course," said he gallantly. "You couldn't have changed for worse."

—George A. Posner

TAKE IT EASY

They were in a fire in a hotel, and the man kept telling his wife: "Now, honey, relax, take it easy, don't get excited, and we'll get out of it O.K."

When they finally reached the sidewalk, he said to her: "Notice how cool I kept through it all?"

"Why shouldn't you be?" she answered. "You forgot your trousers."

—George A. Posner

HOLD IT STILL

A famous matador was fighting in the bull ring in a Mexican border town. Many of the spectators were seeing their first bull fight, and among them was an old cowhand.

The fight had reached the stage where the matador, armed with only a cape, was taunting the bull, avoiding the animal's horns by fractions of an inch and flipping the cape aside as the bull charged past.

At last the old cowhand could stand it no longer. He arose and shouted: "Buddy, he ain't never going to run into that sack unless you hold it still!"   —Bindery Talk

PARDON ME

The club of a coach known for his locker-room orations had played a very effeminate game for the first half and came off the football field dreading a tongue lashing. They sat in the dressing room, waiting for him to burst in and tell them off. Minute ticked after minute as the tension increased.

Then, just a moment before they had to go out on the field again, there was a sound at the door. Every player straightened.

The door opened and the coach stuck in his head. But only for an instant.

"Pardon me, girls," the coach said, and hurriedly closed the door.   —Bindery Talk

RIGHT TO TALK

A customer complained that the new barber was driving him crazy with his incessant chatter.

The proprietor observed mildly, "According to the Constitution of the United States, he's got a right to talk."

"That may be," admitted the customer, "but the United States has a Constitution that can stand it. Mine can't."

—Louisville Courier-Journal

NOT AS REPORTED

The Rev. Hilary Zwisler, of St. Sebastian's church in Akron, tells about the time an internal-revenue agent visited him on a personal matter.

"While I'm here," the agent said, "I'd like to see your church. I've heard so much about it."

Delighted with the request, the priest took him on a tour of the church. "Well," he asked proudly, "what do you think of it?"

"I'm rather disappointed," the agent said.

"Why?"

"From the amount of money your parishioners list as gifts to your church," answered the agent, "I'd come to believe that the aisles were paved with gold."

—Kenny Nichols, All About the Town

HE DOESN'T HOLD ME

Rev. Oscar Johnson, jovial St. Louis pastor, tells this on himself:

Once, after a change of churches, he met a woman of his former flock and asked, "How do you like your new pastor?"

"Just fine," she beamed. "But somehow or other, he just doesn't seem to **hold** me like you did!"

—John Newton Baker

EDISON'S EXPERIMENT

During his campaign for governor of New Jersey in 1940, Charles Edison, son of the inventor, introduced himself by explaining: "People will inevitably associate me with my father, but I would not have anyone believe that I am trading on the name Edison. I would rather have you know me merely as the result of one of my father's earlier experiments."

—Carl John Bostelmann

WHO MADE YOU?

The principal of the school had a way of dropping in to talk to the graduation class a few days before commencement to test the academic proficiency of the current crop of hopefuls. The teacher, who had been there for many years, seemed to have him pretty well figured out.

She was coaching her class for the event, and said: "Now don't worry, and don't be afraid, boys. He always asks the same questions. He'll ask the boy at the head of the first row—you, Johnny—'Who made you?' And you'll answer, 'God made me.' Then he'll ask the second boy, 'Who were the first people on earth?' Your answer will be, 'Adam and Eve.' And so on."

But just before the principal came in, Johnny asked permission to leave the room.

Looking at the first boy, who in the absence of Johnny, was Jimmy, the principal said: "Who made you?"

"Adam and Eve," replied Jimmy.

"Nonsense," said the principal. "Don't you know God made you?"

"Not on your life," spoke up Jimmy. "The fellow that God made is in the washroom, washing his hands."

—George A. Posner

NEARLY RUINED

I am reminded of the story of a colored revival meeting down home in Kentucky.

The parson said: "Rise and testify what the Lord has done for you."

Various members of the congregation rose and testified. Then the preacher spied a gnarled old fellow 'way in back of the meeting house. "Brother Jones," he called, "I see you back there. Won't you tell us what the Lord has done for you?"

Old Brother Jones bent with rheumatism, stood up painfully, leaned on his crutch and said: "All I can say is — He mighty near ruint me!"   —Alben Barkley

AS LINCOLN SAID IT

When I was a high school student, I was asked to give the Gettysburg Address at a Lincoln's Birthday ceremony. Afterward an old gentleman came up to me. "Son," he said, "I liked the way you gave that speech, but you made the same mistake as everyone else. I heard Mr. Lincoln at Gettysburg so I know what I'm talking about. Everyone says, 'of the people, **by** the people and **for** the people,' but Mr. Lincoln said, 'of the **people,** by the **people,** and for the **people.**' It makes a big difference."

—Ted Hatlen

ANIMAL CRACKERS

Mama Skunk was worried because she could never keep track of her two children. They were named In and Out, and whenever In was in, Out was out; and if Out was in, In was out. One day she called Out in to her and told him to go out and bring In in. So Out went out and in no time at all he brought In in.

"Wonderful!" said Mama Skunk. "How, in all that great forest, could you find him in so short a time?"

"It was easy," said Out. "In stinct."

—This Week Magazine

WORKING AT LAST

The widow O'Reilly returned from the funeral of her lamented husband with a triumphant look upon her face.

"He never did a stroke of work in his life, the spalpeen," she told a neighbor. "But I've got him working for me at last."

"Why, how can that be, Mrs. O'Reilly?" the neighbor asked.

"I had him cremated, and I have his ashes in an hour-glass."

—George A. Posner

UNDER WATER

The captain of a yacht looked so worried that he attracted the attention of a woman passenger on board.

"What's the trouble, captain?" she asked.

"The fact is, madam," was the response, "our rudder's broken."

"Oh, I wouldn't worry about that," said the woman. "Being under water nearly all the time, no one will notice it's gone!"

—George A. Posner

PROPOSAL

Two women, shopping in a super-market, became engrossed in conversation.

"I understand the attendance hasn't been good at your church lately," said one woman.

"That's so," replied the other. "There were so few attending last Sunday, that every time the preacher said 'dearly beloved' I felt as though I'd received a proposal."

—George A. Posner

EXPENSIVE

"You've been paying your son's college expenses for two years, Sam. Tell me, is education expensive nowadays?"

"Language runs the highest," replied Sam. "Last month it was $10 for English, $20 for French, and $115 for Scotch."

—George A. Posner

HIS DREAM

Then there was the chap who had a nightmare and dreamt that he was cast away on a desert island with 1,000 brunettes, 1,000 blondes and 1,000 red heads. What makes it a nightmare was the fact that in his dream he was a girl.

—George A. Posner

PERSEVERANCE

Did you ever watch a pipe smoker? He is continually re-lighting his pipe, although many times it may not actually have died out and all it would need is a little puffing to get it going. Many of us are a good deal like that in our daily lives. We feel that we need a fresh match or a new opportunity in order to achieve our goal, when really all we need is to expend just a little more effort on our present task. We only need to try puffing a little harder.

We have no more right to consume happiness without producing it than to consume wealth without producing it.

—Press Proofs

NEVER WROTE IT

(When the speaker disagrees with the Chairman's point of view)

A man in Philadelphia was reading a prepared address to an industrial convention. Along toward the end he swung into his peroration in this wise:

"The American businessman is tired. He has worked long and diligently in the war effort and in the difficult times which preceded it, and he is weary. He is physically tired and mentally tired. But he isn't nearly as tired as the girls who have to type all this eyewash!"

Then came a long, tense pause while a delighted audience came to its senses and began to yelp its appreciation. The speaker stared at his script in unbelief.

"Why," he blurted, when he found his voice, "I **never** wrote anything like **that!**"   —W. C. in Business Week

SORCERY

Here's to woman: That fair magician who can turn a man into a donkey, and at the same time make him think he's a lion.

—Arthur L. Kaser

TURNING TURTLE

Once upon a time two large turtles and a little one went to a bar to quench their thirst with a mug of sarsaparilla. As they began to drink it, one of the large turtles commented that it was raining. After a lively discussion, it was decided that the little turtle should go home for their umbrella. The little turtle demurred, afraid that if he went the big turtles would drink his sarsaparilla. But they convinced the little fellow they would leave his sarsaparilla alone, and he started after the umbrella.

Three weeks passed, and finally one of the big turtles said: "Let's drink the little guy's sarsaparilla."

"I've been thinking the same thing," said the other, "so let's do it."

From down at the end of the bar near the door, a shrill voice cried: "If you do, I won't go after that umbrella."

—Capper's Weekly

MENTAL HAZARD

A farmer hired a hand and set him to chopping wood. In the middle of the morning the farmer went down to see how the hand was coming along. To his astonishment he found the wood all chopped. Next day the farmer told the man to stack the wood in the shed. This involved a lot of toting and the farmer figured the job would keep the man busy. But by noon he had it done.

On the third day the farmer, thinking he'd give the man a light job for a change, told him to sort out the potatoes in the bin. "Put the good ones in one pile, the doubtful in another, and throw out the rotten ones," said the farmer. An hour or so later he went back to see how the job was coming. He found the hired man passed out cold, with virtually nothing done. After throwing water in the man's face and bringing him around, the farmer demanded an explanation.

"Hell," the man said wearily, "it's making them decisions that's killing me."   —Reader's Digest

HOUSE ON FIRE

Two gentlemen, driving home after a convivial evening, came to a railroad crossing. The gate was down, and while they waited for it to rise they fell asleep. They were rudely awakened by the thunder of a passing express.

Rubbing his eyes, one man exclaimed, "Gosh! Wasn't that a well-lighted village we just passed through?"

"Sure was," replied the other, "and did you notice—the first house was on fire?"   —Adrian Anderson

IT'LL RUIN MY DAY

The farmer's wife died and somehow on the day of the funeral there was a shortage of cars. The funeral director asked the husband of the deceased if he would mind very much riding in the same car with his mother-in-law.

"All right," he muttered, "but it'll ruin my whole day."
          —Alben Barkley

INSTINCTS

Once when Henry Ward Beecher was in the midst of an impassioned flight of oratory, a drunken man in the balcony waved his arms and crowed like a rooster. Instantly Beecher stopped, took out his watch, and remarked: "What, morning already? I wouldn't have believed it, but the instincts of the lower animal are infallible."   —Edgar DeWitt Jones

NERVOUS HUSBAND

It happened in a maternity hospital. A nervous husband paced before the admission desk waiting to register his wife for immediate entrance. He fumbled and fidgeted. Finally he turned to the mother-to-be and asked earnestly: "Darling, are you sure you want to go through with this?"
          —Caravan

WHICH CHAPLAIN?

A reporter boarded the train carrying the Notre Dame team to the Southern Methodist game. Looking for a new slant on a story, he said to the student manager, "I understand that you carry a chaplain to pray for the team."

"That's right."

"Would you mind introducing me to him?"

"Be glad to. Which one do you want, the offensive chaplain or the defensive?" —KVP Philosopher

SECURITY

One day an Indian came into my father's bank in Oklahoma and asked about a loan.

"Me want $200."

"And what security have you?"

"Got 200 horses."

This seemed sufficient security, and the loan was made.

A short time afterward the Indian came back with $2,200 cash, paid off the note and started to leave with the rest of the roll in his pocket.

"Why not let me take care of that money for you?" my father suggested.

Looking Father straight in the eye, the Indian asked, "How many horses **you** got?" —Margie Shannon

GOING TO BITE

A woman who had been bitten by a dog was advised by her physician to write her last wishes, as she might soon succumb to hydrophobia. She spent so long with pencil and paper that the doctor finally asked whether it wasn't getting to be a pretty lengthy will.

"Will!" she snorted. "Nothing of the kind. I'm writing a list of the people I'm going to bite."

—Joseph W. Cochran

VERY MUCH AT SEA

A New York minister invited a contingent of Coast Guard Women's Reserve stationed near his church to a Sunday-evening service. Five hundred and fifty uniformed women marched in that night, settled down to hear a sermon on the life of Saint Paul. When the minister came to the shipwreck scene, he raised his arms dramatically and asked: "Have you ever considered how different the history of the world might now be had not Paul clung to a spar all night?"

The SPARs say the minister still doesn't know why they all broke out into gales of laughter.

—The Rev. Carl Bihldorff

EMPTY THEATRE

This happened in a crowded Hollywood theatre. A wild-eyed man rushed into the manager's office and brandishing a gun, shouted: "There's a man in your theatre with my wife, and I'm going to shoot him!"

While the manager was arguing with him, an assistant slipped quietly out of the office and made his way to the stage. There he called for attention and addressed the audience.

"There's a man in the theatre office with a gun who says he is going to shoot someone who came here with his wife. I'll dim the lights so this guilty couple can leave without being observed."

A few minutes elapsed and then the lights were turned on again. Half the theatre was empty!

—George A. Posner

A DREAM

The eighth Duke of Devonshire once told some friends: "The other night I dreamed that I was addressing the House of Lords. Then I woke up and, by God, I was!"

—Judge David Davies

MISSING THE TRAIN

The train was slowly starting to pull out when two bleary-eyed drunks staggered into the Hollywood railroad station, and madly began trying to board at one door all at once. They tried to help each other, and muddled and befuddled they only managed to tear each other's clothes off in the process. Finally the train, gathering speed, pulled out with two of the drunks aboard while the third, fallen on his fanny on the railroad platform, looked after it in utter dismay. A low, mournful moan came from his lips.

A bystander said sympathetically: "Cheer up! Anyway, two of you managed to get aboard."

"Oh me, oh my, that ain't it," moaned the drunk. "They came to see me off!"   —George A. Posner

ROSES

At a Sacramento garden club, the nurseryman who was speaking on roses stressed the benefit of an early mulch of well-rotted, old cow manure. During the question period a lady in the audience, who had been busily taking notes, raised her hand and earnestly inquired, "You said the bushes should be mulched with old cow manure. Would you mind telling me how old the cow should be?"

—Maybelle M. Ward

SEE ME NOW

A very large man and a smaller one had been long enough at the bar to reach the confidential stage. "Do you know," remarked the large one, "I weighed only three and a half pounds when I was born?"

"No!" said the small man incredulously. "And did you live?"

"Did I live? Boy! You should see me now!"

—R. Constantian

THE SOURCE OF JOY

To woman: That true source of our joys! The mother, the sister, the wife, the true, sympathetic friend! Without her the first man found the Garden of Eden but a desert; for her, kings have given up their thrones, generals have left their armies, and the course of empire has turned aside. When she ceases to exist, the human race will no longer survive. She is to man "the rainbow in his storms of life, the evening beam that smiles the clouds away and tints the morrow with prophetic ray!"   —James A. Cooper

WHO'S DRIVING?

Two thoroughly inebriated men were driving like mad in an automobile. "Shay," one fumbled his words, "be sure to turn out for that bridge that's comin' down the road toward us."

"What do you mean, me turn out?" the other retorted. "I thought you were drivin'."   —Donald MacGregor

CRIPPLED!

A drunk was walking along the curb with one foot on the sidewalk and the other in the gutter. A cop followed him for two blocks and then said, "Come along, buddy, and I'll help you home. You're drunk."

"Thank God!" said the drunk. "I thought I was a cripple."   —Harlan E. Read

HITTIN' MORE PEOPLE

Two men finished their drinks at the tavern, said good-bye to their friends and began the 40-mile drive to the city. After a while one of them observed, "We're gettin' closer to town."

"What makes you think so?" countered the other.

"Well," reasoned the first, "we're hittin' more people."   —Donald MacGregor

REWARDS OF LEARNING

A man will remain a ragpicker as long as he has only the vision of a ragpicker. We should have ambition to do our best, and refuse to accept our second best. Doing easy things does not tax us, neither does it challenge us. It is a good plan to tackle one hard job every day. If we do this, we will find that we have exercised our will power, our mind, and our body to good purpose. One of the rewards of learning to do hard things is the capacity for doing still harder things.

—Press Proofs

A PANE

Introducing a local pastor at a Kansas City meeting, the chairman apologized to the gathering for being unable to obtain the first two speakers invited. "I feel a little like a bundle of old rags stuffed in a broken windowpane," the minister remarked slyly as he started his lecture.

First to reach him at the conclusion of his talk was a little old lady who hastened to assure him, "Oh, Doctor, you're not old rags; you're a pane!"   —AP

HOMESICKNESS

A Russian who had managed to get across the Red border was being questioned and searched by the police in his new country.

"What's this?" the police asked, when they found a bottle of pills.

"Oh, that's for headaches," the Russian said.

"And what's this?" they asked about another bottle of pills.

"That's for toothaches."

They came to a picture of Malenkov and demanded, "But what's this?"

"That," said the Russian, "is for homesickness."

—Earl Wilson, Post-Hall Syndicate

RUSSIANS IN PARADISE

In Paris they tell about Malenkov reporting to Premier Stalin that it had just been verified that Adam and Eve were Russians.

"What if the Voice of America calls this merely propaganda when we announce it?" Stalin demanded. "What definite proof have we?"

"The best in the world," Malenkov replied. "Adam and Eve had no clothes. They had no dwelling. All they had to eat was apples—and they believed they were in Paradise. They must have been Russians."   —New York Times Magazine

TOGETHER AGAIN

The late Senator William Alden Smith of Michigan used to tell about the introduction he was accorded at a farmers' picnic in his home state. "Senator Smith will now talk for an hour," the chairman said, "after which the band will call you together again."   —G. Lynn Sumner

NO TIME TO THINK

At the Paris conference a reporter asked a hurrying diplomat what he thought about a certain international problem. "Don't bother me now," snapped the diplomat. "I must make a speech. This is no time to think."

—Walter Winchell

WEDDING CAKE

A health lecturer was enlarging on the dangers of certain foods. Pointing at a rather harassed-looking listener, he demanded: "What is it? We all eat it at some time or another, yet it's the worst thing in the world for us. Do you know?"

It appeared that the little man did know, for he replied in a husky whisper: "Wedding cake!"   —Montreal Star

HIS DEFINITION

The professor was endeavoring to give a definition of woman. After clearing his throat, he began: "Woman is, generally speaking . . ."

"Stop right there, professor," interrupted a low-brow; "if you talked a thousand years you'd never get any nearer to it than that."

The professor tried it again. "Woman is, generally speaking . . ."

"Yes, she generally is," murmured a poor married man in the front row. —Arthur L. Kaser

PLAYING SAFE

A young Philadelphia couple were recently married and immediately following the ceremony left for a honeymoon trip to northern Indiana. Here they decided to put up at a summer hotel for a while on the shore of one of Indiana's beautiful lakes. Upon their arrival there they employed a colored man to look after their luggage, the bridegroom giving him explicit instructions about removing all the labels from their trunks so that no one would know that they were newlyweds. He tipped the colored man generously to insure against that gentleman letting it leak out that they were just recently married.

Two or three days later, whenever the bride left her room she noticed that everyone rushed to get a view of her. She informed her husband of the guests' strange actions and he, thinking that the colored man had broken his word, called the latter to the carpet.

"Hones' to goodness, boss, I ain't tol' nobody a-tall dat you-uns was jes' married. De fac' am, boss, dat I tol' dem you-uns wasn't married a-tall, but was jes' good friends."

—Arthur L. Kaser

I WOULD RATHER

I would rather be toasted than roasted;
I would rather be patted than struck;
I would rather have cash when I need it,
Than to need it and just trust to luck.

I would rather be smiled at than laughed at;
I would rather have one friend than none;
I would rather be **buried,** a dead one,
Than live and be **classed** as one.

—Arthur L. Kaser

IT'S A GOOD DOG NOW

A minister in an eastern town usually preached for an hour at a time. Recently one of his sermons only lasted ten minutes. At the conclusion of the brief remarks he explained:

"Friends, I regret that I cannot say more this morning. My dog this morning playfully ate the portion of the sermon that I have not delivered. Let us pray."

After the service a man who was a member of another church shook hands with the minister and asked:

"If you please, sir, I would like to know whether that dog of yours has pups. If so, I want to get one for our minister."

—Arthur L. Kaser

PHILOSOPHY

Don't kick because you have to button your wife's waist. Be glad your wife has a waist, and doubly glad you have a wife to button a waist for. Some men's wives have no waists to button. Some men's wives' waists have no buttons on to button. Some men's wives' waists which have buttons on to button don't care a button whether they are buttoned or not. Some men don't have any wives with buttons on to button.

—Arthur L. Kaser

HOW LONG?

Woodrow Wilson was once asked how long he took to prepare a ten-minute speech. He said, "Two weeks."

"How long for an hour speech?"

"One week."

"How long for a two-hour speech?"

"I'm ready now."

—The Public Speaker's Treasure Chest

CAN'T AFFORD IT

George O'Brien's favorite story is about the two psychiatrists who met:

"You're fine," said one. "How am I?"

Then they got down to serious talk.

"I'm not feeling so well," said the first. "So could you give me a going over?"

"But you know the biz. Can't you diagnose yourself?"

"What! At the prices I charge? I can't afford it."

—George A. Posner

THREE VISITS

To my departed uncle: Who, the first time he went to church, had water thrown on him; who, the second time he went to church, had rice thrown on him; who, the third time he went to church, had dirt thrown on him.

—Arthur L. Kaser

GOOD BOSS

"A good boss is one who makes his men think they have more ability than they have, so they consistently do better work than they thought they could."   —Charles E. Wilson

THE FELLOW WHO'LL TAKE MY PLACE

Here is a toast that I want to drink to a fellow I'll never
know,
To the fellow who's going to take my place when it's time
for me to go.
I've wondered what kind of a chap he'll be and I've wished
I could take his hand,
Just to whisper, "I wish you well, old man," in a way he'd
understand.

I'd like to give him the cheering word that I've longed at
times to hear;
I'd like to give him the warm hand-clasp when never a friend
seems near.
I've learned my knowledge by sheer hard work, and I wish
I could pass it on
To the fellow who'll come to take my place some day when
I am gone.

Will he see all the sad mistakes I've made and note all the
battles lost?
Will he ever guess of the tears they caused or the heartaches
which they cost?
Will he gaze through failure and fruitless toil to the under-
lying plan,
And catch a glimpse of the real intent and the heart of the
vanquished man?

I dare to hope he may pause some day as he toils as I have
wrought,
And gain some strength for his weary task from the battles
which I have fought.
But I've only the task itself to leave with the cares for him
to face,
And never a cheering word may speak to the fellow who'll
take my place.

Then here's to your health, old chap; I drink as a bridegroom
  to his bride;
I leave an unfinished task for you, but God knows how I
  tried.
I've dreamed my dreams as all men do, but never a one
  came true,
And my prayer to-day is that all the dreams may be realized
  by you,

And we'll meet some day in the great unknown—out in the
  realm of space;
You'll know my clasp as I take your hand and gaze in your
  tired face.
Then all our failures will be success in the light of the new
  found dawn—
So I'm drinking your health, old chap, who'll take my place
  when I am gone.

—Author Unknown

HERE'S A ROCK

A little girl had been particularly naughty all day and her
exasperated mother finally sent her out in the back yard to get
a switch off the peach tree. Considerable time elapsed and the
child didn't return, so the mother called out the door for the
child to come into the house at once, and "bring that switch
with you." The youngster, her lips puckered and quivering,
meekly appeared with her hands behind her back.

"Well?" the mother said.

"I couldn't weach the peach tree," the child said, and then,
holding out one hand, added, "but here's a wock you can
frow at me."

—Tom Fesperman, Charlotte, N. C. News

LIKE A CLOCK

Here's to women: So much like a clock—pretty hands,
pretty face, pretty movement, and hard to regulate when they
get out of order.   —Arthur L. Kaser

RACE

The man in the witness chair, being instructed to tell the story in his own words, proceeded to do so, the tempo of his speech increasing by the minute. He grew hoarse, he started to perspire, he loosened his collar—but raced on, his sentences becoming less and less coherent. The court reporter, his fingers growing numb as he took down page after page, finally took a split second to glance at the man above him. The witness half rose and pointed a trembling finger at the reporter. "You!" he gasped. "Won't you stop a minute, please? I'm going to have to rest a little if I have to keep up with you!"

—Mary Alkus

IT LOOKED EXACTLY LIKE HER PENNY

The well-known president of a well-known university was walking along a well-known street in the well-known city of Boston, when his attention was attracted by a grubby little girl who was on her knees in the gutter, poking and scratching amongst the dead leaves which had accumulated at that particular point.

"What is the matter, little girl?" he asked.

The child raised a grimy tear-stained face to his and blubbered, "I've lost my p-p-penny."

"That's too bad," said the old gentleman as he too joined in the search, "but don't cry. We're sure to find it."

But they didn't. Their joint efforts were fruitless. The penny was not to be found.

"Never mind, little girl," said the kindly old man. And taking a penny from his pocket, he held it out to her. "Here is a penny."

The child straightened up and gazed at the coin in astonishment. Then, her cheeks crimson and anger blazing in her eyes, she snatched the penny from his hand.

"You durned old crook!" she yelled. "You had it all the time!"

—Arthur L. Kaser

THEN WHAT?

Mark Twain, in an after-dinner speech at a certain Wagnerian society, once said: "Gentlemen, lately I've been taking a great deal of interest in the works of Wagner. I've been to orchestra concerts to hear his music played. I've stayed at home to study his compositions in full score. The conclusion I've arrived at, gentlemen, is that Wagner's music is really not half so bad as it sounds."   —Arthur L. Kaser

TERRIFIC DATE!

"Terrific date last night," Fred told Bill at the office one morning. "Blonde. Really gorgeous. After the dance we went out and parked by the lake. I asked her for a kiss. She said she would if I'd put the top down so we could enjoy the moonlight. So I went to work and got the top down in about an hour and—"

"An hour?" Bill exclaimed. "I can get mine down in two minutes."

"Sure," replied Fred, "but **you** have a convertible!"
                      —R. W. Tupper in Reader's Digest

TAXES

Henry Suburban is aroused in the morning by his alarm clock (price $6, plus $1.32 tax). He walks across the floor of his $8,000 house (annual property tax $240) and switches on the electricity ($3\frac{1}{2}$c tax on each dollar of his monthly bill) which lights the bulb (price 20c, plus 2c tax). Hardly a thing Henry touches is not taxed: cuff links (price $3.50, plus 77c tax), toaster (price $20.50, plus $1.74 tax), refrigerator (price $300, plus $25.52), cigarette (price per pack 10c, plus 7c federal tax, plus 4c state tax). Even Henry's wife, whom he kisses good-by, cost Henry a $2 marriage license, to say nothing of the tax on the lipstick he wipes off.   —Press Proofs.

SOUNDS ALL RIGHT

A wedding party was disturbed by the crying of a baby belonging to one of the women guests. One of the young ladies present remarked to the bridesmaid, "What a nuisance babies are at a wedding!"

"I should say so," returned the latter, and added without very full consideration, "When I send out the invitations to my wedding I shall have printed in the corner, 'No babies expected.' "   —Printing Trade News

ANOTHER VERSION OF IT

An automobile dashed along the country road. Turning a curve, it came suddenly upon a man with a gun on his shoulder and a weak, sick-looking dog beside him. The dog was directly in the path of the motor car. The chauffeur sounded his horn, but the dog did not move until he was struck. After that he did not move.

The automobile stopped and one of the men got out and came forward. He had once paid a farmer ten dollars for killing a dog that belonged to another farmer. This time he was wary.

"Was that your dog?" he asked.

"Yes."

"Looks as if we killed him."

"Reckon on how it looks thata way."

"Very valuable dog?"

"Not so very."

"Will five dollars satisfy you?"

"Yes."

"Well, then, here you are." He handed a five-dollar bill to the man with the gun and added pleasantly, "I'm sorry to have broken up your hunt."

"I wasn't goin' huntin'," replied the other as he pocketed the bill. "I was just goin' down to the woods to shoot the dog."

—Arthur L. Kaser

SATISFACTORY EXPLANATION

The accountant who always made out Mr. Bungleton's income-tax reports looked coldly at his client and said: "My dear sir, will you kindly explain this one claim for deduction—nearly $800 for repainting the front attic window of your house?"

"Well," replied Bungleton, "I thought I could do the job myself. And I was doing fine until a gust of wind started the ladder to skidding. Then I dropped the paint bucket and grabbed for the window sill. But the paint bucket happened to land upside down on a cute little blonde girl that works as a secretary. She was wearing a new fur coat, and said I'd have to buy her another—or she'd sue me. I took her into the furrier's and was buying her a new one, but a friend of my wife's happened to see me. By the time I got home, my wife was at the lawyer's. And I had to pay him another $50 for calling the divorce off . . . Does that clear everything up?"

—Wall Street Journal

LAPLANDER

It was rush hour and the subway car was jammed. A big, blond giant of a man, hanging carelessly onto a strap, lost his balance when the car jerked, landing squarely in a forbidding-looking woman's lap. Before he could apologize, she blurted indignantly, "You! You big Swede!"

"Lady, I'm not a Swede," he replied calmly. "I'm a Laplander!"   —F. L. Hower in Reader's Digest

WOMAN'S WORLD

When a man is born, people ask, "How is the mother?" When he marries, they exclaim, "What a lovely bride!" And when he dies, they inquire, "How much insurance did he leave her?"

—Northwestern Mutual Life Insurance Bulletin

RATHER ODD

A woman approached a famous psychiatrist and said, "I do wish you'd see my husband. He blows smoke rings through his nose and it frightens me."

"I see nothing wrong with that," said the doctor. "I don't know that it's so terribly unusual for someone to blow smoke rings through his nose."

"But," complained the woman, "my husband doesn't smoke!"   —Howie Lasseter

DODGER FAN?

The patient was being carefully questioned by the skilled psychoanalyst. "What do you dream about at night?"

"Baseball."

"Don't you dream about anything else?"

"Nope, just about baseball, night after night."

The analyst was extremely puzzled. "Don't you ever dream about women?" he asked.

"What? And miss my turn at bat!"   —Stan West

THAT'S ONCE

When anyone asked my grandfather the secret of his 50 years of serene married life, he always told this story:

Right after our wedding, we started out to my ranch, with Jenny up behind me on the mare. Suddenly the mare stumbled. "That's once," I said. After a while she stumbled again. "That's twice," I said. And a few miles later on she stumbled the third time. "That's three times," I said, and put Jenny down on the ground, pulled out my gun and shot the mare dead.

Jenny got sore because I had killed a perfectly good horse, and she read the riot act, real mad.

I waited until she was completely unwound. Then I said, "That's once."   —Helen Peters in True

CREDIT

A department store had been sending out duns for several months to one customer who owed a lot of money and who, apparently, had no intention of paying. Finally, in desperation, the store threatened to turn his account over to a collection agency.

A few days later, the store received a reply from the man: "If I'm still alive, you'll have your money one week from today."

When the week passed and no money was forthcoming, the store inserted this death notice in the local paper: "John Johnson died today at his home in this city. Funeral arrangements later. Please omit flowers."

The next day Mr. Johnson arose from the dead and walked into the store. He paid his bill in full.   —Press Proofs.

CURIOUS

A mild little man walked into the local internal-revenue office, sat down, and beamed on everyone in sight.

"What can we do for you?" asked the collector.

"Nothing, thank you," replied the little man. "I just wanted to meet the people I'm working for."   —Cape Argus

MIGHTY POPULAR

There was a sad incident one day in the heart of the Ozark Mountains. A farmer's mule kicked his mother-in-law to death. A tremendous crowd turned out for the funeral, but it was made up almost entirely of men. The minister commented, "This old lady must have been mighty popular because so many people have left their work to come to her funeral."

"They're not here for the funeral," explained the farmer. "They're here to buy the mule."   —Kroehler News

ROUNDABOUT WAY

At a concert in Detroit, quarters were decidedly cramped and the late, beloved Madame Ernestine Schumann-Heink, as soloist, had to make her entrance from the rear, down thru the orchestra with its maze of music stands. All went well until she came to the orchestra where her familiarly large proportions began knocking over music racks.

"Go sideways, Madame," said Conductor Gabrilowitsch, in an excited stage whisper.

Ernestine wrinkled her brow, gave a puzzled look from left to right, and called back to the conductor in a hoarse whisper:

"Himmel! I **have** no sideways!"   —Press Proofs.

JUST FOR LAUGHS

A woman came into the millinery department of Harold's department store in Minneapolis recently and tried on all the frothy, giddy bonnets she could find. Finally Miss Grace Benson, the buyer of the department, asked: "Did you find anything you liked?"

"I didn't come in to buy," replied the customer, "I just came in for laughs."

—Cedric Adams in Minneapolis Sunday Tribune

HOW TO RUN MY BUSINESS

I'm standin' on da corner minding my own business when a bum comes up to me and snarls: "Gimme a buck!"

So I ups ta him and says: "Whadda you mean a buck?" And he says, "You heard me, buddy." And I says, "Look! If you ast me for a dime or a quarter—or a half a dollar, even—but a buck! You must be outa your mind!"

And then the bum says, "Get this, buddy, you can cough up the buck or not—that's up to you—**but don't try to tell me how to run my business!**"   —Jimmy Durante

EVERYBODY OFF!

I'm lyin' on the park bench takin' my siesta—as is my wont
—when along comes a bunch of flies and settles on my nose.
I lets 'em loiter—live and let live is my motter.

Den a bee comes along—lights on my nose and stings me.
"Dat does it!" I says. "Dere's always gotta be a smart aleck in
every crowd. Now—just for that—EVERYBODY OFF!"

—Jimmy Durante

LONG SWIM

John Carmichael, the Chicago baseball writer, tells the
story about a woman who divorced her husband and obtained
custody of their 12-year-old son. When she remarried after a
year or so, her ex-husband was somewhat concerned about the
boy. "How do you get along with your stepfather?" he asked
the lad the first chance he got.

"Fine," said the youngster. "He takes me swimming every
morning. We go out to the lake, and he rows me out to the
middle, and then I swim back in."

"Isn't that a pretty long swim for a boy your age?" asked
the father.

"Not too bad. Really, the only tough part of it is getting
out of the sack."

—Joe H. Palmer in New York Herald Tribune

NOT TOO CAREFUL

I was hitchhiking along a country road in Wisconsin when
an automobile stopped with four elderly women in it. One of
the ladies rolled down the back window and asked me if I
were a burglar or a hijacker. When I assured her that I was
neither, she opened the door and let me in. "I hope you didn't
mind my questioning you," she said. "You know, one can't be
too careful these days."

—Fred A. Risser in Reader's Digest

RELAX

Four years ago an old gentleman who probably never drove an automobile in his life taught me a motoring lesson I'll never forget. In my first car, a stripped-down roadster, I raced up to a stop light just as he started to cross. He jumped back in alarm as I screeched to a stop and I called out, "Relax, Pop. I missed you, didn't I?"

Angrily but with dignity the old man strode to my car, lifted his cane and swung it at my head. I easily dodged the blow. "Hey, take it easy!" I cried.

"Now, **you** just relax, son," he replied. "I missed you, didn't I?" As he went on across the street he turned to remark more kindly, "Worry counts for something, my boy."

—Richard F. Toob in Reader's Digest

HOW MUCH?

My uncle, helping a farmer prepare his tax return, examined his ledger. There were no debit or credit columns, but instead the entries read: "Sold eggs $2.68" or "Bought feed $16.92." Most of the items were easy to interpret, but one reading simply "Horse $10" stumped my uncle. "Did you buy the horse for ten dollars or sell him?" he asked.

"Well," said the farmer, "it's like this: I bought that ornery animal for ten dollars. He right away kicked down two stalls, and that cost ten dollars. Then I used him to pull a car out of a mud rut, and got paid ten dollars. Once I sold him for ten dollars, but he caused such a peck of trouble that I bought him back for ten dollars. I used him to take some kids for a ride, and they gave me ten dollars. Finally the fool horse wandered into the road, and a guy hit him and killed him. He paid me ten dollars, but I had to turn around and pay ten dollars to have the carcass hauled away. And you know," said the farmer, "I must of lost track somewhere, 'cause I can't figure whether that durn horse ended up owing me or me owing him."

—Helen T. Morrison in Reader's Digest

GULLIBLE GULLS

In our friendly neighbor city of St. Augustine great flocks of sea gulls are starving amid plenty. Fishing is still good, but the gulls don't know how to fish. For generations they have depended on the shrimp fleet to toss them scraps from the nets. Now the fleet has moved to Key West.

The shrimpers had created a Welfare State for the St. Augustine sea gulls. The big birds never bothered to learn how to fish for themselves and they never taught their children to fish. Instead they led their little ones to the shrimp nets.

Now the sea gulls, the fine free birds that almost symbolize liberty itself, are starving to death because they gave in to the "something for nothing" lure! They sacrificed their independence for a handout.

A lot of people are like that, too. They see nothing wrong in picking delectable scraps from the tax nets of the U. S. Government's "shrimp fleet." But what will happen when the Government runs out of goods? What about our children of generations to come?

Let's not be gullible gulls. We Americans must preserve our talents of self-sufficiency, our genius for creating things for ourselves, our sense of thrift and our true love of independence.

—The Barnett National Bank of Jacksonville, Fla.

HELPLESS HUSBAND

Two women were discussing their husbands in that indulgent tone appropriate to the subject. "Henry is perfectly helpless without me," said one. "I don't know what would become of him if I went away for a week."

"John, too," sighed the other. "The way I have to look after that man! Why, whenever he sews on buttons or darns his socks, I always have to thread the needle for him."

—Balance Sheet

FREEDOM'S THE KEY

When you must choose between two contrary courses of action, look carefully at each one in turn, and ask yourself this question: "Will it increase or diminish the freedoms of my fellow men?" If it offers to enlarge the scope of individual freedom, then it can never be the wrong course, because whatever else may be its weakness, it is leading, at least, in the right direction. But if it would curtail your freedom—even in the smallest degree—then it can never be the right course; because no matter how far and how fast it may help you to travel, you will only be running the ball towards the wrong goal.

—Benjamin F. Fairless,
Chairman of the Board, U. S. Steel

EXAGGERATION

The old colonel's weakness was exaggeration. One evening at the general store he was talking about his wonderful bull, Jeff Davis. "Ol' Jeff delights to race that new streamlined train," he said. "Every mawnin' he waits at the no'th end of the back forty and races it to the south fence. Beats it every time."

A doubter interrupted: "I'm laying $100 that he can't do it, and I'll be over in the morning to see for myself—with witnesses."

Honor at stake, the colonel covered the wager.

Next morning the doubter and his witnesses turned up at daybreak. The colonel was nowhere to be seen, and a hired man informed the delegation: "Cun'l just phoned me from Washington—he's up there on Gov-ment business."

"He couldn't be," scoffed the doubter. "The trains don't run that fast. How'd he get there?"

"Cun'l tol' me," the hired man replied solemnly, "he rode ol' Jeff."   —Lillington, N. C., Harnett County News.

DIRTY WINDOW

A husband said to his wife, "Have you heard the story about the dirty window?"

"No," she replied.

"Well," he said, "you couldn't see through it anyway."

His wife asked a friend later, "Have you heard the story about the window you couldn't see through?"

"No," said her friend.

"Oh, well," said the wife, "it's too dirty to tell anyway."

—Chuck Acree, MBS

JUST BEING TACTFUL

The veteran bellhop was briefing a new man on the routine of his job. "Above all, always be polite and use tact," instructed the older man.

"I get the polite stuff, but explain the 'tact,'" said the younger.

"Well, now, I'll give you an example. One day I happened to open a door and there was a lady sitting in the bathtub. I shut the door quickly and said, 'Beg your pardon, sir.' The 'beg your pardon' was just politeness, but the 'sir' . . . that was tact."

—Snap Shots

THE HAPPY MAN

If you observe a really happy man, you will find him building a boat, writing a symphony, educating his son, growing double dahlias, or looking for dinosaur eggs in the Gobi desert. He will not be searching for happiness as if it were a collar button that had rolled under the radiator, striving for it as the goal itself. He will have become aware that he is happy in the course of living his life twenty-four hours each day.

—Press Proofs

TOO MANY HANDS

It is recorded that Emperor Frederick the Great, King of Prussia, had a difficult time, as all government heads do, in balancing his country's budget. On one occasion he gave a banquet, inviting persons of note to discuss the situation. He explained his dilemma, and asked how it came about that, altho the taxes were high, not enough money was on hand to meet expenses.

At last an old general, seated at the other end of the long banquet table, arose and fished a large lump of ice from his punch bowl. He held the ice in his hand for a moment, then passed it on to his neighbor, and asked that it be passed from hand to hand until it reached the emperor.

This was done, and by the time the lump of ice reached Emperor Frederick, it was reduced to the size of a small walnut. The general sat down. The lesson was obvious—there were too many hands in the government.   —Press Proofs

WRONG NUMBER

The husband and wife were having breakfast, the former ensconced behind the newspaper.

"You had a very restless night, dear," said his wife, "and what's more, you kept murmuring a woman's name in your sleep. Now who is Daisy?"

"Oh—er," he stammered, "the fact is, my dear, Daisy is a filly I backed yesterday. It won, ten to one and here is your share." He handed his wife five dollars, and hid himself once more behind his newspaper. In the evening, when he returned to dinner, his wife once more returned to the attack.

"By the way, dear," she said, "you know that horse you backed yesterday? . . ."

"Yes," he grunted.

"Well," she continued, "she rang you up on the phone this afternoon."   —Montreal Star

A SILLY QUESTION GETS A SILLY ANSWER

At the dinner given by President Syngman Rhee of Korea for President Eisenhower, Dr. Howard Rusk, professor of rehabilitation and physical medicine at New York university, told the story of the two farm boys who were puzzled by fingerbowls at their first dinner in a swank city hotel.

"Can't be for drinking because we got a glass of water right here," said the first farm boy. "Let's ask the waiter."

The second farm boy protested that questioning such a rigid character would lead to no good, but the first farm boy insisted and posed his question.

"That, sir, is a bowl of tepid water for washing one's fingers should they be soiled during the course of the repast," said the waiter haughtily. "After washing the extremities are dried on the serviette."

"See, what did I tell you?" the second farm boy observed. "You ask a silly question and you get a silly answer."

—Chicago Tribune

JUST LIKE A HUSBAND!

Everyone in the office was curious when the elderly new employe asked everyone to just call him "Lucky." They held back for a while, but eventually he was asked how he came to have the nickname "Lucky."

"Back some 15 years ago," he answered, "my wife and I were living in our 21-room mansion overlooking the Gulf of Mexico. One day while I was away from home a violent storm came up and blew my house and my wife away."

"How awful," one of the listeners exclaimed.

"Then your nickname is one of irony," another ventured.

"On the contrary," he laughed. "With the house gone I was able to get my homemade cabin boat out of the basement workshop. It had been bothering me for years!"

—Wall Street Journal

SWITCHED

(When speakers or the program has been changed around)

Patrick Murphy's cat became such a pest to the neighbors, howling the whole night through, that Maggie Murphy ordered Pat to dispose of it. "Do it gently," said Maggie. So Pat took the cat to the basement and chloroformed the animal. Then he wrapped the carcass in a clean piece of paper. "Take it down, town," said Maggie, "and when you come to the river bridge, throw it over the railing."

"Sure and I will," said Pat, and he was on his way.

As Pat was strolling down the street, the wrapped cat tucked under his arm, he met his next door neighbor, Dennis O'Keefe, in front of Casey's tavern.

"Sure and if it ain't me neighbor, Murphy," said O'Keefe.

"And sure if it ain't O'Keefe," said Murphy. "Let's go into Casey's and have one."

O'Keefe also had a bundle under his arm, and the two men entered the tavern, where they placed their respective bundles on the bar.

"Here's to your future success," said Murphy, adding, "By the way, Dennis, what have you got in that package?"

"What have I got?" said O'Keefe. "I've got the finest ham that ever came out of Brady's butcher shop. We are going to have a feast tonight—boiled ham and cabbage. I see you also have a bundle, Pat."

"Sure, and it's a package I'm going to deliver for Maggie," said Murphy.

Further reference to the bundles was not brought up, and the men lingered at the bar. After about an hour or so O'Keefe said, "Well, Murphy, I must be gettin' along. The old lady is waitin' for the ham."

Then each man picked up a package and departed—Murphy towards the bridge, and O'Keefe to his home.

When Pat returned home, he heard a horrible commotion going on over at O'Keefe's house. "What in the devil is goin' on over there?" Pat said to Maggie.

"They're havin' a fight. Mrs. O'Keefe has been raving like a mad woman for the past half hour. She keeps on yellin' somethin' about a cat."

"Well, let other people fight their own battles," said Pat. And then with a cunning look in his eyes he added, "Maggie, I brought you a present."

"You brought me a present! What is it?"

Pat looked in the direction of the O'Keefe house and then with a chuckle said: "The finest ham that ever came out of Brady's butcher shop!"   —Horton Smith

FRANK CRITICISM

About five years ago I was selected to give an eulogy on the life of a very dear friend of mine, George Gray, who died suddenly. It was a civic memorial ceremony, held several days after the good man's funeral.

Practically every one in town was present, and speaker after speaker got up and gave short preludes on George's good deeds during his lifetime. As I was the principal speaker, my talk naturally was of some length. I had spent a great number of hours in preparation and rehearsal, as I wanted to do justice to both George and to myself before such a distinguished and vast audience.

It took me over an hour to make my full delivery, which nearly exhausted my strength, as the evening was warm. When I had concluded and had stepped down from the podium, I was greeted by a number of my friends with warm hand clasps and congratulations. After I had accepted a number of these felicitations with gratitude, I noticed that my dear friend, Walter Bellows, stood apart from the group.

I walked over to him and said, "Walter, how did you like my talk?"

"Bill," he said, stroking his chin meditatively, "it would have been much better if you'd have died and George Gray had given the eulogy."   —Robert Eaton

IF I HAD KNOWN

If I had known the burden that you bore
That morning when I met you on the street,
Could I have seen beneath the smile you wore
That cloudy day when first we chanced to meet.

I should have quite forgot the cares I had
And given you a cheery word to make you glad.
If I had known your heart was aching so
With loneliness and yearning for a friend,
And known what road, alone, you had to go,
Had dreamed what bit of gladness I might lend,
I would have been the help I meant to be
If I had really known you needed me.

Had I but known God led you there that day
To wait for me, that I might ease your pain
And walk with you, a mile along the way.
Until you felt your load grow light again.
Then would my blinded eyes be made to see,
If I had known you counted so on me.

—Author Unknown

GIVE HIM CREDIT FOR TRYING

"Here's the latest news from Russia," announced the American sportscaster. "A Russian made an endurance run of 100 miles in the fantastic time of 24 hours. To top it off, he ran over rough fields, through streams and through dense woodland. It was as much an obstacle run as it was an endurance run."

The radio audience was astounded by the news as the announcer paused for a few seconds to let the statement sink in.

"But," he resumed, "the run was made in vain. He was caught and returned to Russia."   —Wall Street Journal

IN KALAMAZOO

(When someone fails to answer a question or tries to evade an issue.)

It would appear to me that John is beating it around the bush tonight. I have asked him several times to explain just exactly what his proposal is, and I'm afraid that he is giving us nothing but double talk. This reminds me of the story of a beautiful young lady, blonde of course, who attended a formal dinner in her honor at one of the best golf clubs in the northern part of our state. The men were in full dress and the ladies were all in evening formals, with bare arms and swishing gowns. The young lady was seated beside the chairman, who lost no time in picking up a conversation with such a beauty.

"It certainly is a pleasure to sit along side of you this evening, Miss Clausen," said the chairman in a patronizing tone of voice.

"The pleasure is all mine," the girl responded, reaching out her lovely bare arm to pick up an olive. "But I nearly missed the dinner," she added.

"Is that so?" said the chairman, inching over to her.

"Yes, I was vaccinated several days ago, and I've had quite a time of it."

The chairman looked again at the girl's snow-white arms, and scrutinizing every inch of those graceful contours, curiously asked, "Where were you vaccinated?"

Miss Clausen dropped her eyelids and demurely replied: "In Kalamazoo." —Fuller Marlow

HOMEMADE

A group of tiny tots were overheard discussing their arrival in this big world. The versions differed somewhat. Billy claimed that his folks had bought him in a department store; Tommy said the stork brought him; Diane said the doctor had brought her. Then a very tiny miss piped up, but rather modestly, "My folks were too poor to buy me; I was homemade." —Bindery Talk

TRAIN PULLS OUT

To this day there's one thing that disturbs Senator Claghorn. One election year some time ago, he had been giving a rousing oration on the value of soybeans to the city folk on the back platform of the train which had stopped in Paducah. He was just getting warmed up and had finished a particularly searing statement against his opponent, when all of a sudden, with a creak and a groan, the train started to pull out of the station. This set off a tumult of roaring and yelling from the assembled crowd.

The Senator has been trying to figure out ever since . . . was the applause for him . . . or was it for the engineer?

—Roger Hart

DIDN'T HEAR A WORD

(When someone is singing or a band is playing in an adjoining room.)

The music that is being played at the meeting down the hall is very lovely, but at a time like this when we have some important matters to bring up in our gathering, it is also distracting. It reminds me of Heck Walters from Montana, who made his first trip east last summer. Heck took in all of the sights down east and was amazed at what he saw in the big city.

A tour through the campus of one of the colleges was on Heck's itinerary. Heck strolled along the walks that twined about the ivy-covered buildings, until he came to the college chapel where chimes were pealing out a melodious hymn. As Heck's ears by training were tuned only to a two-note clang of the bell on Great Northern number ten that passed through his town twice a day, he was amazed at the variations of tones in the chapel bells. As he stood there craning his neck at the tower from which the melody was bursting forth, the rector of the chapel walked up and greeted him.

"My good man," said the rector. "I see that you are enjoying the heavenly messages of our bells. It is a great consolation to stand here beneath this ivory tower and receive these spiritual blessings. Doesn't it appear to you that those lilting notes, lingering momentarily on the leaf of ivory and then flitting away through the quiet summer air, are as realistic as if the heavenly angels were up there speaking to you in the vibrating tones of ethereal music? Don't you agree to that, my good man?"

Heck lowered his craned neck and turning to the rector said: "Sorry, but those damn bells were making so much noise, I didn't hear a word you said." —Horton Smith

APRIL FOOL

Little Tommy Tucker was playing nimbly around the house, while his mother was busy in the kitchen, helping to get together the family dinner. Suddenly little Tommy dashed into the kitchen calling excitedly in a piping voice, "Mother! Mother! Come, quick! There's a strange man in the dining-room kissing the maid!"

Mother Tucker wiped her hands on her apron and made a hurried exit out of the kitchen. Just as she was in the proximity of the dining-room, little Tommy squealed again, "April Fool! It's only Dad!" —Horton Smith

WHO WAS HE?

The Sunday-school class was composed of three-year-olds. The teacher asked: "Do any of you remember who St. Matthew was?" No answer.

"Well, who was St. Mark?" Still no answer.

"Surely someone must remember who Peter was?"

The little faces were full of interest, but the room was quiet. Finally, a tiny voice came from the back of the room.

"I fink he was a wabbit." —Bindery Talk

MARVELOUS JOB

(When someone is holding back some information)

Gentlemen, I feel that Bill is holding something back, that he has more information to give us, but for some reason or other he has elected to keep it secret. This recalls to my mind a story about a lawsuit that took place some years ago against a railroad.

At a certain railroad crossing, which was attended by watchman Patrick O'Flannigan, a serious accident happened when an automobile crashed into an oncoming train.

The matter came up later in the courts when the owner of the automobile brought suit against the railroad company. After other evidence pertaining to the matter had been placed before the court, the attorney for the railroad company called watchman Flannigan to the witness stand. When Patrick had completed his testimony he was greeted as he left the witness chair by the attorney for the railroad company, who ushered him into the hallway, where he extended congratulations to watchman O'Flannigan.

"You certainly did a marvelous job, Pat, in describing how you stood at the crossing, waving your lantern. It saved the day for us."

"Well," said Pat, "I was gittin' over the wavin' part all right, but I was scared out of me wits that that attorney was goin' to ask me if me lantern was lit."

—Karl Kirsten

BUOYISH

The two starlets watched as the aging actor noted for his vanity swam far out from the shore.

"Gee," said one, "he's taking quite a chance for an old man."

"Listen," said the other, "with his swelled head and inflated ego he wouldn't be any safer with water wings."

—Wall Street Journal

PLUG FOR HIS BUSINESS

(The chairman remarks after a speaker throws in a few plugs for his own business.)

That was a very fine talk, Bill. I am sure that all of us enjoyed it immensely, especially the part about your store, which reminds me of the six-year-old boy who went to church for the first time accompanied by his father. The lad was an ardent devotee of television, and he was well acquainted with the procedure of a television program, having spent the greater portion of his waking hours squatting before the screen.

"Well, son," said the father. "How did you like the church services?"

The lad thought for a moment and then replied: "The music was okay, but the commercial was too long."

(Pause.)

Well, it would be too much to expect Bill to overlook such a good opportunity as this to put in a plug for his business.

—Hillary Williams

A TABLE GROANS

Robin Hart, the Globe's new reporter, was an exceptional reporter. He had picked up the tricks of the newspaper profession rather rapidly. Because of his precocity he constantly was under the scrutiny of the city editor who delighted in catching young Hart in a mistake, although he rarely did so.

"About the story of last night's banquet," sternly asked the editor, "you wrote it, didn't you, Hart?"

"Yes, I did," replied the cub.

"What about this expression in the story," said the editor, "'the banquet table groaned?' It's pretty difficult to hear a banquet table groan, isn't it?"

Shot back young Hart, "I don't think so, sir, those stories the after-dinner speakers told would make any table groan."

—Roger Hart

FAMINE AND ITS CAUSE

(Use on two fellows, one fat and one thin, who are friends and who are in the audience.)

On my way here tonight I met Bill Jones and Jack Smith, standing in the outer hall, engaged in a conversation. Bill, as all of you people know, is a man of considerable girth, while Jack Smith is very much of an attenuated fellow, ten pounds lighter than a straw hat. As I was hurrying through the hall, I heard Bill say to Jack: "To look at you, Jack, one would think that there was a famine in the country."

To which Jack replied: "And to look at you, Bill, one would think that you were the cause of it."

—Horton Smith

IT PAYS TO ADVERTISE

One day last week I picked up a copy of our local news— The Blade—and much to my annoyance a spider was crawling across the pages. I said to my wife, "Mary, what does Bill Jones, the publisher of The Blade, mean by permitting a spider to be delivered to our house with his newspaper?"

"I don't know," said my wife unconcerned, adding, "It appears to be a trivial matter."

"Trivial matter, nothing. It's an omen of bad luck," I replied. "I am going to write Bill a letter, asking for an explanation." Which I did.

A few days later I received a reply from the publisher which read as follows: "Finding a spider in your newspaper is not necessarily a sign of bad luck. You most likely noticed, if you followed the actions of the spider on the newspaper page, that it swiftly ran across it, looking for a merchant who does not advertise in our paper. You probably noticed also that the spider suddenly vanished. The explanation is that the spider hurriedly went to the store of a non-advertiser, where he spun a web across the front door, and thereby will live an undisturbed life ever after."

—William Powell

HEAD SHOT OFF

**(When someone keeps jumping to his feet,
offering objections or complaints.)**

During the course of the meeting Jack Owens has been on his feet half of the time, objecting to this and objecting to that. While on the other hand we haven't heard a word from Bill Smith. He has been as quiet as a mouse. The conduct of these two gentlemen this evening reminds me of an incident that happened in the Pacific during the last war.

Patrick O'Flannigan, Michael O'Toole and Terry O'Keefe were in the same infantry company. During the heat of a battle a Jap shell came over the lines and took off Mike O'Toole's arm. Mike went running to Pat O'Flannigan and cried out: "Pat, Oi've had me arm shot off!"

Pat looked at Mike and said: "Quit you're bellyaching! Look at Terry up on the hill. He had his head shot off and he ain't saying a word." —Kirk Kirsten

HOW DO YOU DO IT?

Last spring I had the honor of making the principal talk before the graduating class of Roseville High School. It was a momentous occasion for me, and I really put it on for the youngsters. I presented a sure-fire formula for the success in life of every young man and young woman who has completed a course in high school study. I said, "Young men and young women, I am a self-made man. What I have done you can do. But remember this—there is one faculty that is absolutely necessary for success in life—and that is pluck. What I am today, and what I hope to be tomorrow depends upon one thing. And what is that one thing? That one thing, my young people, is pluck, pluck and more pluck! That, boys and girls, is my secret which I pass onto you free of charge."

From the back of the auditorium a young voice called out: "Tell us how and whom to pluck." —Jack Cosgrove

SMART CHICKENS

This report, recently smuggled from behind the iron curtain, has to do with a trio of Soviet chicken farm managers. Summoned before a checker-upper from Moscow the first man was asked what he fed the chickens.

Smiling happily he replied, "Corn, sir."

"Corn!" roared the brass. "Off to Siberia with you! Corn is used to feed people."

And as the unhappy farmer was dragged away the government man asked the same question of the second manager. Trying to avoid the trap he answered, "We feed our chickens cornhusks, sir."

He, too, was arrested. Cornhusks were used, it seemed, to make cloth.

"And you?" he asked the third man. "Me? Oh, I just give the chickens the money and tell 'em to go buy their own food." —Wall Street Journal

BUSINESS IS BUSINESS

The clergyman felt annoyed to find that an old gentleman fell asleep during the sermon on two consecutive Sundays. So after service finally he asked the boy who accompanied the sleeper into the vestry:

"My boy, who is that elderly gentleman you attend church with?"

"Grandpa."

"Well, if you will keep him awake during my sermon I'll give you five cents each week."

For the next two weeks the old gentleman was attentive to the sermon. The third week, however, found him soundly asleep again.

The vexed clergyman sent for the boy. "Didn't you promise to keep him awake if I paid you five cents a week?"

"Yes, but Grandpa now gives me a dime not to disturb him." —Montreal Star

GETTING OFF LIGHT

(When a speaker dresses down someone at the meeting—or a member is criticized for something or other.)

I imagine that John feels that we have ganged up on him tonight because so many of us have dressed him down for his report on the activities of his committee. Apparently in the opinion of most of us here, John is somewhat in the position of the darky down South who was being lynched. In the minds of the citizens of this Southern town, this darky was guilty of a crime of great magnitude, so a masked band captured the man and rushed him out in the darkness of the night to an isolated pine on a mountain top.

After the ceremonies were duly performed and the colored man was swaying from a rope in the cool mountain breeze, the leader of the mob heard a rustle in the bushes nearby. Hurrying over to the thicket, he extracted a dark, scared-to-death fellow, whose white eyeballs stood out like two phosphorous moons in the blackness.

The leader of the mob grabbed the darky by the neck and shook him until his head was vibrating in conjunction with the chattering of his knees.

"What did you see?" asked the leader of the mob, placing a gun against the man's shaking ribs.

"I'se done seen nothing," said the trembling darky.

"Are you sure you didn't?" asked the leader of the mob.

"I'se positive," answered the darky.

"Now see here," said the leader, again placing the muzzle of his gun against the fellow's ribs, "Don't you think that man up there hanging on that rope got just what was coming to him?"

The terrified darky looked up at the corpse swinging from the tree and in a paroxysm of fear said, "He's a gettin' off light."

(Pause.)

So perhaps John is getting off light.

—Hillary Williams

YESTERDAY DOESN'T COUNT

Some time ago the firm with which I am associated put on a strenuous sales drive. Every one in the organization participated, as we wanted to show Old Man Cockle, our president, that he had an up-to-date fighting bunch of employees.

One Thursday afternoon we gathered around the sales-manager's desk to count up the score of Wednesday's sales. There was a smile of victory on every one's face for it looked as if we had run up a record.

"By George, if we didn't," yelled the salesmanager, as he jumped to his feet waving a tabulation of yesterday's sales.

"I'll wire old man Cockle!" I said enthusiastically.

"Go ahead," said the salesmanager. "Give him the good news."

I immediately dictated the following wire to old man Cockle: "Sales soared to a new high yesterday, all previous records shattered."

Then we sat around the office, holding post mortems, praising this man's work and that man's ingenuity, and also wondering what old man Cockle would say when he got the telegram.

"We ought to be hearing soon," I said to the salesmanager.

"We certainly should," he replied.

Suddenly a Western Union boy came in the front door waving a telegram. Every one jumped from his seat to get the message. I got there first, and the boy handed me the telegram. It was from old man Cockle all right.

"What does it say?" chorused a group of employees.

"Hurry up, read it!" yelled the salesmanager.

Nervously I tore open the yellow envelope, held the message up to the light and read old man Cockle's reply which tersely asked, "What have you done today?"

—Jack Cosgrove

AD BRINGS ACTION

Two years ago I was on a tour of some of the small towns in the northern part of the state, covering an extensive speaking engagement. As it was necessary for me to be away for some time, I took my dog, Blackie, along. I was deeply attached to Blackie and he was my constant companion.

While stopping at the Grand Hotel in the little town of Grove Valley, I had the misfortune to lose Blackie. I had left him in care of the hotel proprietor, but somehow or other he escaped, and could not be found in the vicinity. I suddenly decided that I would place an advertisement in the local paper, hoping that some kind-hearted dog lover would find him and return him to me.

I hurried over to the offices of the Grove Valley Bugle, where I found a staff of three persons putting the paper to bed.

"I want to place a lost and found advertisement," I said to the editor, who was sitting on a stool wearing a green eye shade and chewing tobacco. Two other rural gentlemen of the press were busy reading proof of the outcoming edition.

"It's just past the deadline," said the editor, "but we'll stop the presses and put her in fer ya."

"All right," I said, and then gave him a description of the dog. "Make it a fifty-dollar reward," I added.

After I had returned to the hotel, I thought the matter over and decided that I should have added, "No questions asked." It would be safer. Some culprit might have stolen the dog and be fearful about returning it. So I went back to the paper. When I arrived inside the office, no one was on hand but a freckle-faced office boy, who stood staring out a window at the distant fields.

"Where's everybody?" I asked.

The lad ran his hand through his touseled hair and said, "Out looking for the dawg!" —Robert Dillon

IMAGINATION

Last night as I arrived home from the office, I was met at the door by my little five-year-old daughter, Mary. After the little darling had given me a big hug and a kiss, she said to me, "Daddy, I've been drawing today."

"So my little girl's been drawing," I said, as I hung up my hat. "What have you been drawing?" I casually asked, at the same time looking around for the evening paper.

"I've been drawing everything," said little Mary. "I've been drawing roosters. I've been drawing a cat. I've been drawing a dog. But now I'm going to draw something really hard."

"You are?" I said, as I opened the paper to the sports section. "What are you going to draw that's so hard?"

"I'm going to draw a picture of God," the child said simply.

"Why, Mary!" I exclaimed as I put down my paper, "you can't draw a picture of God. You have never seen him. No one has. Why, no one knows what God looks like."

Little Mary bit the end of her pencil for a moment and then quickly said to me, "Everybody'll know when my picture gets finished."   —William Hurley

HUSKY BABY

An old-timer named Andy Haskins had a shack, and he made most of the record fish catches in his vicinity during 40 years. He had a big record book containing dates and weights to impress visitors.

One summer a young married couple camped in a luxurious lodge three miles above old Haskins' place. A baby was born at the lodge and the only scales the father could obtain on which to weigh the child was that with which Andy had weighed all the big fish he had caught in 10 years.

The baby tipped the scales at 35 pounds!

—Ottawa Journal

A BOOMERANG!

Many years ago I took a whirl at politics. I took just one whirl. That was my last. I learned an early lesson.

I was running for the office of state senator against a fellow by the name of Pete Smith. It was a bitter campaign. I stumped my district, making speeches before every conceivable kind of a gathering. Usually Pete Smith was on hand at the same meetings, retaliating in kind to every attack I made upon him.

One evening before a woman's organization of strict decorum, I launched my surprise of the campaign. I stood up before the ladies assembled and told how Pete Smith in his early days used to be a bartender—how he sold demon rum across the mahogany, and how he was a very lowly bartender at that. Then I cried out, "Do you good ladies want that kind of a man to represent you in our great state senate?"

I sat down, pleased with myself, and eagerly looked over my audience of women who had turned to one another with nodding heads and moving lips, apparently concluding that my opponent was poor material for a senator. I figured that Pete Smith was a dead duck.

When Pete Smith stood up to speak, the atmosphere was very chilly, indeed. The ladies sat with their arms folded and heads tilted back as if they were trying to pull as far away as possible from that sinner Smith. Pete Smith cleared his throat and began to talk. "Ladies of the sixth district. What my opponent, Bill Jones, says is true. A number of years ago I was a bartender and I sold whiskey. I also remember that my opponent, Bill Jones, was one of my best customers. Many a time I stood on one side of the bar and sold whiskey to Bill Jones on the other side. But there is a difference between us now. I have left my side of the bar, but my opponent, Bill Jones, sticks to his side as tenaciously as ever."

—George Dixon

THE UMBRELLA

(When the meeting assembled during a heavy rainstorm)

I want to congratulate this audience for its very fine attendance this evening. Very few of us were prepared for the sudden outburst of rain that poured out of the sky as we were making our way here. Most of you got soaked to the skin, being without raincoats or umbrellas. I was more fortunate; I got an umbrella.

As I came in the door, Bill Jones said to me, "Where did you get that umbrella?"

"Well," I said, "I was standing over on the next corner, protected by an awning and contemplating how I would get over to the meeting without getting drenched, when I spied a fellow walking down the street under an umbrella. Thinking that it was someone who would be going to our meeting, I called out to the man: 'Hey! Where did you get that umbrella?' The man dropped his umbrella and ran. That's how I got it."

—Horton Smith

HE SHOULD HAVE SAID IT SOONER

Billie Burke was enjoying a transatlantic ocean trip when she noticed a gentleman at the next table was suffering from a bad cold.

"Uncomfortable?" she asked sympathetically.

The man nodded.

"I'll tell you just what to do for it," said Miss Burke. "Go back to your stateroom. Drink lots of orange juice. Take five aspirin tablets. Cover yourself with all the blankets you can find. Sweat the cold out. I know what I'm talking about. I'm Billie Burke of Hollywood."

The man smiled warmly and said, "Thanks. I'm Dr. Mayo of the Mayo clinic."

—The Journal of the American Medical Association

DAD TAKES A BACK SEAT

A number of years ago my little girl came into the living room and after jumping upon my knee said, "Daddy, I have to tell you something."

"If you have, out with it, little lady," I said, flipping the pages of the evening paper.

"You won't like it," she said sheepishly.

"I won't like it," I said. "Why won't I like it?"

"'Cause it's not nice about you, Daddy. That is, it's not as nice about you as it is about Mother," she said.

"Come on now, out with it," I repeated. "I want to finish reading the stock market quotations."

Little Mary paused for a moment and started to move her little lips. "Well," she said, "I'm much nearer to Mother than I am to you, 'cause I'm Mother's little girl, and I'm only related to you by marriage."   —Arthur Barry

HIGH LIVING

A man was complaining that he had just bought a prefabricated house and that it had, in the end, cost him $40,000.

Friend—"Forty thousand! Isn't that an awful lot to pay for a prefab?"

Home-owner—"Yes. It wasn't so much to begin with, but I told the factory I wanted it right away, and they sent it to me airmail."   —Ottawa Journal

GOOD ADVICE

"When you speak of Heaven, let your face light up, let it be irradiated with a heavenly gleam, let your eyes shine with reflected glory. But when you speak of Hell—well, then your ordinary face will do."   —Charles H. Spurgeon

CROOKS IN WASHINGTON

We all know that there are times when even the best-intentioned acts from Washington are viewed with a jaundiced eye. I heard a story the other day about a farmer out in Texas who had undergone the most appalling series of misfortunes. His barn had burned down. Then his wife had broken her leg. His children all got whooping cough. Then he himself got sick. Then a tornado blew down most of the rest of his farm. At this point, in desperation, not knowing where to turn, he sat down and wrote a letter to The Lord. He explained his troubles, and asked the Lord if He could send him just $500 to help him out.

The letter eventually found its way to the Dead-letter Office in Washington. Eventually it was opened by a young bureaucrat, who was so moved by the plight of the Texan that he decided he would do something about it personally. So he passed the hat around the office, and among his friends, and finally, after a great deal of effort, he had managed to get $450 together, but he just couldn't stretch it to $500. So he put the $450 into a government envelope and mailed it to the Texan, feeling quite pleased with this work of kindness.

To his surprise, some time later another letter turned up in the Dead-letter Office in the same handwriting. The same beneficient bureaucrat opened the letter and read, "Dear Lord: Thanks very much for the money, but I thought I ought to tell you that those crooks in Washington kept out $50 of it."

—Arthur Larson, Under Secretary of Labor

NO CHOICE

If you are dissatisfied with what I have said this evening, my only comment is that which a little girl made to her mother, who chided her because God would not be pleased with her sleepy prayer: "Well, it's the best He will get out of me tonight."   —William Walter Phelps

WAS MY FACE RED!

I was attending a dinner one day last winter, when I was given an unusual setback by one of my fellow speakers. We had all taken our places and ravenously we began to partake of the food that was being placed on the table with great rapidity by a score of waiters. When the meat course arrived, I cut off a good slice and stabbing it with my fork, held it up before my friend, Abe Cohen, who was sitting beside me.

"Abe," I said, dangling the meat before his eyes, "is this pig?"

Abe looked at the meat swaying on the end of my fork, wiped his mouth with a napkin, and then softly said, "What end of the fork are you talking about?"   —George Dixon

GOOD PREACHER

"A good preacher should get religion like a Methodist; experience it like a Baptist; be sure of it like a Disciple; stick to it like a Lutheran; pray for it like a Presbyterian; conciliate it like a Congregationalist; glorify it like a Jew; be proud of it like an Episcopalian; practice it like a Christian Scientist; propagate it like a Roman Catholic; work for it like a Salvation Army Lassie; enjoy it like a colored man."

—Dr. Edgar DeWitt Jones

THOSE LAWYERS !

A woman in the midst of divorce proceedings was complaining to a friend about the boring conferences she had to go through and all the legal red tape.

"Oh," said her friend, "don't talk to me about lawyers and the law. I've had so much trouble over my property that sometimes I wish my husband hadn't died."

—Wall Street Journal

UPKEEP IS THE DOWNFALL

A well-known economist tells about his experience before an audience when he spoke for almost an hour on the intricate make-up of our economic system. He felt that he had done a pretty good job in explaining the complicated subject in simple phraseology. After he sat down the chairman who had introduced him got up and said:

"Ladies and gentlemen, what our speaker has been telling you is that, if your outgo exceeds your income, then your upkeep will be your downfall." —Lawrence M. Brings

BUT HE CAN'T TRUST HIMSELF

A rather absent-minded minister who depends on his wife to keep his engagements diary and see to his travel needs turned up at the barrier of the local station, and was perturbed to discover that he'd mislaid his ticket.

"That's all right, sir," said the collector, beckoning him through. "We can trust you."

"But I must find it," exclaimed the minister, becoming even more flustered. "I must know where I'm going!"

—The Montreal Star

MINOR DETAIL

A highway traffic officer stopped an American motorist and said, "I'm giving you a ticket for driving without a tail light."

The surprised motorist got out and investigated. Immediately he began to wail his dismay. "Come now," said the officer, "it's not as bad as that."

The motorist explained. "It's not the tail light I'm worried about. What became of my trailer?" —Ottawa Journal

PEDDLING HIS WORLDLY GOODS

Two high school students were so much in love they threatened to elope if their families did not sign the necessary papers for an under-age ceremony. When the parents could no longer talk them into deferring marriage until they were older, they reluctantly consented. So a big church wedding was planned by both families.

As the 17-year-old boy stood at the altar and looked adoringly at the 16-year-old girl, he repeated after the minister, "With all my worldly goods I thee endow."

At this point his father whispered to his wife, "Well, dear, there goes Junior's bicycle."   —The Ottawa Journal

EYE TO ECONOMY

Making tests of a homemade brew which a cautious Scot had submitted for analysis, the chemist said: "I'm sorry, but this stuff is dreadful. If you drank this I guarantee you would be blind for life. You'd better let me destroy it."

"No need to do that," said the Scot, stretching out a hand for the bottle. "My old friend McTavish has been blind for years. I might as well give it to him for a birthday present."   —Montreal Star

SUCCESS

That man is a success who has lived well, laughed often and loved much; who has gained the respect of intelligent men and the love of children; who has filled his niche and accomplished his task; who leaves the world better than he found it, whether by an improved poppy, a perfect poem or a rescued soul; who never lacked appreciation of earth's beauty or failed to express it; who looked for the best in others and gave the best he had.   —Robert Louis Stevenson

NO INTERFERENCE

The essential role of government in this new era of labor relations, is not control, not interference, but service.

This policy of non-interference reminds me of the favorite story of my grandfather, Theory Larson. My grandmother called him Theory, because he so seldom worked. He was riding one day in an old-fashioned street-car, the kind that had a heavy iron bar running up and down the middle of the entrance door. A very fat lady with a basket of clothes tried to board the car, and in so doing she got hopelessly stuck in the door and couldn't move either forward or backward. My grandfather, who had a delightful sense of humor, just laughed and laughed until he almost cried. The fat lady became quite indignant at this, and shouted. "If you was half a man, you wouldn't sit there laughing; you'd help me out of here." My grandfather shouted back, "And if you was half a woman, you wouldn't be stuck in that door."

I'm afraid Grandpa carried non-interference a little too far there; I think he could have been of a little more service, without being accused of interference.

—Arthur Larson, Under Secretary of Labor

STILL BELIEVES IN GOD

All I can say is that all this reminds me of the time in Milwaukee when a young friend of mine, who was a preacher, asked me to substitute for him one Sunday morning. I was glad to do so, since I at one time had ambitions to be a minister. I preached a vigorous sermon on the subject of atheism. I denounced atheism in every way I knew how. I ridiculed atheism. I disproved atheism. I trampled all over atheism, and by the time I was through I had thoroughly demolished atheism. After the service, I was talking to a sweet little old lady, and asked her what she thought of my sermon. "Young man," she said, "you're a mighty convincing talker, but I still believe in God."   —Arthur Larson, Under Secretary of Labor

ACOUSTICS

As I walked into the hall this evening and shook hands with your chairman, I casually asked him: "How are the acoustics in this hall?"

"Excellent," he answered, "excellent! The speakers can hear every cough."   —Sylvester McGovern

OVERHEARD IN THE HALL

Just as I entered the hall this evening, I overheard a conversation by two of our guests. One fellow said to another fellow, pointing at me: "That's our principal speaker. At his last talk in Pineville he had the audience in the aisles."

"Applauding?" asked the second fellow.

"No," said the first fellow. "Stretching and yawning."

—Rome Roberts

AESOP MODERNIZED

The King of Beasts had just been told off by his lady lioness for speaking out of turn, and he went into the jungle to indulge his grouch on the other wild folk. Seizing a tough old warthog, he shook him up and growled, "Who is king of the jungle?"

"You are, mighty one," said the warthog.

A little later he grabbed a big ape and knocked him against the nearest tree, saying, "And who do you think is king here?"

"No one but you, great Leo," whimpered the ape.

Then the lion met a big bull elephant coming toward him. Blocking the elephant's path he asked the same question. In reply the big pachyderm wrapped his trunk around the lion, slammed him against the ground and then threw him against a boulder twenty feet away.

"Darn it!" said the lion as he pulled himself to his feet. "Just because you don't know the answer isn't any reason why you should get rough!"   —The New Age

CHARITABLE

Pray do not find fault with the man who limps
    Or stumbles along the road,
Unless you have worn the shoe he wears
    Or struggled beneath his load,
There may be tacks in his shoes that hurt,
    Though hidden away from view,
Or the burden he bears, placed on your back,
    Might cause you to stumble too.
Don't sneer at the man who's down today,
    Unless you have felt the blow
That caused his fall, or felt the same
    That only the fallen know.
You may be strong, but still the blows
    That were his, if dealt to you
In the self-same way at the self-same time
    Might cause you to stagger too.
Don't be too harsh with the man who sins
    Or pelt him with words or stones,
Unless you are sure, yes, doubly sure,
    That you have no sins of your own.
For you know, perhaps, if the tempter's voice
    Should whisper as soft to you
As it did to him when he went astray,
    'Twould cause you to falter too.

                —Author Unknown

YOU CAN'T WIN

If you run after money, you're money mad; if you keep it,
you're a capitalist; if you spend it, you're a spendthrift; if you
don't get it, you are a ne'er-do-well; if you don't try to get it,
you lack ambition; if you get it without working for it, you're
a parasite; and if you accumulate it after a lifetime of hard
work, people will say you are a fool who never got anything
out of life.   Anderson (S. C.) Independent

AN ANALYSIS OF CENSUS FIGURES

Population of the U. S.	153,000,000
Those over 65	41,000,000
Left to do the work	112,000,000
Those under 21	54,000,000
Left to do the work	58,000,000
Government employed	25,000,000
Left to do the work	33,000,000
In the armed forces	10,000,000
Left to do the work	23,000,000
In state or city work	19,000,000
Left to do the work	4,000,000
In hospitals or asylums	3,800,000
Left to do the work	200,000
Bums who won't work	175,000
Left to do the work	25,000
In pens and in jails	24,998
Left to do the work	2

You and I—and I'm getting tired!

—Farm News Show

SUBJECT FOR STUDY

The circuit rider was asking the hillbilly girl if he could speak to her father.

"Naw, sir," said the girl, "Daddy's in the pen."

"Well then," said the minister, "What about your mother?"

"Mamma's in the county sanitarium," said the girl, "she was seein' things."

"Perhaps I could speak to your brother," said the minister.

"Naw," said the girl, "he's away at Harvard."

"Oh," said the minister, brightening, "That's fine, what is he studying?"

"He ain't studying nothin'," said the girl, "they're studying him."

—Bindery Talk

REASON FOR REFLECTION

A hillbilly, not being away from home much, took a trip to the city. While there in a department store he picked up a hand mirror, looked in it and said, "Dang, if that ain't my pappy's picture."

In his excitement he had it wrapped, hurried home, gave it to his wife and told her he had found his pappy's picture.

She unwrapped the mirror and looked in it. "That ain't your pappy," she said, "that's one of them good-for-nothing, lowdown gals you were running around with in the city."

—Ottawa Journal

A SHADOW OF THE ORIGINAL

An antique collector, passing through a small village, stopped to watch an old man chopping wood with an ancient ax.

"That's a mighty old ax you have there," remarked the collector.

"Yes," said the villager, "it once belonged to George Washington."

"Not really," gasped the collector. "It certainly stood up well."

"Of course," admitted the old man, "it's had three new handles and two new heads." —Wall Street Journal

NO DETOUR

A teacher was explaining to her third grade children the joys and wonders of heaven. After several convincing minutes, she asked how many wanted to go to heaven. All but one little girl raised their hands.

"Mary Lou," the teacher asked, surprised, "don't you want to go to heaven?"

"I want to go all right," Mary Lou replied, "but my mother told me to come straight back after school."

—Wall Street Journal

EXPENSIVE DIET

The new minister was enthusiastic about foreign missions, and one of his first tasks was to call upon parishioners whom he knew to have money.

"I'm sorry," said one wealthy farmer, "but it's no use asking me. I don't approve of foreign missions."

"But surely," the minister persisted, "you know that we are commanded to feed the hungry."

"That may be," came the grim reply, "but can't we feed 'em on something cheaper than missionaries?" —Ottawa Journal

PLAY BY PLAY

A bachelor, left in charge of his infant niece, was faced with a crisis. He frantically called a young acquaintance, who was a parent, and who solved the problem in this man-to-man fashion.

"First, place the diaper in position of a baseball diamond with you at bat. Fold second base over home plate. Place baby on pitcher's mound. Then pin first and third to home plate."

—Tracks

SUPERFLUOUS COMPLAINTS

The congressman had made a speech on a controversial subject which brought him a flood of telegrams. When a reporter asked for an analysis of these, he held up a small stack of them in each hand.

"These 10 support my speech, and these six oppose it. The rest"—he pointed to a big box overflowing with wire—"are indecisive."

The reporter showed disbelief. "You mean all those over there show no definite opinion one way or the other?"

"No, I don't mean that," smiled the congressman. "They probably contain some very strong opinions. But they're from addresses outside of my district."   —Wall Street Journal

THE EASY WAY

With his usual long-windedness, the bore was describing one of his miraculous escapes.

"There was I," he said, "on a lonely road, miles from anywhere, with a blazing car. What do you think I did?"

One weary listener stifled his yawns long enough to reply: "Took a long breath and blew it out."   —Montreal Star

SOBER OUTLOOK

A poet was out meditating in the country when a farmer came along and looked at him curiously.

"Ah," said the poet, "perhaps you, too, have seen the golden red fingers of dawn spreading across the eastern sky, the red stained sulphurous islets floating in a lake of fire in the west, the ragged clouds at midnight, blotting out the shuddering moon?"

"No," replied the farmer, "not lately. I've been on the wagon for over a year."   —Montreal Star

TOO LITERAL

A newlywed groom came home one evening with a package of sausage and suggested that the bride prepare them for breakfast. "How do you cook them?" his bride inquired timidly.

"Fry 'em just like fish," instructed the husband patiently.

Next morning the bride sat at the breakfast table and apologized. "I hope you enjoy the sausages, dear, but there wasn't much left of them after I cleaned the insides out."

—Ottawa Journal

RAIN WOULD BE BETTER

I recall, when I gave the very first speech of my career, I was talking to a group of farmers in South Dakota. I had a very carefully prepared and memorized speech, and delivered it in my best public-speaking-class style. After it was all over, I was talking to one of the farmers in the crowd, and asked him what he thought of the speech. "Well," he said, "It wasn't too bad, but a half hour of rain would have done a damn sight more good." —Arthur Larson, Under Secretary of Labor

A HOT DEAL

Robinson had died and gone below. Hardly had he settled down when a hearty hand slapped him on the back, and into his ears boomed the familiar voice of a persistent traveler who had pestered him on earth.

"Well, Mr. Robinson," said the traveler, "I'm here for that appointment. You'll remember that every time I came into your office to interest you in my proposition, you told me you'd see me here first." —Montreal Star

CHECKING UP

The boy went into the neighborhood grocery and asked if he could use the phone.

"Sure, son, go ahead," said the proprietor. He could not help overhearing the conversation.

"Hello. Dr. Brown?" said the boy on the phone. "Do you need a boy to take care of your lawn this summer? Oh, you already have a boy. Well, is he any good? Does he give you satisfaction? Oh, so he's all right—well, thanks very much."

The grocer said, "So you didn't get the job? That's too bad."

"Oh, I already got the job, I was just checking up on my-self." —Wall Street Journal

SPREADING HERSELF

I don't suppose it was intended that I should entirely cover the subject in all its magnitude tonight. I have been generous to suppose that I was asked to speak in the spirit of the small boy in the country who came in and told his mother that he had set the old hen on two dozen eggs. "Why," she said, "you don't expect her to hatch two dozen, do you?" He said: "No, but I just wanted to see the darned old thing spread herself."

—Horace Porter

THE BEGINNING OF SALESMANSHIP

When Adam and Eve opened up the Garden of Eden, Adam never dreamed that there was any necessity for advertising, and never conceived of there being any such thing as sales-manship. He knew he had the only woman in the world, a low overhead and, in fact, everything went along all right until a salesman came along with a red apple and a wonderful selling talk. Eve fell for that selling talk, and on that day salesmanship and advertising originated. —Edward S. Jordan

GOOD FOR THE EGO

A gentleman passing the St. James's club the other day noticed a sleek limousine at the curb, a uniformed chauffeur standing expectantly beside it. A seedy-looking old chap sauntered up, nodded to the chauffeur and said in a patronizing tone, "I won't be using the car this afternoon, Fergus. I think I'll walk."

The chauffeur touched his cap respectfully and answered, "Very good, sir."

Curious, the gentleman asked the chauffeur who the man was.

"Haven't the faintest idea, sir," was the reply. "He's been coming along like that once or twice a week for months. Always says the same thing. Guess it kind of makes him feel important." —The Montrealar

ENTIRELY BY CHANCE

At last a notorious and dangerous burglar had been caught while on one of his jobs. His captor was a middle-aged woman, alone at the time, who felled him with a dining room chair as he crept through the house. Her comment on the excitement was printed in the following day's paper:

"It was 2 o'clock in the morning and I was sitting at my bedroom window when I saw this sneaky creature make his way through the back yard. I had locked all the doors so I knew just what he was going to do, come through the kitchen window which had the loose screen. I was all prepared for him. I hid in the dining room and waited until he went by me, then I picked up a chair, and hit him with all my might. Naturally, of course, I thought it was my husband." —Wall Street Journal

WRONG THING TO SAY

"I'm going over to comfort Mrs. Brown," said Mrs. Jackson to her daughter Mary. "Mr. Brown hanged himself in their attic a few weks ago."

"Oh, Mother, don't go; you always say the wrong thing."

"Yes, I'm going, Mary. I'll just talk about the weather. That's a safe enough subject."

Mrs. Jackson went over on her visit of condolence.

"We have had rainy weather lately, haven't we, Mrs. Brown?" she said.

"Yes," replied the widow. "I haven't been able to get the week's washing dried."

"Oh," said Mrs. Jackson, "I shouldn't think you would have any trouble. You have such a nice attic to hang things in."

—Don O. Shelton

HOWLING WILDERNESS

A politician had prepared a speech and tried to commit it to memory. The opening sentence was as follows:

"Ladies and gentlemen. One hundred years ago tonight the place where I now stand was a howling wilderness."

Here he paused and tried in vain to recall the next sentence of his prepared speech.

Sparring for time he said, "I repeat it for the sake of emphasis. One hundred years ago tonight the place where I now stand was a howling wilderness."

He paused again and tried to recall the next lines of his prepared speech, but they simply would not come, and then he said: "And I wish the Lord that it was a howling wilderness now and I was in the middle of it."

He then sat down.

—A. F. Sheldon

THIS IS ON ME

Two Texans strolled into a Cadillac salesroom after a hearty meal.

A salesman showed them various styles, but it developed that each of them had one or more of the various models. In desperation the salesman thought of two Cadillacs which had been goldplated for a special auto show. The Texans were interested.

"Have you got one of these?" the first Texan asked.

"Nope," said the second Texan. "They sure are pretty."

"We'll take both of them," said the first Texan, reaching for his checkbook. "How much for the pair?"

"Now wait a minute," protested the second Texan reaching for his checkbook. "This is on me. Remember, you bought the lunch." —Gov. Allan Shivers of Texas

TRYING TO BE HELPFUL

I was addressing a large group of banks in Louisville when the microphone ceased to function. Raising my voice, I asked a man in the back row if he could hear.

"No," said the man. Whereupon a man in the front row stood up.

"I can hear," he shouted to the gent in back. "And I'll change places with you." —Homer Livingston,
President, American Banker's Ass'n.

THE CHAMPION

No presidential candidate has ever equaled the speech-making marathons of William Jennings Bryan.

In his 1896 campaign against William McKinley, he created a world's record by speaking 19 times in one day, with a daily wordage total of between 60,000 and 100,000. Again opposing McKinley in 1900, he broke his own record by speaking

21 times in a day. And in 1908, against William Howard Taft, he set an all-time mark with 36 long speeches within 24 hours.

Traveling on slow moving trains, Bryan slept only three hours a night, waking at 5 a.m. to work more than 20 hours at speaking, writing or giving interviews. He insisted upon being awakened at any time people gathered at stations along the route.

To maintain strength, he ate six meals a day. At night, he rubbed down his giant body with gin, at the same time exhorting his aids against internal use of alcohol.

—Wall Street Journal

ENTERPRISING HENRY

At a recent political meeting, the speakers were much disturbed by a man who called constantly for a Mr. Henry. Whenever a new speaker came on this man bawled out, "Henry! Henry! I call for Mr. Henry!"

After several interruptions of this kind, a very young man ascended the platform and began to speak, when again came the call for Mr. Henry. The chairman now rose and remarked that it would oblige the audience if the gentleman would refrain from any further calls, as Mr. Henry was now speaking.

"Is that Mr. Henry?" cried the disturber of the meeting. "Why, that's the little cuss that told me to holler!"

—The Kablegram

THE TOASTMASTER

The ideal toastmaster is one who can be witty, appropriate, and brief, and who, fully informing himself about the speaker, knocks him in a good-natured way that enables the speaker to get back in his opening remarks and so get off to a flying start.

—Frank E. Carpenter

SERVICE SUPREME

A careful man I ought to be;
  A little fellow follows me;
I do not dare to go astray
  For fear he'll go the self-same way.

I cannot once escape his eyes,
  Whate'er he sees me do he tries.
Like me he says he's going to be
  The little chap who follows me.

He thinks that I am good and fine,
  Believes in every word of mine.
The base in me he must not see,
  That little chap who follows me.

I must remember as I go
  Thru Summer's sun and Winter's snow
I am building for the years to be;
  That little chap who follows me.

—Author Unknown

INSULT ADDED TO INJURY

In the good old days of romance and adventure a king's jester one day found His Majesty bending over a basin and washing his face.

In a spirit of fun the jester gave the king a resounding kick on that part of his sacred person situated directly behind his stomach.

Deeply enraged, the king ordered the immediate execution of his audacious jester, but finally consented to pardon him if he would make an apology more outrageous than the original insult.

The condemned jester reflected for a moment and then remarked: "Will Your Majesty please forgive me? I did not know it was you. I thought it was the queen."

—James Madison

THE ASSAULT

In a cheap little side street saloon, the sailor had suddenly picked up an empty whiskey bottle and banged it resoundingly upon the bartender's head. Now he stood in court to answer for his offense.

"My client admits he struck the bartender," said the sailor's lawyer, "but he acted under the influence of liquor, and pretty poor liquor at that."

"But he does admit assaulting the man," insisted the court.

"Yes," replied the attorney, "but your honor, consider this fact—the man first assaulted my client with its contents."

—Wall Street Journal

PERSUASIVE POWERS

I feel somewhat like the colored man who, when called upon to make a public address, declared: "My body rises up, but my mind sits down."

Perhaps I'd feel a bit more confident if I had the persuasive powers of a lawyer who was called in by an old maid so that she could make her last will and testament.

She declared, "I want to give $3,000 to the Art Museum, $1,000 to my nephew, $1,000 to the YMCA, and $1,000 to the library."

"What about the remaining $500?" asked the lawyer.

The old maid replied, "I have never had a sweetheart, and I'll give that to anyone who will kiss me and make love to me."

"I'll do it," said the lawyer. So he hurried home and explained matters to his wife. That very evening he showed up at the old maid's home.

At nine o'clock his wife became nervous and called him on the phone.

"It's all right, dearie," he explained. "She has cut off the Art Museum and the library, and if you'll let me stay another hour she'll drop the YMCA."

—James Madison

DENSE CROWD

Chief Justice Warren, when governor of California, began a political address with: "Ladies and gentlemen, I'm pleased to see this dense crowd here tonight." A voice from the back shouted, "Don't be too pleased. We ain't all dense!"

—Sacramento Shopping News Times

"The American Congress is strange," a Russian actor once reported after sitting in the spectator's gallery of the House of Representatives. "A man gets up and speaks and says nothing. Nobody listens—then everybody disagrees."

—Liberty Magazine

WHAT COLOR?

A visitor to an insane asylum was stopped by one of the inmates who seemed to be in a playful mood, for he cupped his hands as though he were holding something in them and challenged the visitor, "What do you think I've got here?"

"A million dollars?" guessed the visitor, eager to co-operate.

The inmate stole a look at the palms of his hands and answered triumphantly, "No, guess again."

"An airplane?"

"No," said the inmate after another peek.

"Is it a horse?" the guest finally ventured.

Furtively the inmate eyed his cupped hands again. Then he looked up coyly and asked, "What color?"

—Eddie Cantor

BETTER PREPARED

A preacher who had written his sermon carefully found himself at the church without his manuscript. "As I have forgotten my notes," he began his sermon, "I will rely on the Lord for guidance. Tonight I will come better prepared."

—Religious Digest

NOT FOR AMATEURS

A banquet was given in my honor by a native king of Samoa. When the time came to say the nice things about me, the king still remained squatted while a professional orator, brought in for the purpose, laid it on. After a long speech of complete praise, I started to get up to express my thanks, but the king drew me back. "Don't get up," he said. "I have provided an orator for you. In Polynesia we don't believe public speaking should be engaged in by amateurs."

—Dr. Victor C. Heiser

THE DIFFERENCE

The celebrated English clergyman and wit, Sidney Smith, was discussing the relative importance of two prominent men. "There is the same difference between their tongues," he observed, "as between the hour and the minute hand on a clock. The one goes twelve times as fast, the other signifies twelve times as much." —Christian Science Monitor

NO REAL MEAT

The rather flattering introduction reminds me of the story of Uncle Eben. "Some ministers," drawled the old darkie, "uses big words de same as a turkey spreads his tail feathers. Dey makes a elegant show, but they don't represent no real meat." I am greatly indebted to my friend for his gracious words. —The Kablegram

MY FIRST BIRTHDAY SPEECH

I have had a great many birthdays in my time. I remember the first one very well, and I always think of it with indignation. Everything was so crude, unaesthetic, primeval. Nothing like this at all. No proper appreciative preparation made; nothing really ready. Now, for a person born with high and delicate instincts—why, even the cradle wasn't whitewashed—nothing ready at all. I hadn't any hair, I hadn't any teeth, I hadn't any clothes, I had to go to my first banquet just like that.

Well, everybody came swarming in. It was the merest little bit of a village—hardly that, just a little hamlet, in the backwoods of Missouri, where nothing ever happened, and the people were all interested, and they all came. They looked me over to see if there was anything fresh in my line. Why, nothing ever happened in that village—I—why, I was the only thing that had really happened there for months and months and months; and although I say it myself that shouldn't, I came the nearest to being a real event that had happened in that village in more than two years. Well, those people came; they came with that curiosity which is so provincial, with that frankness which also is so provincial, and they examined me all around and gave their opinion.

Nobody asked them, and I shouldn't have minded if anybody had paid me a compliment, but nobody did. Their opinions were all just green with prejudice, and I feel those opinions to this day. Well, I stood that as long as—you know I was courteous, and I stood it to the limit. I stood it an hour, and then the worm turned. I was the worm; it was my turn to turn, and I turned. I knew very well the strength of my position. I knew that I was the only spotlessly pure and innocent person in that whole town, and I came out and said so. And they could not say a word. It was true. They blushed; they were embarrassed. Well, that was the first after-dinner speech I ever made. I think it was after dinner.

It's a long stretch between that first birthday speech and this one. That was my cradle song, and this is my swan song, I suppose. I am used to swan songs; I have sung them several times.   —Mark Twain

JUMPING AT CONCLUSIONS

Now I want to tell a story about jumping at conclusions. It was told to me by Bram stoker, and it concerns a christening. There was a little clergyman who was prone to jump at conclusions sometimes. One day he was invited to officiate at a christening. He went. There sat the relatives—intelligent-looking relatives they were. The little clergyman's instinct came to him to make a great speech. He was given to flights of oratory that way—a very dangerous thing, for often the wings which take one into clouds of oratorical enthusiasm are wax and melt up there, and down you come.

But the little clergyman couldn't resist. He took the child in his arms, and, holding it, looked at it a moment. It wasn't much of a child. It was little like a sweet potato. Then the little clergyman waited impressively, and then said: "I see in your countenances disappointment of him. I see you are disappointed with this baby. Why? Because he is so little. My friends, if you had but the power of looking into the future you might see that great things may come of little things. There is the great ocean, holding the navies of the world, which comes from little drops of water no larger than a woman's tears. There are the great constellations in the sky, made up of little bits of stars. Oh, if you could consider his future you might see that he might become the greatest poet of the universe, the greatest warrior the world has ever known, greater than Caesar, than Hannibal, than—er—er (turning to the father) what's his name?"

The father hesitated, then whispered back: "His name? Well, his name is Mary Ann."   —Mark Twain

SALESMANSHIP

When Adam and Eve opened up the Garden of Eden, Adam never dreamed that there was any necessity for advertising, and never conceived of there being any such thing as salesmanship.

He knew he had the only woman in the world, a low overhead and, in fact, everything went along all right until a salesman came along with a red apple and a wonderful selling talk.

Eve fell for that selling talk, and on that day salesmanship and advertising originated. On the same day we had the beginnings of Hart, Schaffner & Marx—now the greatest clothing manufacturers in the world.

When Noah saw the waters rising and conceived the idea of the first great ocean liner, he advertised the fact that he was sorry he could provide accommodations for but two of each of the living species. That's alluring advertising.

I do not know how many extra rooms he had, but the conversation that he gave out has been duplicated by every hotel clerk I ever met in my life. There is always a shortage of rooms in the best hotels. And that's salesmanship.

—Edward S. Jordan

SUCCESS

Success is in the way you walk the paths of life each day;
It's in the little things you do and in the things you say.
Success is not in getting rich or rising high to fame;
It's not alone in winning goals which all men hope to claim.
Success is being big of heart and clean and broad of mind.
It's being faithful to your friends and, to the stranger, kind.
It's in the children whom you love and all they learn from you;
Success depends on character and everything you do.

—Author Unknown.

WHY AM I UP HERE?

My position here on the platform this morning rather unexpectedly reminds me of a story of two Norwegians which I heard the other day who had had a rather heavy evening of drinking. They were on their way home across the Brooklyn Bridge to Brooklyn. It was a bright moonlit night. The moon was reflected in the water. They were leaning over looking at the river, and Olie said, "What is that bright thing down in the water?" And his friend Hansen said, "Well, that is the moon down there. Don't you see the moon?"

"The moon!" said Olie. Well, if that is the moon down there, what in hell am I doing up here?"

That is the way I feel this morning.

As the chairman has explained to you, Secretary Mitchell was unavoidably and unexpectedly required to be out of town today and has asked me to extend his greetings to you and make these closing remarks to summarize the conference and send you home with a challenge to action.

—Arthur Larson

The opening of an address delivered by Arthur Larson, Under Secretary of Labor, at the President's Conference on Occupational Safety at Washington, D. C.

RAIN WOULD HAVE BEEN BETTER

My first speech was made to a group of South Dakota farmers. I had a carefully memorized talk, and delivered it in my best public-speaking-class style. After it was all over, I asked one of the farmers what he thought of it.

"Well," he said, "it wasn't too bad. But a half-hour of rain would have done a damn sight more good."

—Arthur Larson

GOING MY WAY

I am a traveler on a one-way journey through life and never expect to retrace my steps or come this way again. My yesterdays are poignant recollections of tasks neglected or undone, mixed with pleasant memories of the few things done well. My tomorrows hold a promise of opportunity to do bigger and better things. My present is being lived in the valley of struggle and pain, and sharing the load of others.

Since I pass this way but once, my hope is that men, women and children may be glad that I came and regret that I am leaving. As I journey with my fellow men, may I be privileged to bring joy where once sorrow ruled; smiles to replace tears; to plant a flower of kindness in those hearts where once weeds of despair grew.

As I follow the noble pattern of the Apostle Paul, may I never falter as I press toward the mark for the prize of the high calling; but, should I stumble and fall, may the grace of God lift me and start me forward, going my way. — Anonymous

SIGNIFICANT HISS

I am reminded of the famous speaker who was rudely interrupted as he approached the dramatic climax of his talk by someone in the audience who hissed loudly and long.

But he soon regained his composure and calmly said: "There are only three things that hiss—a goose, a snake, and a fool. I suggest that you now arise and be identified."

—Henry Johns

MEETING OF THE BORED

During the announcements period the minister of the church stated that there would be a meeting of the Board at the chancel immediately after the services. When the group gathered a stranger was discovered in their midst and the minister asked him: "There's a misunderstanding, isn't there? You are not a member of this Board."

"Oh, pardon me," replied the stranger, "I must have misunderstood you. I thought you announced that there was to be a meeting of those who were bored." —Arthur L. Kaser

BIG MONEY

When we compare social gatherings such as we have here this evening with social affairs of forty or fifty years ago we fully realize how times have changed. When we were kids, ten cents was big money. Yes, my friends, dimes have changed.

—Arthur L. Kaser

GIVE US A CHANCE

It was the next day after I had been master of ceremonies in our town. I ran into one of our most influential citizens. He said to me: "We would like to compliment you on your job as master of ceremonies. When are you going to give us a chance?"

—Arthur L. Kaser

YOU NEVER CAN TELL

I never had the courage to talk across a long, narrow room. I should be at the end of the room facing the audience. If I attempt to talk across a room I find myself turning this way and that, and thus at alternate periods I have part of the audience behind me. You ought never to have any part of the audience behind you; you never can tell what they are going to do. So I'll sit down. —Mark Twain

BROTHER OR SISTER?

(When the Chairman whispers to another for information about the man he is going to introduce.)

I want to beg your pardon for hesitating a moment. I was not quite sure about the name and occupation of the next gentleman I am going to introduce. I am still not certain I didn't hear all of the details from the obliging fellow at my left. In this respect I am somewhat in the position of a minister, who upon a moment's notice was called in to officiate at a funeral, substituting for the regular pastor who was ill. When the minister arrived at the church, the services already were in progress. The organ was playing the customary hymn, accompanying a soprano voice. Abruptly it came time for the minister to preach. He stepped up to the pulpit, opened his book, and then remembered that he didn't know the sex of the deceased. "Heavens," he said to himself, as he craned his neck trying to figure out whether a man or a woman was layed-out in the coffin. But the lid of the coffin obstructed his view. All he could see was flowers.

Finally in desperation, just as the last peal of the organ rumbled around the rafters of the church, the minister leaned over to a close-by mourner and whispered in the vernacular of the pulpit: "Brother or sister?"

The mourner whispered back: "Cousin."

(Pause.)

So I have about as much information about the next speaker as the minister had about the deceased. If I make any blunders, I know that you will excuse me.

—Harold Butterworth